EGALITARIANISM

Some people are worse off than others. Does this fact give rise to moral concern? Egalitarianism claims that it does, for a wide array of reasons. It is one of the most important and hotly debated problems in moral and political philosophy, occupying a central place in the work of John Rawls, Thomas Nagel, G. A. Cohen, and Derek Parfit. It also plays an important role in practical contexts such as the allocation of health care resources, the design of education and tax systems, and the pursuit of global justice.

Egalitarianism is a superb introduction to the problem of contemporary egalitarian theories. It explains how rival theories of egalitarianism evaluate distributions of people's well-being, and carefully assesses the theoretical structure of each theory. It also examines how egalitarian theories are applied to the distribution of health and health care, thus bringing a deceptively complex philosophical debate into clear focus. Beginning with a brief introduction to basic terminology, Iwao Hirose examines the following topics:

- Rawlsian egalitarianism
- luck egalitarianism
- telic egalitarianism
- prioritarianism
- sufficientarianism
- equality and time
- equality in health and health care.

Including chapter summaries, annotated further reading, and a glossary, this is an ideal starting point for anyone studying distributive justice for the first time, and will also be of interest to more advanced students and researchers in philosophy, economics, political theory, public policy, and public health.

Iwao Hirose is Associate Professor at the Philosophy Department and the School of Environment, McGill University, Canada. He is the author of *The Ethics of Health Care Rationing* (with Greg Bognar, Routledge, 2014) and *Moral Aggregation* (2014).

NEW PROBLEMS OF PHILOSOPHY
Series Editor: José Luis Bermúdez

'Routledge's New Problems of Philosophy series has a most impressive line-up of topical volumes aimed at upper-level undergraduate and graduate students in philosophy and at others with interests in cutting edge philosophical work. The authors are influential figures in their respective fields and notably adept at synthesizing and explaining intricate topics fairly and comprehensively.'
— John Heil, Monash University, Australia, and Washington University, St Louis, USA

'This is an outstanding collection of volumes. The topics are well chosen and the authors are outstanding. They will be fine texts in a wide range of courses.'
— Stephen Stich, Rutgers University, USA

The New Problems of Philosophy series provides accessible and engaging surveys of the most important problems in contemporary philosophy. Each book examines a topic or theme that has either emerged on the philosophical landscape in recent years, or a longstanding problem refreshed in light of recent work in philosophy and related disciplines. Clearly explaining the nature of the problem at hand and assessing attempts to answer it, books in the series are excellent starting-points for undergraduate and graduate students wishing to study a single topic in depth. They will also be essential reading for professional philosophers. Additional features include chapter summaries, further reading and a glossary of technical terms.

Also available:

Analyticity
Cory Juhl and Eric Loomis

Moral Epistemology
Aaron Zimmerman

Fiction and Fictionalism
Mark Sainsbury

Embodied Cognition
Lawrence Shapiro

Physicalism
Daniel Stoljar

Self-Knowledge
Brie Gertler

Noncognitivism in Ethics
Mark Schroeder

Semantic Externalism
Jesper Kallestrup

Consequentialism
Julia Driver

Images
John V. Kulvicki

Attention
Wayne Wu

Forthcoming:

Imagination
Fabian Dorsch

Emergence
Patrick McGivern

Disjunctivism
Matthew Soteriou

Cognitive Phenomenology
Elijah Chudnoff

Perception
Adam Pautz

Metaphysics of Identity
André Gallois

Modal Epistemology
*Otávio Bueno and
Scott Shalkowski*

Social Metaphysics
Amie L. Thomasson

Consciousness
Rocco J. Gennaro

Relativism
*Maria Baghramian and Annalisa
Coliva*

Abstract Entities
Sam Cowling

EGALITARIANISM

Iwao Hirose

Routledge
Taylor & Francis Group
LONDON AND NEW YORK

First published 2015
by Routledge
2 Park Square, Milton Park, Abingdon, Oxon, OX14 4RN

and by Routledge
711 Third Ave., New York City, NY. 10017

Routledge is an imprint of the Taylor & Francis Group, an informa business

British Library Cataloguing in Publication Data
A catalogue record for this book is available from the British Library

Library of Congress Cataloging in Publication Data
Hirose, Iwao.
Egalitarianism / by Iwao Hirose. -- 1 [edition].
pages cm. -- (New problems of philosophy)
Includes bibliographical references and index.
1. Equality--Philosophy. 2. Distributive justice. I. Title.
HM821.H57 2014
305--dc23
2013050292

ISBN: 978-0-415-78318-7 (hbk)
ISBN: 978-0-415-78319-4 (pbk)
ISBN: 978-1-315-77200-4 (ebk)

Typeset in Joanna and Scala Sans
by Taylor & Francis Books

MIX
Paper from
responsible sources
FSC
www.fsc.org   FSC® C013056

Printed and bound in Great Britain by
TJ International Ltd, Padstow, Cornwall

To my mother

CONTENTS

Acknowledgements   x
Preface   xii

Introduction   1

1   Rawlsian egalitarianism   15

2   Luck egalitarianism   41

3   Telic egalitarianism   63

4   Prioritarianism   86

5   Sufficientarianism   112

6   Equality and time   136

7   Equality in health and health care   152

Concluding remarks   179

Glossary   186
Bibliography   190
Index   202

ACKNOWLEDGEMENTS

My analysis of egalitarian theories of distributive justice could not have been properly shaped without long and lively discussion with my colleagues and friends over many years. Those colleagues and friends are Matt Adler, Gustaf Arrhenius, Ralf Bader, Greg Bognar, Dan Brock, John Broome, Krister Bykvist, Erik Carlson, the late Jerry Cohen, Roger Crisp, Norm Daniels, Nir Eyal, Marc Fleurbaey, Axel Gosseries, Nils Holtug, the late Susan Hurley, Karsten Klint Jensen, Gerald Lang, Kasper Lippert-Rasmussen, Adina Preda, Wlodek Rabinowicz, Andrew Reisner, Ben Saunders, Shlomi Segall, and Larry Temkin. I want to thank them for helping me to understand many aspects of egalitarian theories of distributive justice. Some of them gave me detailed written comments on an early draft and helped me to improve the presentation and arguments for the final manuscript. Those were Martin Peterson, Adina Preda, Andrew Reisner, and Shlomi Segall. Three anonymous readers for Routledge also sent me many constructive comments. My special thanks go to each of them.

I was fortunate to have a chance to discuss a full draft of this book at two research centers: the Centre for the Study of Equality and Multiculturalism at the University of Copenhagen in October 2012 and Manchester Centre for Political Theory at the University of Manchester in May 2013. I am grateful to Richard Child, Morten Ebbe Juul Nielsen, Søren Flinch Midtgaard, Nils Holtug, Karsten Klint Jensen, Xavier Landes, Kasper Lippert-Rasmussen,

Tom Potter, and Liam Shields for their detailed comments, helpful suggestions, and friendly criticisms.

Two institutions provided me with a fantastic environment for writing this book. I wrote most of the first draft in an office with a breathtaking lake view at Villa Brocher in Hermance in spring-summer 2012, and prepared the final manuscript on the Left Bank of the Seine in spring-summer 2013. I thank Fondation Brocher and Fondation Maison des Sciences de l'Homme for offering such ideal environments for research, and the staff members of these foundations for enabling me to concentrate on writing the book.

I would like to extend my thanks to my research assistants, Emma Ryman, Joseph van Weelden, and Rebecca Acheson, who helped me to improve the manuscript. I would also thank Tony Bruce and Adam Johnson at Routledge for their patience and professional advice.

Finally, I gratefully acknowledge the financial support from the Canadian Institutes of Health Research and the Social Sciences and Humanities Research Council of Canada.

PREFACE

This book presents some of the main ideas of broadly defined egalitarian theories of distributive justice in contemporary moral and political philosophy. The literature on egalitarianism is enormous. Therefore, I could not address every aspect of that literature. Among many important aspects, this book is focused on the evaluative aspect of egalitarian distributive principles. By the evaluative aspect, I mean the study of the relative goodness, or ordering, of states of affairs. This means that I will not discuss other important aspects of egalitarianism, e.g. feminism, democratic equality, global justice, the notion of well-being, interpersonal comparability of well-being, and so on. I am under no illusion that this book is a complete reference in the area of distributive justice.

This book is primarily designed to serve as a textbook for advanced undergraduate and graduate students in philosophy and political theory. However, it is also aimed at reaching a wider audience. Although an elementary level of knowledge and analytical skills in normative ethics and political philosophy are assumed, presentation is pitched at a level accessible to students in economics, politics, sociology, public policy, public health, medicine, and any other discipline concerned with the distribution of human well-being.

Distributive justice is an area not only of philosophy, but also of several other academic disciplines. For example, the formal analysis of economics is extremely important and valuable for understanding the structure of egalitarian theories of distributive justice. However, it intimidates some people. I believe that the most fruitful way to present theories of distributive justice is to integrate the results of economics and political theory into philosophical analysis. Therefore, I decided to include some of their results in an informal way. Many universities have offered an integrated undergraduate program in Philosophy, Politics, and Economics (the PPE Program) in recent years, and this book should be particularly suitable for a course in such a program.

The literature on contemporary egalitarianism is massive, specialized, intricate, and complex. This fact sometimes discourages some students from digging into serious theoretical analysis of egalitarian distributive justice. Yet egalitarianism has been, and will certainly remain, one of the central issues in moral and political philosophy, and many students within and outside philosophy are interested in understanding egalitarianism, whether it be for the purposes of endorsing it, or applying it to practical issues. This book aims at bridging this gap. It offers an overview and critical analysis of the literature on egalitarianism of the last roughly 40 years.

The biggest challenge that I took up in this book was to add a chapter on distributive justice in health and health care. Students often find it difficult to articulate abstract philosophical analysis in practical contexts even when they understand theories of distributive justice very well. In order to show how egalitarianism can be relevant and put into practice, I chose the context of health and health care. The issue of the distribution of health and health care has established itself as a distinctive area of research. Greg Bognar and I are in the process of publishing *The Ethics of Health Care Rationing* with Routledge, and I would recommend reading it if you are interested in further exploring the ethical issues arising from the distribution of health and health care. However, theories of egalitarian justice can be applied to many other areas. My hope is that readers endeavor to do further research in egalitarianism, both in theory and in practice, after reading this book.

INTRODUCTION

Egalitarianism refers to many philosophical ideas – probably too many. In this book, I cannot discuss all the ideas that are labeled as egalitarianism. So it is a good idea to start by clarifying what I shall discuss and what I shall not. This introduction is intended to identify the subject matter, aims, and structure of the book. First, I will offer a definition of egalitarianism, which I will examine throughout this book. Second, I will clarify some philosophical ideas that might be classified as egalitarianism by some people but will not be discussed in this book. Third, I will identify the goal and structure of the book. Fourth, I will define the basic philosophical terms to be used throughout the book. Fifth, I will introduce some technical terms that are used in the literature on distributive justice.

What is egalitarianism?

Some people are worse off than others. Does inequality among people with equal moral worth give rise to a moral concern? Proponents of egalitarianism claim that it does. Here is the definition of egalitarianism that I will examine in this book:

> *Egalitarianism*: a class of distributive principles, which claim that individuals should have equal quantities of well-being or morally relevant factors that affect their life.

It is difficult to define a philosophical concept without provoking con-
troversies. Some people would find my definition of egalitarianism to be
too broad because it includes too many distributive principles, while others
would find it to be too narrow because it excludes too many. In this
introductory section, I will first attempt to make sense of this definition
and elucidate what is excluded from it. By doing this, we can identify the
subject matter of the book.

Distributive principles are the rules that serve as criteria for normative
judgments concerning the distributions of the morally relevant factors of
different individuals in society. Some distributive principles such as the
utilitarian distributive principle are not concerned with the distribution of
people's well-being or morally relevant factors. The egalitarianism that I will
examine in this book is a specific class of distributive principles which
endorse equality of well-being or morally relevant factors among different
people.

Proponents of egalitarianism endorse equal distribution of something.
The egalitarianism I will analyze in this book endorses equal distribution of
people's *well-being*. It is not concerned with the equality of entities with no
moral standing. The fact that one leg of a table is shorter than others causes
inconvenience, but does not give rise to a moral concern. Egalitarianism is
concerned with the equality of entities with moral standing. What are the
entities with moral standing? This question leads us to a substantive disagreement concerning my definition of egalitarianism. Some people think
that all sentient animals including non-human animals have moral standing
and therefore that egalitarianism should be concerned with the equality of
all sentient animals. But, for the sake of simplicity, I will take egalitarianism
to be concerned with the equality of human beings.

Some people are shorter than others. Is egalitarianism concerned with
equality of height? I do not think so. Egalitarianism is concerned with some
morally relevant factor that humans possess. When there are inequalities of
morally relevant factors among different individuals, egalitarianism speaks
to them. What is the morally relevant factor that humans possess? I call it
well-being. I shall use the notion of well-being in the broadest sense. I take
the notion of well-being to be a placeholder for what egalitarianism aims to
equalize. This means that I will leave the notion of well-being unspecified.
This way of using the notion of well-being is not uncontroversial. Let me
explain briefly why I make such an assumption.

Let me start by introducing a piece of philosophical jargon. It is
equalisandum. Equalisandum refers to the preferred concept of morally

relevant factors to be equalized among different individuals. The equalisandum has a wide spectrum of possible accounts. On one end of the spectrum, the equalisandum is an objectively identifiable good, or a list of objectively identifiable goods, such as income, Rawls's social primary goods, Dworkin's resources, and so on (the *objective list view*). On the other end of the spectrum, the equalisandum is a person's mental states such as pleasure, desire-satisfaction, preference-satisfaction, and so on (the *mental state view*). Some people locate the equalisandum between these extremes: the capability to function, opportunity for welfare, and so on. There are many accounts of the equalisandum, and there is no consensus concerning what is the best account.

The issue of "equality of what?" is fundamental in ethics. No theory of distributive justice is complete unless the appropriate account of the equalisandum is established. Conventionally, it is believed that whenever we discuss distributive justice, we must resolve (1) the issue of the best account of the equalisandum, (2) the issue of how the equalisandum is measured, and (3) the issue of the interpersonal comparability of the equalisandum. This implicitly suggests that we cannot discuss distributive principles unless we settle these three difficult issues. I believe, however, that a lot of meaningful philosophical analysis of distributive principles can proceed without committing to a particular account of the equalisandum. In order to focus on the issues of various distributive principles, I simply bracket off the whole debate concerning the best account of the equalisandum. This is why I assume the broadest notion of morally relevant factors, which enables me to be neutral with respect to the competing accounts of the equalisandum and discuss distributive principles independently of different accounts of the equalisandum. Throughout this book, I will use well-being as a shorthand for morally relevant factors unless I clearly note otherwise.

The definition of egalitarianism I have presented is broad because it includes some principles that sometimes are not thought to be egalitarian in a strict sense. More specifically, it includes what have become known as prioritarianism and sufficientarianism in the broadly defined category of egalitarianism. Strictly speaking, these two principles are not meant to be versions of egalitarianism, because they are not concerned with equality as such. At least, proponents of these principles say so. However, I will include these principles in the broadly defined category of egalitarianism as I explain in chapters 3 and 4.

What is not egalitarianism?

I defined egalitarianism in terms of equality of people's well-being or morally relevant factors that affect their life. This definition may appear too narrow because it does not cover cases where other senses of equality crop up. Equality before the law (sometimes labeled as legal egalitarianism) is such an example. Equality before the law holds that each individual or group is subject to the same laws, with no individual or group having special legal privileges. This is a normative claim and concerned with equality between individuals or groups. But it is not concerned with equality of well-being. Therefore, I will not discuss this type of egalitarianism in this book. Another example is political equality. Political equality holds that all citizens should have the equal right to participate in the government, and to choose or remove public officials by voting. One of the specific claims is "one person, one vote." This is also a normative claim and concerned with equality between individuals, but it is not concerned with equality of well-being. Therefore, it is not a version of what I call egalitarianism.

There are at least four well-known distributive principles that are not egalitarian in the sense I defined above, yet some people think that these are egalitarian in some sense. The first example is utilitarianism. Utilitarianism can be defined in various ways. Take classical utilitarianism. Classical utilitarianism contends that an act is right if and only if it maximizes the total sum of people's well-being in a given society. When we calculate the total sum, we assign equal weight to each person's well-being and simply add up different people's well-being. Classical utilitarianism endorses assigning equal weight to every person's well-being, and it might be claimed that it is egalitarian. However, it is not concerned with how people's well-being is distributed. Thus, I do not consider it as a form of egalitarianism.

The second example is libertarianism. The best-known libertarian distributive theory is Robert Nozick's side-constraint theory (Nozick 1974). His side-constraint theory consists in three principles. The first is the principle of acquisition: a person owns his or her labor, and by "mixing his or her labor" with a previously unowned part of the natural world thereby comes to own it. The second is the principle of transfer: a transfer of holdings is just if and only if it is voluntary, a principle that would seem to follow from respect for a person's right to use the fruits of the exercise of his or her self-owned talents, abilities, and labor as he or she sees fit. The third is the principle of rectification: the proper means of setting right past injustices in acquisition and transfer. According to Nozick, insofar as the requirements of these three principles are met, any distribution of well-being should be tolerated. Any attempt to equalize people's well-being should be seen as unjust. Thus, libertarianism is not concerned with equality of well-being. The defenders of libertarianism generally argue that distributive principles, which impose demands of equality, conflict with more important moral demands such as those of liberty or respect for self-ownership.

The third is the Marxist principle of justice or communism. Sometimes, the Marxist principle of justice is associated with a form of egalitarianism. The Marxist principle of justice, as I understand it, attempts to realize a society in which the bourgeoisie's domination of the proletariat is abolished. The Marxist principle of justice, if it is realized in a certain way, may well end up with a state of equal well-being. However, its primary goal is to abolish the capitalist structure of production and eradicate the bourgeoisie's domination of the proletariat. It does not necessarily aim at equality of well-being. Thus, I do not include the Marxist principle of justice in the category of egalitarianism here. Nor do I include Karl Marx's famous slogan in the Critique of the Gotha Program: "from each according to his ability, to each according to his needs." According to this slogan, in a communist society, every person should contribute to society to the best of his or her ability and consume from society in proportion to his or her needs. There is a sense in which this slogan might be called a version of egalitarianism. Yet, again, it does not aim at equality of well-being. Thus, I do not see it as a version of egalitarianism.

The fourth is the proportionality principle. In its most general form, it holds that we should distribute more to the person who has the stronger claim than to one who has the weaker claim. Additionally, there are different ways to distribute. For example, consider the following problem that is found in the Talmud: "Two hold a garment; one claims it all, the other claims the half. What is an equitable division of the garment?" The solution provided in the Talmud is that we give the first claimant ¾ and the second claimant ¼. The idea is that the dispute is over only half of the garment, and that claimants share the disputed part equally and the first claimant receives the undisputed part (this method is known as the Shapley value in game theory). This is one way to distribute the garment among competing claimants. There is another well-known way to distribute. That is the Aristotelian proportionality principle, according to which the garment should be distributed in proportion to the degree of legitimate claims. It implies that we should give the first claimant ⅔ and the second claimant ⅓. Both the Talmud and the Aristotelian proportionality principle are concerned with fair distribution of benefits, not equality of well-being. Therefore, I do not include the proportionality principles in the category of egalitarianism.

Goals and organization

My general goal in this book is to offer an account of the foundational, structural, and practical features of egalitarian theories in contemporary moral and political philosophy. More specifically, I aim to outline my understanding of (1) how equality of well-being can be justified, (2) how egalitarian distributive principles evaluate the distributions of people's well-being, and (3) what kind of philosophical problems arise when abstract egalitarian principles are applied in particular contexts. By contemporary moral and political philosophy, I mean moral and political philosophy after John Rawls's *A Theory of Justice* (Rawls 1971). Even if I confine my analysis to this limited time period, the literature of contemporary egalitarianism is still enormous, specialized, intricate, and complex. Although I tried to make this book as comprehensive as possible, it is impossible to cover all the topics. So I chose seven topics, which I take to be central in the literature of contemporary egalitarian theories of distributive justice, which I then divided into three broadly defined parts. The first part is about foundations of egalitarianism. The second part is about the theoretical structure of substantive distributive principles. The third part is about the applications of egalitarianism in particular contexts.

The first part (chapters 1 and 2) examines two influential theories that offer grounds for egalitarianism. When we discuss distributive justice in general and the equal distribution of well-being in particular, the following question immediately arises. Why does unequal distribution of well-being give rise to a moral concern? There are two influential theories that ground egalitarian distributive principles. These are John Rawls's theory of justice as fairness and luck egalitarianism.

In chapter 1, I will critically examine Rawls's difference principle. As I said above, contemporary moral and political philosophy starts with Rawls's *A Theory of Justice* (Rawls 1971). Strictly speaking, Rawls's difference principle does not aim at equality of well-being. Rather, it identifies under what conditions socioeconomic inequalities are justified. He thinks that, given his account of justice as fairness, socioeconomic equality does not require justification, whereas socioeconomic inequalities require justification. How could he reach this conclusion? I begin by explaining the criticisms of utilitarianism, which Rawls takes to be the most serious rival view. Then,

I will outline Rawls's argument for the difference principle and the basic features of his difference principle. As is widely known, both proponents and critics of egalitarianism criticize his difference principle. I will sketch their criticisms. I conclude chapter 1 by examining two recent distributive principles inspired by Rawls's theory of justice: Thomas Nagel's unanimity and T. M. Scanlon's version of contractualism.

In chapter 2, I will consider the other influential foundational theory of egalitarianism. That is luck egalitarianism. Luck egalitarianism originates from Ronald Dworkin's resource egalitarianism, and was further developed by Richard Arneson and G. A. Cohen. Luck egalitarianism attempts to include the notion of responsibility in an egalitarian theory of distributive justice. By distinguishing the bad effects of luck that are beyond one's control from those within one's control, luck egalitarianism distinguishes inequalities that should be reduced from inequalities that do not require reduction. Luck egalitarianism is motivated partly by criticism of Rawls's difference principle. However, it has become a foundational theory of egalitarianism in its own right. In chapter 2, I will outline the basic claims of, and objections to, luck egalitarianism.

The second part (chapters 3 to 5) examines how various egalitarian distributive principles evaluate the distribution of people's well-being. More specifically, it focuses on three principles: Telic egalitarianism, prioritarianism, and sufficientarianism. The literature of egalitarianism saw a radical change in the mid-1990s. With the publication of Derek Parfit's paper, "Equality or Priority?," the landscape of philosophical discussion about egalitarianism changed completely (Parfit 1995, 2000). Parfit's paper is massively influential. In that paper, he raised objections to what he calls telic egalitarianism and put forward his proposed priority view, or prioritarianism. Many of the debates concerning Parfit's paper revolve around the contrast between telic egalitarianism and prioritarianism. However, more recently, what has become known as (and is horribly named) sufficientarianism appears to be a credible alternative to telic egalitarianism and prioritarianism. The second part of this book will examine the theoretical structure of these distributive principles.

In chapter 3, I will examine the theoretical structure of two versions of telic egalitarianism. I will first introduce Parfit's characterization of telic egalitarianism (the intrinsic view) and his objections to it (the leveling down objection and the scope objection). I will then consider an alternative characterization (the aggregate view) that is familiar to economists, and compare it with Parfit's intrinsic view.

In chapter 4, I will move on to Parfit's prioritarianism. In recent years, prioritarianism has become very popular among philosophers. Strictly speaking, it is not egalitarian, because it does not aim at equality. Nevertheless it has a built-in bias towards equality. First, I will explain how the leveling down objection motivates prioritarianism. Second, I will characterize prioritarianism as the conjunction of three conditions – non-relationality, the Pigou-Dalton condition, and Pareto – and offer the most general formula of prioritarianism. Third, I will compare the theoretical structure of prioritarianism with that of telic egalitarianism, and consider the advantages and disadvantages of prioritarianism.

In chapter 5, I will critically assess sufficientarianism. Most generally, sufficientarianism contends that priority should be given to benefiting those below a threshold level of well-being. It is supposed to be an alternative to telic egalitarianism and prioritarianism. To illustrate its intuitive appeal, I will begin by introducing the results of experimental economics, in which many subjects favor a version of sufficientarianism. After this, I will offer a philosophical analysis in the following way. First, I will explain the philosophical motivations for, and the basic claims of, sufficientarianism. Second, I will provide an exact characterization of sufficientarianism. Third, I will show that the theory would give priority to the worse off both below and above the threshold.

The third part of this book (chapters 6 and 7) concentrates on two selected topics of egalitarianism. The analysis in the first and second parts is very abstract. When a philosophical analysis is put in particular contexts, additional philosophical problems arise. This is why the analysis of egalitarianism becomes very complicated. There are many contexts in which egalitarianism encounters additional difficult problems. I chose two such contexts. The first is the context of intertemporal distributive judgments. The second is the context of the distribution of health and health care.

In chapter 6, I will discuss two topics. The first topic is about the temporal unit of distributive judgment. When we evaluate the distribution of people's well-being, should we consider the distribution of people's well-being at specific times, or the distribution of lifetime well-being? In a series of thought-provoking papers, Dennis McKerlie carefully analyzes this question. The question is a surprisingly difficult one. In the first half of this chapter, I will explain what telic egalitarianism and prioritarianism have to say about the temporal unit of distributive judgment. The second topic concerns the distribution of future people's well-being. Future people will come into existence, but considered in the abstract they will have no properties that instantiate their well-being. In one possible future state, there will be a set of abstract people. In another possible future state, there will be a different set of abstract people. There might or might not be an overlap between these sets of future people. The evaluation of future states with different population sizes is called population axiology. Since Derek Parfit posed the "repugnant conclusion" and the "mere addition paradox," discussion of population axiology has grown very rapidly and become one of the most difficult problems in contemporary moral philosophy (Parfit 1984). In the second half of this chapter, I will merely explain what kind of distinctive problems population axiology poses for telic egalitarianism and prioritarianism.

In chapter 7, I will examine how egalitarian theories of distributive justice operate in the domain of health and health care. Many people think that health, and therefore health care, is very important in our lives. So, therefore, is the distribution of health and health care. In this chapter, I will distinguish health and health care clearly. In the first half of this chapter, I will consider how the Rawlsian theory and luck egalitarianism approach the issue of health inequality. In the second half, I will sketch how egalitarianism can be employed in the allocation of scarce health care resources.

What is left out?

The literature on contemporary egalitarianism is so large that, regrettably, I had to leave out several major topics. I want to point to two such topics that I take to be particularly important.

The first topic is democratic equality. Roughly, according to democratic equality, the point of equality is not to aim for equality of goods. Rather, it is to secure the social, political, and economic conditions of everyone's freedom to participate in democratic self-governance, so that each person stands to every other as fundamentally equal. In short, what democratic equality aims for is a relationship between equals. If democratic equality is a plausible objective, then two obvious points follow. First, egalitarian principles, which I will examine in this book, miss the point of equality, thus being misguided. Second, democratic equality permits some unequal distributions of goods insofar as everyone stands equal to everyone else. The idea of democratic equality has become prominent in the recent literature of political philosophy and includes a broad spectrum of positions (Anderson 1999; Christiano 1996; Daniels 2012; Scheffler 2003b). I shall briefly discuss Norman Daniels' version of democratic equality in the context of equality in health and health care in chapter 7. However, in this book, I will simply set aside the topic of democratic equality because I cannot provide a fair analysis in one or two chapters.

The second topic that I leave out is the general issue concerning the grounds of equality. Why does inequality among people with equal moral worth give rise to a moral concern? This question is so fundamental that a comprehensive study of egalitarianism cannot afford to ignore it. In this book, I will address this question in several chapters. However, I will leave out the large literature of global justice, in which this question is the central problem. There are enormous global inequalities. Billions of people suffer from acute poverty and die from preventable disease while a small fraction of the world population lives an affluent life. However, there is no global government or transnational authority that enables us to redistribute resources from the rich to the poor. How can we argue for a reduction of global inequality in such an environment? In recent years, the literature on global justice has grown rapidly, and the question of the grounds of equality has been examined carefully in this literature. Initially, my plan was to add one chapter devoted to the literature on global justice in order to address the issues affecting the grounds of global justice. However, the literature on global justice is so large that I had to drop the topic from this book. I just want to point to several important monographs in this literature: Caney (2005), Gilabert (2012), Pogge (2008), Sen (1999), and Tan (2012).

It is not my contention that these topics are less important than those I discuss in the book. Due to the lack of space, I had to concentrate on a limited number of topics. I am under no illusion that this book is anything but an incomplete study of egalitarianism.

Philosophical terminology

Throughout this book, I will make some assumptions about basic normative concepts. At the outset, I should clearly state these assumptions.

First, I will distinguish two categories of ethical theories: teleology and deontology. I will follow John Rawls's influential characterization (Rawls 1971: 24). It is common to associate teleology with Aristotle's philosophy, according to which final causes exist in nature. In this book, however, I will not use teleology in the Aristotelian sense. I will use teleology in Rawls's sense. According to Rawls's characterization, teleology is the view that rightness or wrongness is determined by goodness and badness. The chief example of teleology is utilitarianism. According to utilitarianism, the rightness or wrongness of an act is determined by the amount of good that the act brings about, and the relevant good is people's pleasure or happiness. Rawls's characterization includes any theory that determines rightness or wrongness by appeal to the good and bad. Deontology, on the other hand, is the view that the rightness or wrongness of an act is determined independently of good and bad. Examples of deontology include Robert Nozick's side-constraint theory and Kantian ethics. For example, according to Kantian ethics, very roughly speaking, an act that treats a person merely as a means is wrong, regardless of how much good such an act would bring about.

Although Rawls's characterization of teleology and deontology is influential, it can be challenged. Think of the following case. Classical utilitarianism is an example of teleology and holds that an act is right if and only if it maximizes the total sum of pleasure. It requires assigning an equal weight to every person's pleasure. The equal weight of people's pleasure is a sort of constraint on how people's pleasure should be aggregated. And yet that constraint does not come from the concept of good or bad. It may be argued that giving equal weight to every person's pleasure is a constraint that is neither good nor bad. Thus, when classical utilitarianism assumes a certain constraint, it is not a matter of goodness or badness (see Kymlicka 1988).

Second, I will distinguish consequentialism and axiology. Consequentialism holds that an act is right if and only if it brings about the best outcome. It is one of the teleological theories: rightness or wrongness is derived from the relative goodness of states of affairs. Axiology is confined to the relative goodness of states of affairs. It merely ranks the states of affairs in terms of relative goodness. Almost all versions of consequentialism imply axiology, but not *vice versa*. That is, almost all consequentialist theories include some versions of axiological theories, but some axiological theories do not necessarily commit their proponents to teleological theories. For example, some axiological theories would judge that a state of affairs x is strictly better than y, but nonetheless judge that it is wrong to bring about x, because bringing it about violates some important deontological constraint such as basic rights. In contrast, teleological theories would judge that it is right to bring about x on the basis that x is strictly better than y.

Third, as I mentioned earlier, I will take the notion of well-being to be as broad as possible so that I can be neutral with respect to competing notions of well-being. Well-being can be an objectively identifiable list of goods. It can also be some mental states such as pleasure, happiness, desire-satisfaction, preference-satisfaction, and so on. When I talk about other notions of the equalisandum (such as Rawls's social primary goods and Dworkin's resources), I will clearly note this.

Fourth, let me clarify what I mean by state of affairs, outcome, and act. For these words, I will follow Leonard Savage's definitions (Savage 1972). A state of affairs is a complete description of the world. An outcome is one of the states of affairs that an act brings about. More formally, an act is a function that maps a set of states of affairs onto an outcome. Some philosophers use outcomes and states of affairs interchangeably. But I want to clearly distinguish these terms. Axiological theory ranks the possible states of affairs in terms of goodness, and identifies the best state of affairs. Teleological theory ranks the possible states of affairs in terms of goodness, and holds that the act, which brings the best state of affairs into an outcome, is the right act. Deontological theory holds that the rightness or wrongness of an act can be determined independently of the ranking of states of affairs in terms of goodness.

Technical terminology

Egalitarianism is a topic within economics as well as philosophy. The formal methods of economics have made a significant contribution to the formal aspects of egalitarianism. However, the formal terminology can be intimidating. Although I will minimize the use of formal terminology, it is useful to introduce some basic technical terms here. Technical terms first crop up in the context of the measurement of well-being. This is because distributive justice requires some sort of measurability and interpersonal comparability of well-being. An ordinal measure of well-being refers to the relative level of well-being. We simply rank a person's states. A cardinal measure assigns some numerical scale to a person's well-being. However, the numbers do not have any independent meaning. Five (5) units of well-being are simply better than three (3) units of well-being. The number can be negative, for example, -10. Notably, -10 does not mean that the person is in a state of suffering, or below the level worth living. Nor does 0 mean non-existence.

The distinction between ordinal and cardinal measures is a separate issue from that of interpersonal comparability. A cardinal measure does not imply interpersonal comparability of well-being. An ordinal measure can be interpersonally comparable. There are different types of interpersonal comparability. *Level comparability* means that the level of a person's well-being can be compared with that of another person. That is, it is possible to judge that one person is better off than another, but we cannot judge how much better off he or she is. *Unit comparability* means that the gain or loss of a person's well-being can be compared with that of another person. *Full comparability* means that both the level and unit can be compared interpersonally. For example, as we will see in chapter 1, Rawls's difference principle assumes an ordinal measure and level comparability. For Rawls's purposes, it suffices to compare the level of social primary goods of different social groups (the difference principle does not need to identify the gains and losses for social groups) and to identify which group is the worst off (the difference principle does not need to identify how badly off those individuals in the worst off group are). Interpersonal comparability is one of the most difficult issues in measurement theory. However, in this book, I shall simply assume full comparability unless I clearly note otherwise.

When we talk about teleological and axiological theories, we refer to the ordering, or ranking, of states of affairs. To be precise, let me define a betterness ordering in axiology and teleology. Let X be a finite set of states of affairs. Define a betterness relation on X such that, for all x and y in X, x is at least as good as y. Throughout this book, I will assume that the betterness relation constitutes a complete weak ordering, i.e. that it is reflexive, transitive, and complete. A betterness relation on a set X is reflexive if and only if, for all x in X, x is at least as good as x. It is transitive if and only if, for all x, y, and z in X, (1) x is at least as good as y and (2) y is at least as good as z together imply (3) that x is at least as good as z. It is complete if and only if, for all x and y in X, either x is at least as good as y or y is at least as good as x.

A betterness relation on X can be represented by a real-valued function U such that, for any pair of x and y in X, $U(x) \geq U(y)$ if and only if x is at least as good as y. That is, one state of affairs has a greater value than another if and only if it is better. Note that the value of $U()$ merely represents the betterness ordering: it does not signify a quantity of good. The condition of a real-valued function representing a given ordering does not determine one single function. If U represents an ordering, then any strictly increasing function V of U also represents that ordering. The condition of representing an ordering determines a real-valued function uniquely only up to strictly increasing transformations.

Further reading

Surprisingly, there are few comprehensive books on egalitarianism. The most comprehensive to date is Temkin (1993). White (2007) is a book aimed at entry-level undergraduate students in political theory. For a concise overview of egalitarian theories of distributive justice, see Arneson (2007), Temkin (2009), and Vallentyne (2007). If you are not afraid of math, read Roemer (1998b) and Tungodden (2003). In this book, I will bracket off the notion of well-being, but anyone engaged in the study of distributive justice must consider the notion of well-being very seriously. I would recommend reading Griffin (1986) and Sen (1985, 1999). I did not provide any detailed discussion concerning measurement theory and interpersonal comparability of utilities. The classic work on measurement theory in the non-natural sciences is Krantz et al. (1971) while F. Roberts (1985) is more accessible. Fleurbaey and Hammond (2004) is a comprehensive survey of the issue of interpersonal comparability. The volume edited by Elster and Roemer (1991) contains many important papers on interpersonal comparability of well-being.

1

RAWLSIAN EGALITARIANISM

In every field, there are one or two important figures nobody can afford to ignore. In the contemporary literature on distributive justice in general, and egalitarianism in particular, we cannot avoid John Rawls's *A Theory of Justice*, whether or not we agree with his arguments. The contemporary debate concerning egalitarianism starts with his theory of justice. In this chapter, I will examine Rawls's difference principle and the other broadly defined contractualist distributive principles of Thomas Nagel and T. M. Scanlon. I will not attempt to summarize or assess Rawls's whole theory of justice or the far-reaching ethical theories of Nagel and Scanlon. Rather, I will concentrate on a small part of each of their projects. Since their respective theories are intended as alternatives to utilitarianism, it is necessary to begin with a short introduction to the utilitarian theory of distributive justice. Section 1.1 outlines the basic features of the utilitarian theory of distributive justice. Section 1.2 elucidates the theoretical structure of Rawls's distributive principle: the difference principle. Section 1.3 describes the typical objections leveled against the difference principle. Section 1.4 examines the recent arguments of Thomas Nagel and T. M. Scanlon, which are each inspired by Rawls's contractarianism, in the context of the distribution of goods.

Let me make one quick terminological remark. As for the distinction between contractarianism and contractualism, I will follow Stephen

Darwall's definition (see the introduction to Darwall 2002). According to Darwall, contractarianism refers to the idea that morality is a set of social practices that self-interested, rational actors adopt in their common interest. On the other hand, contractualism refers to the idea that morality is a set of principles that mediate relations of mutual respect between free and equal persons. Both contractarianism and contractualism see morality as a kind of agreement or contract. The difference is that contractarianism takes the underlying motivation to be rational self-interest whereas contractualism takes it to be mutual respect between equals.

1.1 Utilitarianism, the dominant distributive principle

John Rawls (1971) famously complained that the predominant systematic theory in modern moral and political philosophy has been some form of utilitarianism. There are various versions of utilitarianism. I will only focus on the formal features of two versions: classical and average utilitarianism. Classical utilitarianism holds that an act is right if and only if it maximizes the total sum of people's well-being (i.e. the value of $(w_1 + w_2 + w_3 + \ldots + w_i + \ldots + w_n)$ in the n-person case, where w_i denotes the numerical representation of well-being of person i. Average utilitarianism holds that an act is right if and only if it maximizes the average of people's well-being (i.e. the value of $1/n(w_1 + w_2 + w_3 + \ldots w_n)$ in the n-person case).

There are six formal features that are shared by classical and average utilitarianism. The first is consequentialism. Consequentialism is the view that the rightness or wrongness of an act is determined solely by the goodness of its consequences. In contrast, non-consequentialism is the view that the rightness or wrongness of an act can be determined independently of the goodness of its consequences. According to utilitarianism, the rightness or wrongness of an act is determined by the overall goodness of the outcome that the act brings about, and the goodness of the outcome is determined by the total sum or average of people's well-being. Needless to say, utilitarianism is also axiological because it ranks states of affairs in terms of goodness.

The second formal feature is welfarism. Welfarism is the view that the relative goodness of states of affairs is determined by people's well-being and nothing else. Welfarism is a version of axiology. It is not equivalent to consequentialism. Consequentialism does not imply welfarism, because some versions of consequentialism determine the relative goodness of states of affairs on the basis of people's well-being and the value of something else which cannot be reduced to the value of well-being. For example, some environmental ethicists would claim that the relative goodness of states of affairs is determined by the total sum of people's well-being and the value of the natural environment, and that it is right to bring about the best state of affairs. These people are consequentialists because they contend that the rightness or wrongness of an act is determined by the goodness of its consequence. And yet, they are not committed to welfarism, because they consider, for example, the value of the natural environment in addition to people's well-being when they estimate the goodness of the consequences of an act.

Welfarism does not imply consequentialism, either, because some welfarists may well accept some deontic constraints. For example, some welfarists would say that a state of affairs is strictly better than another in terms of people's well-being, but claim that it is wrong to bring about that state, because bringing it about violates some important deontic constraints. Thus, welfarism is not equivalent to consequentialism. Welfarism is a particular type of axiological theory, which ranks states of affairs solely on the basis of people's well-being.

The third is impartiality. Impartiality holds that the permutations of personal identities do not affect our judgment about the relative goodness of outcomes. That is, two states are equally good if they differ only with regard to the identities of the people in question. For example, consider two states of affairs in the two-person case. One state of affairs is $(10, 5)$, and the other $(5, 10)$. The bracketed numbers show the well-being levels of person 1 and person 2 respectively. Impartiality implies that $(10, 5)$ and $(5, 10)$ are equally good. If, for example, $(10, 5)$ is judged to be better than $(5, 10)$, person 2 has a legitimate ground for complaining about such a judgment because his or her interest is not considered in the same way. Some people might think that impartiality is not the correct word to refer to this feature, and hence that impartiality must refer to something different, for example, fairness or equal treatment (economists call this feature anonymity). This does not raise a serious concern. It is merely a matter of naming. The relevant feature could be called by a different name, and retain its meaning. However, for the present purpose, I use impartiality for the feature, which entails that permutations of personal identities do not change our distributive judgment.

The fourth is that utilitarianism satisfies the Pareto principle. The Pareto principle holds that if a state X is strictly better for some person than another state Y and X is worse for no person, then X is strictly better than Y. For example, compare $X = (10, 5)$ and $Y = (9, 5)$. State X is strictly better for person 1 than Y, and no worse for person 2; X is thus said to be

Pareto-superior to Y. However, the scope of the Pareto principle is quite limited. Compare $X = (10, 5)$ and $X' = (6, 9)$. X is strictly better for person 1 but worse for person 2. Likewise, X' is strictly better for person 2 but worse for person 1. Thus, neither is strictly better than the other in terms of the Pareto principle. These two states of affairs are said to be *Pareto-incomparable.*

However, the Pareto principle becomes quite powerful when it is combined with impartiality. Compare $X = (10, 5)$ and $Y = (4, 10)$. As such, X and Y are Pareto-incomparable. That is, the Pareto principle is silent about the relative goodness of these two states of affairs because each state of affairs is strictly worse for either one or the other person. However, the conjunction of impartiality and the Pareto principle gives the result that X is strictly better than Y. Here is a proof. Imagine another state of affairs $Y' = (10, 4)$, which is derived by a permutation of personal identities from Y. By impartiality, Y' is equally as good as Y. By the Pareto principle, X is strictly better than Y'. Consequently, X is strictly better than Y. Thus, in some cases, the conjunction of impartiality and the Pareto principle can rank two states of affairs that are Pareto-incomparable (though the conjunction of impartiality and the Pareto principle still cannot rank $X = (10, 5)$ and $X' = (6, 9)$).

The fifth formal feature is strong separability (Broome 1991). Utilitarianism adds up the value of different people's well-being in order to estimate the goodness of a state of affairs. This feature implies the following: roughly speaking, the relative goodness of states of affairs depends on the relative goodness of the well-being of the people who are affected by the choice of outcomes. Table 1.1 shows four states of affairs, and each state of affairs shows the well-being level of six individuals. Consider two binary comparisons: A and B, and then C and D.

In a comparison of A and B, only persons 1 and 2 are affected by the choice of states of affairs. The well-being of the other people is unaffected, no matter which state of affairs is brought about. Likewise, in a comparison of C and D, only persons 1 and 2 are affected by the choice, and the other

Table 1.1

	1	2	3	4	5	6
A	2	2	2	2	2	2
B	1	4	2	2	2	2
C	2	2	1	1	1	1
D	1	4	1	1	1	1

persons are unaffected. The state of persons 1 and 2 is the same in A and C and in B and D. The idea of strong separability is that the relative goodness of A and B must be consistent with the relative goodness of C and D because it is the relative goodness of the well-being of persons 1 and 2 that makes the difference between A and B as well as between C and D. That is, the relative goodness of A and B and the relative goodness of C and D should be determined by the relative goodness of (2, 2) and (1, 4). More precisely, strong separability holds that A is better than B if and only if C is better than D, and that B is better than A if and only if D is better than C. Now if we do some simple math, we can easily verify what utilitarianism, be it classical or average, judges: B is better than A, and D is better than C. Thus, utilitarianism satisfies strong separability.

Some people may disagree with strong separability. For example, they may judge that A is better than B, but that D is better than C. I will come to such judgments when we discuss telic egalitarianism in chapter 3. The notion of strong separability captures the feature of what I will call non-relationality. Non-relationality is where the relation between different people's well-being does not matter in determining the goodness of a state of affairs. If one judges that A is better than B but that nonetheless D is better than C, one cares about the relation between different people's well-being, and thus makes a relational distributive judgment. However, utilitarianism is not concerned with the relation between different people's well-being, and thus, it is non-relational. Whether or not a theory is committed to non-relationality depends on whether it satisfies the strong separability I characterized above. This notion of strong separability will become important when we characterize prioritarianism in section 4.2.

The sixth is the cardinal and interpersonally comparable measure of well-being. It should be obvious enough that, in order for utilitarianism to be able to add up the value of well-being, some cardinal measure is required. It should also be obvious enough that, in order to add up the value of different people's well-being, some sort of interpersonal comparability is required. Quite often, proponents of utilitarianism simply assume cardinality and full comparability. That is, they assume that we can measure the value of well-being in terms of a numerical scale and compare both the level and unit of different people's well-being. However, full comparability is not absolutely necessary for utilitarianism. Cardinal unit comparability suffices to make judgments about the relative goodness of states of affairs. For example, compare two simple states of the two-person case: X = (10, 15) and Y = (12, 14). One way to judge the relative goodness of these two states of affairs is to compare the sum of the two people's well-being. That is, we compare $10 + 15 = 25$ and $12 + 14 = 26$, and judge that Y is better than X. This way of comparing requires cardinal, full comparability. However, there is another way. That is, we can compare the net gain and loss. If we choose Y rather than X, person 1 will have 2 units of gain, and person 2 will have 1 unit of loss. By choosing Y, we can obtain 1 unit of net gain on balance. Thus, we only need to compare the net gain and loss for each person. Strictly speaking, we do not need to compare the level of different people's well-being, and thus do not require full comparability.

These are six formal features of utilitarianism. What does utilitarianism have to say about the distribution of people's well-being? What utilitarianism is concerned with is the total sum or average of people's well-being. Therefore, it is not concerned with how people's well-being is distributed. For example, compare X' = (1, 9) and Y' = (5, 5). Classical and average utilitarianism judge that X' is equally as good as Y' because the total sum and average of the two people's well-being is the same. However, there is a huge amount of inequality in X' whereas there is perfect equality in Y'. Utilitarianism does not take the distribution of well-being into account. This is why utilitarianism is non-egalitarian. I think this is straightforward and easy to understand.

However, there are two senses in which utilitarianism can be seen as egalitarian, First, utilitarianism is said to be egalitarian in the sense that it gives equal respect and weight to each person's well-being. One of the slogans of utilitarianism, known as Bentham's dictum, is "everybody to count for one, nobody for more than one." It is true that there is some notion of equality in utilitarianism. But if this interpretation is correct, nearly every ethical theory is egalitarian in one way or another. Amartya Sen takes this interpretation and asserts that, "every normative theory of social arrangement that has at all stood the test of time seems to demand equality of something – something that is regarded as particularly important in that theory" (Sen 1995: 12–13). According to Sen, even the side-constraint theory of Nozick (1974) is egalitarian because it demands equality of libertarian rights. I shall not dispute the truth of Sen's interpretation of egalitarianism. I will simply assume that we are interested in a more substantive interpretation of egalitarianism and that in this sense utilitarianism is not egalitarian, as it is not concerned with the distribution of well-being.

The second sense is more substantive. Utilitarianism can be considered to be egalitarian in the sense that in practice it demands the transfer of resources from the better off to the worse off up to the point where everyone's rate of marginal pleasure becomes the same. The idea behind this claim is *diminishing marginal utility*. Diminishing marginal utility implies that, for each unit of resources consumed, utility increases at a decreasing rate. For each person, the first unit of resources provides the greatest utility gain, the second unit the second greatest gain, and so on. An extra unit of resources never decreases the absolute level of utility, but it adds a strictly smaller utility. The notion of utility is usually understood as some mental state such as pleasure, happiness, or preference-satisfaction. For example, I derive an awful lot of pleasure from having a first sports car, but less pleasure from a second sports car, even less from a third sports car, and so on. My absolute level of pleasure never decreases but the marginal pleasure diminishes, as I possess additional cars. This is the basic idea of diminishing marginal utility. It is assumed that everyone's utility diminishes in the same way (i.e. the utility function is the same for all individuals).

On the basis of diminishing marginal utility, utilitarianism can make an egalitarian claim in a practical context. We all know that a large number of people in developing countries suffer from a lack of sufficient nutrition, clean water, basic health care, basic education, and so on. Their suffering is severe. On the other hand, people in developed countries enjoy a high level of wealth that is more than enough to maintain a pleasant level of life. Even if $1,000 were taken away from my bank account, my life would not see enormous suffering. But $1,000 could save at least several people from acute suffering and preventable premature death. If we transfer resources from people in developed countries to people in developing countries, especially the poorest countries, we can reduce the suffering of a large number of people at relatively small cost to people in wealthy countries. The reduction of suffering in developing countries would easily offset the reduced level of pleasure for a relatively smaller number of people in developed countries, and thus result in a large net gain of pleasure (or net loss of suffering) in the world. Thus, some advocates of utilitarianism, most famously Peter Singer (1972), contend that, on the basis of diminishing marginal utility, it is right to transfer resources from developed countries to poorer countries because such a transfer increases the total pleasure.

It is true that utilitarianism exhibits an egalitarian upshot in this context. However, utilitarianism does not aim at equality of pleasure as such. In principle, its primary goal is to maximize the total sum or average of people's pleasure. A more equal global distribution of resources happens to increase the total sum or average of pleasure. In other contexts, utilitarianism can be radically anti-egalitarian precisely because diminishing marginal utility is a commonsensical condition of mental states. Consider a situation where almost all people in the world are above the level of suffering and people in developed countries can derive an enormous amount of pleasure from consuming luxury commodities and services. In this situation, there is no reason for utilitarianism to transfer resources from richer countries to relatively poor counties. For utilitarianism, an equalizing transfer of resources would merely be a by-product of pursuing the greatest pleasure for the greatest number, not a goal, ideal, or requirement.

1.2 Rawls's difference principle

In his vastly influential book, *A Theory of Justice*, Rawls proposes a systematic theory that is an alternative to two other types of moral and political theory. One is, needless to say, utilitarianism. The other is intuitionism. By intuitionism, Rawls means theories that (1) consist of multiple basic principles, which may conflict with each other in particular cases, and (2) include no priority rules for weighing these principles against one another. Rawls's project is to put forward a comprehensive non-utilitarian theory without falling into intuitionism. I shall not even attempt to summarize his enormous project here. Rather, I shall focus on the distributive principle in his comprehensive theory of justice.

Rawls takes a society to be a cooperative venture among free and autonomous individuals. Individuals form a cooperative venture because it is mutually beneficial. Every individual should benefit from the cooperative venture. There might be losers and winners. But even the losers should benefit. That is what fair cooperation would require. If everyone, including every loser, could not expect net benefit from the cooperative venture, there would be no incentive to stay in the venture and abide by the basic rules of society. Thus, fairness in cooperation characterizes the basic structure of society. By the "basic structure," Rawls means the major social, economic, and political institutions that distribute fundamental rights and duties and determine the division of advantages from the cooperative venture.

What would the principles that apply to the basic structure look like? Rawls derives such principles from the hypothetical choice of rational individuals in the original position. According to Rawls, some features of actual individuals are morally irrelevant when we choose the basic structure of society. These features are individuals' position in society (wealth, race, class, gender, etc.), natural endowments (intelligence, creativity, physical ability, etc.), conception *duties?*

of the good life (religious beliefs, political ideals), and generation. Imagine that individuals are placed behind a veil of ignorance, which deprives them of information about these morally irrelevant features. This hypothetical situation is called the *original position*. According to Rawls, rational individuals in the original position would unanimously choose the following principles:

> *First principle*: Each person is to have an equal right to the most extensive total system of equal basic liberties compatible with a similar system of liberty for all.
> *Second principle*: Social and economic inequalities are to be arranged so that they are both (a) to the greatest benefit of the least advantaged [*the difference principle*] and (b) attached to offices and positions open to all under conditions of fair equality of opportunity [*fair equality of opportunity*].

There is a *lexical priority* among these principles. The first principle is given priority over the second. The second principle kicks in only when the first makes no difference. Within the second principle, fair equality of opportunity is given priority over the difference principle. The difference principle kicks in only when fair equality of opportunity makes no difference. That is, the difference principle comes into play only when the demands of the first principle and fair equality of opportunity are met.

Often, it is believed that the difference principle is the main distributive principle in Rawls's theory of justice. According to this belief, the first principle and fair equality of opportunity are the constraints on, and pre-requisites for, the promotion of goods, whereas the difference principle attempts to promote the goods of individuals in the worst off group. That is, the first principle and fair equality of opportunity must be satisfied before we attempt to implement the difference principle. It is highly debatable whether this widely held belief is correct. Some people claim that the first and second principles jointly constitute a distributive principle (e.g. Norman Daniels 2003, as we see in section 7.1). However, in what follows, we shall concentrate on the difference principle and set aside its relation to the first principle and fair equality of opportunity.

The difference principle contends that social and economic inequalities are justified only when, and only because, they maximize the expectation of a representative individual in the worst off group in society. Otherwise, social and economic inequalities are not justified. Rawls's default position is to maintain equality of socioeconomic conditions. The difference principle identifies under what conditions socioeconomic inequalities can be fair. This means that Rawls permits inequalities insofar as a certain condition holds. The condition is that inequalities maximize the expectation of a representative individual in the worst off social group. How do we identify the worst off group? According to Rawls, the worst off group is identified by comparing the level of social primary goods. Social primary goods are defined as the list of objectively identifiable goods that every individual would rationally want to have, e.g. wealth, income, liberty, and the social bases of self-respect (as opposed to mental states such as pleasure, happiness, or preference-satisfaction).

Rawls explains the structure of the difference principle by referring to the maximin rule. Let me start by explaining the general form of the maximin rule. The maximin rule is intended to rank states of affairs by the minimum level of good. Here is its formal definition. The maximin rule holds that a state of affairs $X = (w_1, w_2, \ldots , w_n)$ is at least as good as another $Y = (w'_1, w'_2, \ldots , w'_n)$ if and only if $\min(w_1, w_2, \ldots , w_n) \geq \min(w'_1, w'_2, \ldots , w'_n)$, where w_i refers to the good of person i. Note that the maximin rule is about the relative goodness of states of affairs, whereas Rawls's original presentation of the difference principle is not about the relative goodness of states of affairs but rather about the justifiability of social and economic inequalities. That is, the maximin rule is an axiological principle whereas Rawls's original presentation of the difference principle is not. Rawls's difference principle merely identifies under what circumstances social and economic inequalities are permitted. According to the difference principle, if social and economic inequalities do not benefit the worst off group, then these inequalities are not permitted. Thus, the difference principle only distinguishes justifiable and unjustifiable forms of social and economic inequalities, and does not rank states of affairs. The difference principle is nonetheless extensionally equivalent to the maximin rule.

Having emphasized the distinction between the difference principle and the maximin rule, let me focus on five formal features of the maximin rule. First, the maximin rule is a maximizing principle. It ranks states of affairs consistently, and identifies the best state of affairs as the one where the level of the worst off is maximized. Second, the maximin rule is impartial in the same sense as utilitarianism. For example, (10, 5) and (5, 10) are judged to be equally good. Third, unlike utilitarianism, the maximin rule violates strong separability. Look at table 1.1 in section 1.1 again. The maximin rule gives the result that A is strictly better than B, but that C is equally as good as D. This means that the maximin rule violates strong separability. Fourth, the maximin rule does not require unit comparability but only level comparability. The gains and losses for the non-worst off people do not affect our distributive judgment insofar as none of them becomes the worst off. The only information the maximin rule requires is the relative level of the worst off. Fifth, the maximin rule violates the Pareto principle, as the state of the non-worst off groups does not affect our distributive judgment. For example, in the two-group case, the maximin rule judges that (10, 5) and (100, 5) are equally as good because the level of the worst off is the same, whereas the Pareto principle judges that (100, 5) is strictly better than (10, 5).

The last feature leads Rawls to allow a modification to the difference principle. Some people might think it implausible to judge (10, 5) and (100, 5) to be equally good. Rawls then permits the lexicographic extension of the maximin rule or leximin for short (Rawls 1971: 83). Leximin first maximizes the level of the worst off; second, if the level of the worst off is equal across distributions, it maximizes the level of the second worst off, and so on until the last case – that is, if the levels of all the preceding worse off groups are equal across distributions, it maximizes the level of the best off. More precisely, a state of affairs $X = (w_1, w_2, \ldots, w_n)$ is strictly better than another $Y = (w'_1, w'_2, \ldots, w'_n)$ if there exists a position k in $N = \{1, 2, 3, \ldots, n\}$ such that (1) the level of k is strictly higher in X than Y and (2) the level of every position $j < k$ is the same in X as in Y. Otherwise, X and Y are equally good. Leximin satisfies the Pareto principle.[1] To see this, notice that leximin judges that (100, 5) is strictly better than (10, 5).

Regardless of whether the structure of the difference principle is understood in terms of the maximin rule or leximin, the difference principle has two important implications. First, any gain for the worst off group, no matter how small, always outweighs any loss for non-worst off groups, no matter how large. Compare $X = (10, 50, 50, 50, 50)$ and $Y = (11, 20, 20, 20, 20)$. Both the maximin rule and leximin judge that Y is strictly better than X. By choosing Y, the worst off group will see a small improvement, but the other groups must accept an enormous loss. Thus, for the sake of improving the state of the worst off group, both the maximin rule and leximin justify any amount of loss to non-worst off groups. Intuitively, this first implication may be seen as a sign of strong commitment to equality. However, a second implication goes against this intuition. The second implication is that both rules allow greater inequality insofar as the level of the worst off group is improved. Compare $X' = (10, 50, 50, 50, 50)$ and $Y' = (11, 90, 90, 90, 90)$. Both the maximin rule and leximin judge that Y' is strictly better than X', although Y' contains greater inequality. The second implication appears to be radically anti-egalitarian. This is very surprising. Although the difference principle can demand large aggregate losses for non-worst off groups for the sake of the worst off group, it can also tolerate increased inequality.

Rawls offers an argument for the second implication (Rawls 1971: 151). His argument is known as the *Pareto argument*, or the *incentive argument*, for inequality. According to Rawls, allowing qualified inequality gives incentives to everyone to make a greater effort and develop their talents. As a consequence, the size of the pie that can be distributed becomes bigger and the worst off group ends up at the same level or higher than they would otherwise. Rawls contends that it would be irrational to insist upon maintaining complete equality if everyone could end up better off by abandoning it.[2] This is why Rawls's difference principle can tolerate increased inequalities insofar as they maximize the expectation of the representative individual in the worst off group in society.

Rawls himself admits that the maximin rule is unusual (Rawls 1971: 154). He thinks that it is rational to choose only when certain conditions are met. The first condition is that there is no secure basis for assessing the likelihoods of different outcomes. The second is that the chooser has a conception of the good such that he cares very little for what he might gain above a satisfactory minimum. The third is that the other alternatives have possible outcomes that the chooser can hardly accept. According to Rawls, his idea of the original position meets these conditions and therefore it is rational for the parties to choose the maximin rule. Notice that the maximin rule is not equivalent to the difference principle. The maximin rule is a principle in decision theory whereas the difference principle is a rule that governs the basic structure of society. Rawls's argument for the maximin rule is a decision-theoretic explanation for adopting the difference principle. Therefore, it is not correct to refer to these two rules interchangeably.

1.3 Criticisms of the difference principle

There are an enormous number of criticisms leveled against Rawls's difference principle. In this section, I will concentrate on only two types. The first type comes from defenders of utilitarianism, who do not care about the equal distribution of well-being. Call these the *non-egalitarian criticisms*. Since Rawls's principles of justice are meant to be a superior alternative to utilitarianism, it is not surprising that proponents of utilitarianism fight back. The other type of criticism comes, a little surprisingly, from those who do care for equality. Call these the egalitarian criticisms. Rawls's difference principle is motivated by the egalitarian concern. Equal distribution is the default position. If inequalities between groups can ever be permitted, this is only in exceptional cases where the worst off group benefits from inequalities. For the sake of improving the condition of the worst off group, any loss for the non-worst off groups is justified. This seemingly strongly egalitarian claim, however, draws criticism from those who are concerned with equality. Let me start with the non-egalitarian criticisms.

Rawls maintains that his principles of justice are superior to utilitarianism. He claims that the two principles of justice include various advantages. First, the parties have psychological stability because they are able to protect their basic liberties and insure themselves against the worst possible outcomes. Second, the two principles encourage the self-respect of citizens. Finally, under Rawls's principles, the parties can rely on one another to adhere to the principles adopted (the strains of commitment). These advantages all contribute to guaranteeing the members of a society a satisfactory minimum, and consequently, they contribute to the greater stability of the basic social structure.

Defenders of utilitarianism disagree. I shall briefly refer to three specific criticisms although there are also many others. Before we look into these criticisms, it is necessary to understand one of the most sophisticated arguments for average utilitarianism, one which Rawls takes seriously. This is John Harsanyi's (1953, 1955, 1977). His argument appeals to rational choice in a hypothetical situation similar to, but distinct from, Rawls's original position. Harsanyi attempts to establish average utilitarianism through two theorems: the representation theorem and the impartial spectator theorem.

The representation theorem holds that if individual and social preferences satisfy the axioms of expected utility theory and the social welfare function satisfies the Pareto principle, then social utility must be represented by a weighted sum (more precisely, an affine transformation) of individual utilities. It is important to emphasize that this theorem merely establishes the additivity of individual utility, and that the weight of a person's individual utility can be different from the weight of another's at this stage. In order to establish average utilitarianism, it must be shown that the weight of individual utilities is the same $1/n$ for every one of n people. It is in the impartial spectator theorem where he does just that and appeals to rational choice in a hypothetical situation comparable to Rawls's original position. In Harsanyi's case, what individuals are deprived of is information regarding their actual position in society. Individuals are not deprived of information concerning their concept of the good or attitudes toward risk. Thus, Harsanyi's veil is thinner than Rawls's. According to the impartial spectator theorem, if individuals were placed behind the veil of ignorance and they did not know their actual position in society, then they would rationally believe that each of them has an equal chance of being in any of these positions. If society contains n people, individuals behind the veil would rationally believe that the probability of occupying any given individual's position is 1/n. From this, the weight of each individual's utility in the representation theorem must be 1/n in the n-person society. Thus, the two theorems jointly establish average utilitarianism, or so he says. This is a powerful result (see Weymark 1991).

I shall now discuss three types of non-egalitarian criticisms. The first concerns Rawls's epistemological assumptions about the parties in the original position. Critics point out that the informational constraints in the Rawlsian framework are unnecessarily restrictive. It would suffice to deprive individuals of their knowledge of their actual position in society in order to secure their impartial judgment. There is no compelling reason to impose stronger informational restrictions. According to critics, Rawls imposes strong restrictions for the sake of deriving the principles he favors. Even if Rawls's assumptions were reasonable, the situation would not be risky enough for the parties to avoid average utilitarianism and opt for the difference principle.

The second type of non-egalitarian criticism concerns the parties' attitudes toward risk. As Rawls himself admits, the decision-theoretic basis for the difference principle, i.e. the maximin rule, is rational only under certain extreme conditions. In the original position, the parties are supposed to be deprived of their special attitudes toward risk. This seems to imply that the parties are not risk-averse or risk-loving. But Rawls claims that they would support the difference principle, which is generally regarded as extremely risk-averse. Thus, there is a tension between Rawls's assumptions and the standard explanation for choosing the difference principle.

The third type of non-egalitarian criticism is that the parties would care for gains above the level of a satisfactory minimum. According to Rawls, the two principles of justice guarantee a satisfactory minimum to everyone and consequently secure the stability of basic institutions. Proponents of utilitarianism, however, point out that individuals would care for gains *does not come from within*

above the satisfactory minimum. The difference principle, as I discussed earlier, allows any loss for individuals in the non-worst off groups, no matter how large, for the sake of a gain for the worst off group, no matter how small. Insofar as the distribution of primary goods is concerned, the difference principle does not take the non-worst off seriously. This implication instantiates a strong commitment to achieving a satisfactory minimum for all. However, critics contend that individuals would care for gains above the minimum level, and that any theory of justice should take the interest of every person, including that of the non-worst off, seriously. If the non-worst off were never taken into account, the basic structure of society would never achieve stability, contrary to Rawls's claim.

All of these are examples of criticisms from the utilitarian point of view. There are many disagreements between utilitarians and Rawlsians. Yet, it is difficult to judge who is correct. Most likely, the first criticism is the weakest one. This is because the point that proponents of utilitarianism make also applies to their claim regarding the informational restriction. It is true that their informational restriction is less demanding than Rawls's. However, the fact that their restriction is less demanding does not make their argument more plausible. Defenders of utilitarianism must provide a reason why their informational restriction is appropriate, independently of the level of demandingness. The second and third criticisms remain as serious threats to Rawls's argument.

I shall move on to the egalitarian criticisms. I shall only discuss two types. The first concerns the fact that the difference principle permits greater inequalities among social groups insofar as the expectation of a representative individual in the least advantaged group in society is improved. The difference principle is motivated by concern for equality. Society is a cooperative venture for mutual benefit. Even the worst off should benefit from this cooperative venture. And the basic structure of society should be organized so as to benefit every group, including the worst off group. However, the difference principle does not aim at equality as such. As we saw earlier, Rawls appeals to the incentive argument for the permissibility of inequalities. G. A. Cohen (1992, 1995) criticizes Rawls's incentive argument in the following way. Cohen claims that if individuals are motivated by a sense of justice, and if Rawls's distributive principle is motivated by a concern for equality, there is no compelling reason to depart from perfect equality. That is, Rawls's difference principle is motivated by concern for socio-economic equality, but the incentive argument goes against the motivation of the difference principle. Rawls may have thought that inequality-generating incentives are necessary (or at least permissible) to make the size of the pie to be distributed bigger, and thus to benefit the worst off. Cohen, however, points out that such incentives and resulting inequalities are superfluous in an ideally just society whose members conform to the demands of justice.

The second type of egalitarian criticism concerns the fact that Rawls confines the scope of his principles to the basic structure of society and consequently applies the difference principle to representative individuals of groups. The difference principle compares the level of social primary goods that a representative individual of each group possesses. It is not concerned with the distribution of primary goods within each group. There might be a large inequality within each group, and some individuals in the worst off group might be better off than some of those in a better off group. By applying the difference principle to groups, however, Rawls does not take inequalities within each group into account. This is a direct consequence of Rawls's interest. He is interested in the basic structure of society, not in particular judgments in specific situations. Therefore, this criticism is not about the difference principle as such, but its scope.

These two types of criticism are motivated by a concern for equality that is stronger than Rawls's. To be fair to Rawls, his theory of justice consists of two principles, and the difference principle is just one part of his theory. As such, it is not fair to criticize the difference principle in isolation. Nonetheless, these two criticisms make perfect sense. In fact, these two criticisms motivate a different type of egalitarian theory, luck egalitarianism, which we will examine in the next chapter.

I have considered two types of criticism leveled against Rawls's difference principle, coming from different sides. One side is utilitarianism, which is not concerned with equality. The other is egalitarianism, which is obviously concerned with equality. In the next section, we will consider two broadly defined contractualist principles that are strongly influenced by Rawls.

1.4 Post-Rawlsian contractualist theories: Nagel and Scanlon

In this section, I will examine two non-utilitarian theories that grew out of Rawls's theory of justice in general and his difference principle in particular.

The first is Thomas Nagel's unanimity (Nagel 1979, 1991). The second is T. M. Scanlon's contractualism (Scanlon 1982, 1998). Although these two philosophers are strongly influenced by Rawls's theory of justice, they share the same worry about Rawls's general method of justification for the principles of justice. Let me start with their shared worry, and then consider their theories.

Rawls's method of justification includes two stages. First, in order to think of a principle as a candidate for unanimous agreement, I must think of it not merely as acceptable to me but as acceptable to others as well. Second, my judgment that the principle is acceptable must be impartial. In other words, the first stage requires acceptability from each person's perspective, and the second stage requires impartial judgment in order to secure acceptability from each person's perspective. According to Rawls, to judge impartially that a principle is acceptable is to judge that it is one that I would have reason to accept, no matter who I turned out to be. Thus, the justification of principles is made from the point of view of a single rational individual in the hypothetical situation. Nagel and Scanlon agree with the first stage, but not the second. They think that each person's impartial judgment about a principle is quite different from the acceptability of the principle from each person's perspective. The impartially chosen principle may lead us to an unacceptable situation. To see this point, consider the choice situation in table 1.2, which contains two individuals.[3]

Each prospect contains two equally probable outcomes: heads and tails. There are two positions that two individuals could occupy: A and B. Suppose that two individuals are placed behind a veil of ignorance and deprived of information concerning their actual position. That is, neither individual knows if he or she will occupy A's or B's position. They compare two prospects from the impartial point of view. From such an impartial perspective, each individual would judge that prospect X is just as good as prospect Y. Why? Because the chance of getting 1 unit of benefit is the

Table 1.2

	A	B		A	B
Heads	1	0	Heads	1	0
Tails	0	1	Tails	1	0
Prospect X			Prospect Y		

same in X and Y. More precisely, given that the two outcomes are equally probable and that each individual has an equal chance of occupying one of the two positions, the expected good of prospect X is the same as the expected good of prospect Y from each person's perspective.

However, prospect X seems better than prospect Y. Why? Because prospect Y appears to be unfair to the person who would occupy B's position. In prospect Y, the person in A's position receives 1 unit of benefit, regardless of which outcome is brought about. However, in prospect X, A and B have an equal chance of receiving 1 unit of benefit. Therefore, there is an important difference between prospects X and Y. However, Rawls's two-stage justification cannot distinguish between these two prospects. This example shows that impartial judgment does not guarantee acceptability from each person's perspective.

Nagel does not claim that the impartially chosen principle is always acceptable from each person's perspective. He proposes the principle of unanimity (Nagel 1979: 125). Whenever there is conflict of interests, no state of affairs is completely acceptable to everyone. Nagel's unanimity attempts to identify the state that is "least unacceptable to the person to whom it is most unacceptable." How do we find the outcome that is least unacceptable from each person's point of view? We find it through a series of pairwise comparisons. Take a pair of individuals who will be affected by our distributive judgment. Compare the possible gains and losses of these two individuals. The state where the maximum loss for each person is minimized is the less unacceptable one. Perform the same comparison for every pair of individuals affected. By doing so, we can identify the least unacceptable state, considered from each person's point of view separately. For example, consider two states of affairs, X and Y, which show the well-being level of 5 individuals:

$$X = (2, 9, 9, 9, 9)$$
$$Y = (8, 7, 7, 7, 7).$$

First, compare persons 1 and 2. If X is chosen, there will be 6 units of loss for person 1, and 2 units of gain for person 2. According to Nagel's pairwise comparison, the degree of unacceptability from the perspective of person 1 is greater than the degree of unacceptability from the perspective of person 2, simply because the possible loss for person 1 is greater than that for person 2. From the perspective of person 1, Y is less unacceptable. Therefore, Y is the state that is less unacceptable from the perspectives of persons 1 and 2 separately. The same reasoning and judgment applies to the pairwise comparisons between person 1 and each one of persons 3, 4, and 5. Thus, Y remains less unacceptable than X. Nagel's unanimity then concludes that Y is less unacceptable than X.

There is a simpler way to explain and utilize Nagel's unanimity. That is to appeal to the minimax rule in decision theory. The minimax rule tells us to minimize the maximum loss for each person. If X is chosen, the maximum loss for one person is 6 units. If Y is chosen, the maximum loss for one person is 2 units. Thus, if we choose Y, the maximum loss is minimized. For this reason, the minimax rule tells us to bring about Y rather than X. Nagel's unanimity is extensionally equivalent to the minimax rule.

Nagel emphasizes a radical feature in his proposal. His distributive unanimity results in "giving absolute priority to the worst off, regardless of numbers" (Nagel 1979: 123). There are two closely related points here. The first point is that his proposed principle gives absolute priority to benefiting the worst off. This sounds like what Rawls's difference principle contends. But there are three important differences: (a) Nagel's proposal applies to specific cases of distributive judgments, whereas Rawls's difference principle applies to the basic structure of society; (b) Nagel's proposal applies to states of individuals, whereas the difference principle applies to the representative individuals of different groups in society; and (c) Nagel takes the worst off to be the individual who has the greatest potential loss, whereas Rawls takes it to be the group that would have the lowest level of social primary goods.

The second point, which is closely related to the first, is that the loss for the non-worst off individuals does not affect our distributive judgment, no matter how large it is. Compare X and Y again. Nagel's proposal tells us to choose Y, no matter how large the aggregate loss for the other individuals, or no matter how many individuals would have 2 units of loss. It is non-aggregative, just like Rawls's difference principle. Obviously, the total and average well-being is maximized if we bring about X. But neither Nagel's unanimity nor Rawls's difference principle aims to maximize the total or average level of well-being. This non-aggregative feature may appear counterintuitive to many people. However, many contemporary ethicists who attempt to propose an alternative to utilitarianism tend to single out interpersonal aggregation of gains and losses as a source of criticism. For them, interpersonal aggregation opens up the door to utilitarianism, and therefore should be carefully avoided.[4]

Even if we set aside this arguably counterintuitive feature, Nagel's unanimity encounters a consistency problem. Compare three states of affairs, which show the well-being level of three individuals.

$$X = (5, 8, 10)$$
$$Y = (8, 10, 5)$$
$$Z = (10, 5, 8).$$

How would Nagel's unanimity make a judgment? There are two interpretations. The first is that we conduct the pairwise comparisons of states of affairs. First, compare X and Y. According to Nagel's unanimity, X is less unacceptable than Y because X minimizes the maximum potential loss for each person (in this comparison, the loss for person 3). Second, compare Y and Z. According to Nagel's unanimity, Y is less unacceptable than Z. Third, compare X and Z. Nagel's unanimity judges that Z is less unacceptable than X. Consequently, Nagel's unanimity makes a cyclical judgment: X is less unacceptable than Y, Y is less unacceptable than Z; but Z is less unacceptable than X. This is a violation of transitivity, and transitivity is thought to be one of the most basic consistency conditions.

The second interpretation is that we compare the three states of affairs simultaneously. According to Nagel's unanimity, all three states are equally unacceptable because, whichever state is brought about, there is a person who would have 5 units of loss. This means that the three outcomes are indifferent. From this judgment, we can infer a judgment that each outcome is equally as unacceptable as every other outcome. For example, X is equally as unacceptable as Y. And yet, if we apply Nagel's unanimity to the comparison between X and Y, as we saw above, X is less unacceptable than Y. Thus, the principle of unanimity gives us an inconsistent judgment. Either way, Nagel's unanimity encounters the problem of inconsistency.

The source of this inconsistency problem is obvious: the violation of impartiality, which I presented in section 1.1. Utilitarianism and Rawls's difference principle satisfy impartiality, and therefore judge that the three outcomes are equally good. These principles do not encounter the inconsistency problem currently under consideration. However, Nagel's unanimity does not satisfy the condition that I call impartiality (of course, Nagel might claim that his principle satisfies a different condition that he calls impartiality), and this is why it encounters the inconsistency problem.

T. M. Scanlon offers a different basis for making distributive judgments (Scanlon 1982, 1998). His theoretical framework is contractualism. Scanlon's contractualism is quite different from Rawls's contractarianism. Scanlon is concerned with the rightness or wrongness of actions, rather than justice in the basic social structure. He attempts to ground the judgment about the rightness or wrongness of a given action on that act's being justifiable to some particular individual. According to Scanlon's diagnosis, Rawls's theory also grounds the justice of the basic social structure on its justifiability to each person. However, within Rawls's contractarian framework, the basic social structure which is justifiable to all individuals must be the one that self-interested individuals would rationally choose in the original position, where the veil of ignorance deprives them of information about their actual position in society and allows them to make impartial judgments. Scanlon disagrees with Rawls in this respect. Scanlon believes that justifiability is not derived from rational choice behind the veil of ignorance. Rather, Scanlon claims that the justifiability of an ethical principle depends only on various individuals' reasons for objecting to that principle and the alternatives to it.

Scanlon then proposes his version of contractualism. It holds that an act is wrong when and because it is disallowed by principles that nobody could reasonably reject from their individual standpoint. According to Scanlon's contractualism, if there is one person who has reasonable grounds for rejecting a principle, this principle cannot serve as the basis for our ethical judgment, even if it benefits many other people. Whether or not a principle should be rejected does not depend on the total sum or average of people's well-being, or on the number of people who benefit from adopting this principle. It all depends on the reasons a particular person has to oppose that principle in a particular context. This is the basic idea of Scanlon's contractualism.

Scanlon explains how his contractualism operates in the context of distributive judgment (Scanlon 1982: 122–23). He invites us to consider two outcomes: A and E. In A, there is a large inequality. In E, the inequality is much smaller and no one is nearly as bad off as the level of the worst off in A. According to Scanlon, prima facie, the worst off in A has a reasonable ground for objecting to A. However, his objection may be rebutted if an individual in E incurs a large sacrifice for the benefit of some other individual and/or if the absolute level of the worst off in A is pretty high. It seems likely that other considerations can weaken or strengthen the reason to object to A or E that each person has. Thus, Scanlon's contractualism appears far too complicated if it is applied to distributive judgments.

Here is one simplified version of Scanlon's idea about distributive justice. In practice, it is a modified version of Nagel's unanimity. Nagel's unanimity compares the potential loss for each individual with the potential loss for every other individual. Scanlon seems to agree with this. Scanlon, however, wants to consider the absolute level of each person, too. There is a practical way to combine concern for the size of their loss with concern for the

Table 1.3

	1	2	3	4
A	10	5	5	5
B	7	6	6	6
C	10	1	1	1
D	7	2	2	2

absolute level of their state. It is to divide the size of their loss by the absolute level of their state. To understand this method, consider the two binary comparisons in table 1.3: A and B; and C and D. The columns show the state of four individuals.

Utilitarianism judges that A is equally as good as B, and that C is equally as good as D. Nagel's unanimity gives the result that A is less unacceptable than B (hence we should choose A), and that C is less unacceptable than D (hence we should choose C). In contrast, my proposed simplified version of Scanlon's contractualist distributive judgment claims that A is less objectionable than B (hence we should choose A), and that D is less objectionable than C (hence we should choose D). Why?

First, consider the comparison between A and B. On the one hand, the potential loss for person 1 is 3 units, and the level of his or her lower state is 7. The simplified version of Scanlon's contractualism divides 3 units by 7, which yields $^3/_7$. On the other hand, the potential loss for person 2 (and persons 3 and 4) is 1 unit, and the level of his or her lower state is 5. The simplified interpretation divides 1 unit by 5, which yields $^1/_5$. Thus, the grounds for person 1's objection to B are strictly stronger than those for person 2's objection to A (and person 3's and person 4's). Next, repeat the same process of calculation for the comparison between C and D. The strength of person 1's objection to D is $^3/_7$. The strength of person 2's objection to C is $^1/_1$. Thus, the grounds for person 2's objection to C are strictly stronger than those for person 1's objection to D. It is not my intention to insist that this process best represents Scanlon's contractualist distributive judgment. But it helps to understand what his rich and complicated contractualism has to say about distributive judgment.

Just like Nagel's unanimity, Scanlon's contractualism is non-aggregative, or so he says (Scanlon 1982: 123). If one person has reasonable grounds for rejecting a principle, this principle cannot serve as the basis for our ethical judgment even if many other people would benefit from adopting the same principle. This means that the force of a single person's reason to object to a principle cannot be trumped by the claims of other people, no matter how large the number of other people is. This non-aggregative feature marks a clear departure from utilitarianism. Both Nagel and Scanlon emphasize this feature in order to contrast their theory with utilitarianism.

However, this poses a theoretical problem for Nagel and Scanlon. The problem has become known as the *number problem*. The number problem is this. Imagine that you find yourself in a position to choose either saving the lives of five strangers or saving one different stranger. For some reason, you cannot save all six lives. For the sake of argument, assume that there are no morally relevant differences among the six strangers: none of them is a criminal, the president, your spouse, your child, or your friend. John Taurek, who rejects the aggregation of gains and losses for different individuals, claims that it is right to flip a fair coin between the two groups and give an equal chance (i.e. 50 percent) of being saved to each stranger (Taurek 1977). Many people, including Scanlon himself, find Taurek's claim to be counter-intuitive. Intuitively, it is right to save the lives of the five strangers outright. It seems that if you reject aggregation, you must agree with Taurek's counter-intuitive claim. How can we make the case for saving the larger number of strangers with no appeal to aggregation? Utilitarianism and other forms of aggregative consequentialism can answer this question easily: the good of saving the five is strictly better than the good of saving the one, and therefore, it is right to save the five. However, critics of aggregation such as Nagel and Scanlon cannot appeal to this sort of aggregative reasoning.

What would Nagel's unanimity say? If you rescue the one stranger, the five strangers will die. If you rescue the five strangers, the one stranger will die. The loss for each person is the same. Therefore, saving the one is equally as unacceptable as saving the five. Nagel's principle of unanimity does not support either alternative over the other. It would not be opposed to Taurek's coin-flipping. If this is true, then Nagel's principle is counterintuitive.

Scanlon (1998: 232–41) attempts to offer a contractualist argument for saving the five with no appeal to aggregation. His argument is this. First, imagine that the choice is between saving one life and saving another life. In this case, the coin-flip is the principle that nobody could reasonably reject. Now imagine that four strangers are added to one side, and it becomes a choice between saving one life and saving five lives. If you still flip a fair coin, you would give no positive recognition to the presence of four additional strangers. This would be reasonably objected to by each of the four additional strangers. By choosing to save the five strangers, we recognize the presence of four additional strangers. Thus, saving the greater number is a principle that nobody could reasonably reject from an individual standpoint.

On the face of it, Scanlon's argument sounds pretty good. It does not add up different people's gains, and thus is non-aggregative. It only appeals to the positive and equal moral weight of each stranger's life. However, two objections can be raised. First, Michael Otsuka (2000) points out that Scanlon's argument is actually aggregative, or at least compares the gains for groups of individuals. In Scanlon's argument, the presence of four additional strangers in combination with the one stranger is what tips the scales in favor of saving the lives of the five strangers. That is, Scanlon's argument compares a group of five against the one. Thus, Otsuka concludes that Scanlon appeals to a sort of group aggregation.

Second, for the sake of argument, let us agree with the reasoning behind Scanlon's argument. Suppose that the choice is between saving the lives of five strangers and the lives of two strangers. If the choice were between saving the lives of five and the life of one, according to Scanlon's argument, it would have to be the case that we save the five. Now imagine that one different stranger is added to the side of the one. If we still choose to save the five lives, the presence of one additional stranger does not make any difference to what we should do. Therefore, the additional stranger does not receive any positive recognition, and could reasonably reject the principle of saving the greater number. Thus, Scanlon's argument does not establish the case for saving the greater number.

The number problem poses a serious theoretical challenge to modern contractualist theories of distributive judgment. Scanlon's contractualism attempts to express the egalitarian concern by giving absolute priority to benefiting the worst off, no matter how we define the worst off, and ruling out interpersonal aggregation. This is because he wants to contrast his proposed contractualism with utilitarianism. Utilitarianism is not concerned with equality of well-being. It aggregates the gains and losses of different people. Scanlon takes these two features to be essential to utilitarianism. In order to distinguish his alternative, he rejects these two features and puts forward a theory that gives absolute priority to the worst off and disallows aggregation. However, the price of doing so is to produce counterintuitive results in response to the number problem.

Chapter summary

Utilitarianism is not concerned with the distribution of different people's well-being. Rawls points out that the utilitarian theory of distributive justice does not guarantee a satisfactory minimum to the members of society and therefore the basic social structure based on it is unfair and unstable. Rawls then defends the difference principle, which holds that socioeconomic inequalities are justified only when, and only because, they benefit a representative person in the worst off group in society. The axiological structure of the difference principle is analyzed in terms of the maximin rule and leximin. However, the difference principle is criticized by both utilitarians and egalitarians. Nagel and Scanlon put forward their distributive principles, which are Rawlsian in spirit. However, both encounter serious theoretical challenges such as the number problem.

Further reading

The theoretical structure of utilitarianism is nicely summarized in Sen (1979) and the introduction to Sen and Williams (1982). Harsanyi's case for utilitarianism has far-reaching scope. For recent Harsanyi-like results, see Broome (1991) and Gibbard (2008). For the contrast between utilitarianism and Rawls's contractarianism, see Scheffler (2003a). To understand the far-reaching scope of the difference principle, one cannot afford to avoid reading Rawls (1971). B. Barry (1973), van Parijs (2003), and Strasnick (1976) offer detailed analyses of the difference principle. For criticisms of Rawls's derivation of the difference principle, see Arrow (1973), Hare (1973), and Harsanyi (1975). Cohen's criticism of Rawls's incentive argument for inequality has created a large literature on the aim and scope of Rawls's difference principle, which includes J. Cohen (2001), Estlund (1998), Pogge (2000), Scheffler (2006), and Andrew Williams (1998). As we saw in section 1.4, Nagel (1979, 1991) and Scanlon (1982, 1998) are good examples of recent Rawlsian theories. Brink (1993) and Hirose (2014) offer an account of how contractualism operates in the area of distributive justice. If you are not afraid of math, d'Aspremont and Gevers (1977), Gevers (1979), Maskin (1978), K. W. S. Roberts (1980), and Sen (1970) offer clear accounts of the theoretical structure of utilitarianism and the difference principle.

Notes

1 More precisely, leximin satisfies what economists call the *Hammond equity*. See Hammond (1976). There is an extra bonus. Leximin also satisfies strong separability, which the maximin rule violates. Look at the two comparisons

in table 1.1 on page 18. Leximin judges that *A* is strictly better than *B*, and that *C* is strictly better than *D*.

2 On the face of it, Rawls's argument for inequality looks similar to the *trickle-down argument* that is typically endorsed by those who do not care about equality at all. However, it should be distinguished from the trickle-down argument. The trickle-down argument contends that reduced tax rates and other economic benefits to businesses and wealthy people will consequently benefit poorer members of society by improving the economy as a whole. However, there is no guarantee that the trickling-down would benefit poorer members of society.

3 The following example was used by Diamond (1967) originally as a counterexample to the impartial spectator theorem of Harsanyi (1955). But it also applies to any arguments based on rational choice behind the veil of ignorance. This counterexample raises general and fundamental issues concerning the distinction and relative plausibility of *ex ante* and *ex post* decision theories. For discussion of how Diamond's counterexample can be met, see Broome (1991), Epstein and Segal (1992) and Karni and Safra (2002).

4 Nagel thinks that the egalitarian concern should be insensitive to both the aggregate loss for a group of individuals, and also the number of individuals. This is a widely debated issue. In his later work, Nagel (1991) becomes indecisive about the relevance of the number of individuals: he thinks the numbers are a relevant consideration in some contexts. For a comprehensive discussion concerning aggregation of different people's gains and losses, see Hirose (2014).

2

LUCK EGALITARIANISM

Does inequality give rise to moral concern, no matter how it occurs? I suspect that some people are not troubled if an out-of-luck gambler ends up worse off than a non-gambler. However, they may well find it troubling if a person with severe disabilities is worse off than someone with no disability (assuming that the other relevant features of the individuals are the same). For some people, whether inequality is morally relevant depends on how it occurs. Inequality gives rise to moral concern if it reflects a difference in circumstances that is beyond the control of the worse off person. Inequality does not give rise to moral concern if it reflects the differential effects of factors within the control of the worse off people. Luck egalitarianism is a class of distributive views that take this idea seriously. For luck egalitarianism, it matters how inequalities occur. Very roughly speaking, luck egalitarianism claims that inequality is bad or unjust if it reflects differences in factors that are beyond the control or choice of the worse off. It also contends that inequality is not bad or unjust if it results from individuals' calculated choices. In the past 30 years, luck egalitarianism has become a prominent theory of distributive justice, an alternative to Rawls's theory of distributive justice. In this chapter, I shall examine this relatively new position.

The original idea of luck egalitarianism is usually attributed to Ronald Dworkin's constructive criticism of Rawls's theory of distributive justice. Dworkin agrees with many of Rawls's points but thinks that Rawls's difference principle fails to address some important points. According to Dworkin, a plausible distributive principle should both support equality and hold individuals responsible for their calculated choices. Dworkin's basic motivation is to propose a responsibility-sensitive egalitarian theory of distributive justice. Subsequently, on the basis of Dworkin's constructive criticism of Rawls, Richard Arneson and G. A. Cohen each developed what has become known as luck egalitarianism. Dworkin's motivation may strike some people as surprising. The notion of responsibility is sometimes invoked by political conservatives, who reject any form of redistribution. How and why does the notion of responsibility come into play in egalitarian theories of distributive justice?

It is a good idea, then, to start this chapter by explaining Dworkin's assessment of Rawls's difference principle and how his assessment has shaped the general notion of luck egalitarianism. Section 2.1 does just this. Section 2.2 examines the different interpretations of factors beyond people's control. Section 2.3 considers how luck egalitarians draw the line between option luck and brute luck, and how different ways to draw the line can lead luck egalitarianism to radically different formulations. Section 2.4 examines the objections leveled against luck egalitarianism.

2.1 From Rawls to luck egalitarianism

Let us go back to Rawls's argument for the two principles of justice. Some people are more talented than others. Some people are physically stronger than others. Some people are born into a rich family, others into a poor family. These circumstances are given and are beyond people's control, and they affect people's state. Rawls believes that such circumstances are morally arbitrary. He thinks that what is morally arbitrary should not affect the design of the basic structure of society. This is why Rawls came up with the idea of a veil of ignorance to neutralize morally arbitrary factors. In the original position, then, the parties do not know their talents, natural and physical endowments, social position, race, sex, and so on. In such a situation, where morally arbitrary factors are neutralized, the two principles of justice would be unanimously chosen. This is a very rough sketch of how Rawls treats morally arbitrary factors in his theory of justice.

It is not hard to agree with the idea of neutralizing morally arbitrary factors. However, some people would disagree with the way in which Rawls attempts to neutralize morally arbitrary factors. More specifically, it could

deficits
some cannot be made up

be argued that Rawls fails to neutralize them in an adequate way. There are at least two cases where Rawls's way of neutralizing the arbitrariness of natural and social endowments is unsatisfactory. First, the difference principle gives us the result that two groups of individuals with the same bundle of #1 social primary goods are equally well off, even if individuals in one group are untalented, physically handicapped, chronically ill, or have special needs. Individuals with disabilities, for example, require extra resources to obtain the same level of well-being as individuals with no disabilities. It is likely that, in reality, individuals with disabilities are worse off than individuals with no disabilities, even if they possess the same bundle of social primary goods. However, the difference principle judges that these two groups are equally well off. Thus, the difference principle fails to capture the bad effects of arbitrary natural or social endowments.

Second, the difference principle may demand implausible transfers of #2 goods even if inequalities reflect the differences in people's calculated choices. Imagine two groups of individuals with the same natural and social endowments. One group comprises a bunch of gamblers. The other comprises normal office workers, who work hard to build an independent life. Imagine that the gamblers are worse off in terms of social primary goods, compared with the office workers. The difference principle would demand a transfer of goods from the office workers to the gamblers insofar as such a transfer would improve the state of the gamblers. Yet this seems at the very least counterintuitive, and arguably unjust. The gamblers preferred and chose this risky lifestyle. Why must the office workers compensate for the bad consequences of the gamblers' risky choices? Many people would say that it is unfair to the office workers if the loss for the gamblers is compensated for from the pockets of the office workers. They would further claim that the gamblers should be held responsible for the results of their own choice, and that their plight does not give rise to any moral concern. The difference principle does not meet this sort of worry. This is because the difference principle looks at only the end-state distribution, and not at people's intentional choices that led them to the end-state distribution.

Ronald Dworkin (1981) takes these two critical points seriously. He thinks that a distributive scheme should be sensitive to people's voluntary choices about their goals, ambitions, and life projects (thus, being *ambition-sensitive*), and that inequalities resulting from people's intentional choices do not give rise to a moral concern. He also thinks that a distributive scheme should be insensitive to differences in natural and social endowments (thus, being *endowment-insensitive*), and that the disadvantages resulting from differential endowments should be compensated. Dworkin's intention is to propose a distributive principle that can both support equality and also hold individuals responsible for their choices.

According to Dworkin, the idea of an ambition-sensitive and endowment-insensitive distributive principle is best captured by what he calls *resource egalitarianism*. Resource egalitarianism contends that the negative effects of differential endowments should be compensated for by the transfer of resources, and that inequalities of resources resulting from individuals' voluntary choices do not require any transfer of resources from a better off person to a worse off person. Resource egalitarianism can both support equality of resources and hold individuals responsible for the consequences of their choices.

For example, consider the gamblers' case again. The gamblers voluntarily chose the gambler's lifestyle among others. Their choice reflects their own ambitions, preferences, and/or tastes. Resource egalitarianism contends that they should be held responsible for the bad effects of that voluntary choice. Even if unsuccessful gamblers end up worse off than successful gamblers, there is no need for neutralizing the differential effects of their bad luck through the transfer of resources. Thus, Dworkin's resource egalitarianism is ambition-sensitive. On the other hand, his resource egalitarianism demands compensation for the bad states of individuals with physical handicaps. This is because those who are handicapped did not choose to be so and hence cannot be held responsible for the bad effects of their handicap. Dworkin's resource egalitarianism is therefore endowment-insensitive. Dworkin thinks that his resource egalitarianism better captures the idea of neutralizing morally arbitrary factors than Rawls's difference principle.

Some gamblers are unlucky to end up worse off. Individuals with handicaps are also unlucky to end up worse off. Yet, there is an important difference between these two instances of being unlucky. Unsuccessful gamblers voluntarily chose a risky course of life, whereas individuals with handicaps did not. In order to contrast these two senses of being unlucky, Dworkin proposes two types of luck: option luck and brute luck.

> Option luck is a matter of how deliberate and calculated gambles turn out – whether someone gains or loses through accepting an isolated risk he or she should have anticipated and might have declined. Brute luck is a matter of how risks fall out that are not in that sense deliberate gambles. If I buy a stock on the exchange that rises, then my option luck is good. If I

am hit by a falling meteorite whose course could not have been predicted, then my bad luck is brute (even though I could have moved just before it struck if I had any reason to know where it would strike). Obviously the difference between these two forms of luck can be represented as a matter of degree, and we may be uncertain how to describe a particular piece of bad luck. If someone develops cancer in the course of a normal life, and there is no particular decision to which we can point as a gamble risking the disease, then we will say that he has suffered brute bad luck. But if he smoked cigarettes heavily then we may prefer to say that he took an unsuccessful gamble.

(Dworkin 1981: 293)

On one hand, the notion of brute luck captures a type of luck that is beyond a person's control. The person cannot be held responsible for the bad effects of brute luck, and therefore, if he or she is worse off than others, the bad effects of brute luck should be compensated for. On the other hand, the notion of option luck captures a type of luck that is within a person's control. The person should be held responsible for the bad effects of option luck, and therefore, if he or she is worse off than others, his or her bad state does not warrant any compensation.

With this distinction, I can now present the most general definition of luck egalitarianism, one that is sufficiently broad to include almost all versions of luck egalitarianism:

> **Luck egalitarianism:** Inequality is bad or unjust if it reflects the differential effects of brute luck. Inequality is not bad or unjust if it reflects the differential effects of option luck.

Luck egalitarianism thus defined makes two general claims. The first is that the differential effects of brute luck should be neutralized through compensation for the bad effects of brute luck. The second is that the differential effects of option luck do not require any compensation. *N.B.,*

Luck egalitarianism based on the brute/option luck distinction can provide an intuitively correct result in the case of the handicapped person. The person with a handicap did not choose to have the handicap. If he or she is worse off than others, that is the result of bad brute luck, and therefore his or her state should be compensated for. On the other hand, if one gambler is worse off than another gambler or non-gamblers, there is no need for reducing the inequality.

Two quick qualifications are in order. First, notice that luck egalitarianism aims to neutralize the differential effects of brute luck, not the causes of brute luck. For example, luck egalitarianism does not aim to eliminate differences in height, race, or sex. It merely claims that the inequalities resulting from differences in height, race, or sex should be eliminated. Second, I defined the normative feature of inequality by the disjunction of axiological and deontic concepts. If inequality resulting from differential brute luck is bad, the badness of inequality may well be outweighed by the goodness of other considerations. If inequality resulting from differential brute luck is unjust, that inequality should simply be eliminated. Unjust inequality resulting from differential brute luck cannot be tolerated even if that inequality promotes a large amount of goods in society.

The distinction between axiological and deontic luck egalitarianism has the following implication. Some people may claim that the definition of deontic luck egalitarianism does not capture the correct meaning of injustice. Imagine that there are two equally sized villages, A and B, where everyone in these villages is at the same level of well-being. Suppose that a hurricane destroys the houses in village A, but not those in village B, and that people in village A are therefore worse off than people in village B. A hurricane is a natural phenomenon that nobody can control. So the inequality between the two villages reflects the differential effect of sheer brute luck. Is the inequality between the two villages really unjust? According to the deontic version of luck egalitarianism, it is unjust. Nevertheless, some people would claim that it is not unjust. Of course, it is regrettable, and probably bad, that people in village A are worse off than people in village B because of the hurricane. But it is not unjust, because the inequality is not brought about by any social institution. Usually, justice is a normative property concerning social institutions such as governments, markets, social systems, and so on. According to the standard semantics of "just" and "unjust," when inequality is brought about through market transactions or by governments, it is seen as unjust. When inequality is brought about by a natural cause such as a hurricane, it is regrettable. But it is not a matter of justice, but of something else. For example, inequality due to a natural disaster might be bad. That is, inequality due to a natural disaster can be captured by an axiological notion, but not by a deontic notion.

This claim makes perfect sense. However, there is a sense in which luck egalitarianism can take the inequality between people in the two villages to be unjust – this would involve an appeal to what Thomas Nagel calls society's negative responsibility (Nagel 1991: 99–102). The notion of society's negative responsibility contends that society's non-interference requires justification as much as its interference does. Usually, society's interference with matters to do with its members requires justification. Yet, society's non-interference also requires justification. According to Nagel, society has no life of its own to lead. Its task is to arrange the collective life of its members. There are a lot of natural inequalities, such as the inequality between the two villages. According to the notion of society's negative responsibility, society must provide a justification if it does not attempt to neutralize the bad effects of sheer brute luck. If society does not attempt to neutralize the inequality between the two villages, it is choosing to permit the inequality to exist. Proponents of luck egalitarianism can appeal to this idea. There is no satisfactory justification for choosing to permit the inequality between the two villages. Since there is no such justification, the inequality between the two villages is unjust. On the other hand, if inequality reflects people's voluntary choice, there is a justification for inequality. The justification is that those worse off people should be held responsible for the differential effects of their voluntary choice. Thus, luck egalitarianism can provide a justification for non-interference in inequalities resulting from people's voluntary choices, and hence can claim that inequalities resulting from people's voluntary choices are just.

2.2 Unpacking the concept of option luck

As mentioned earlier, there are several factors that distinguish one version of luck egalitarianism from another. One such factor is the currency of equality. Simply put, equality of what? Dworkin, we saw, aims at equality of resources, not equality of what people derive or achieve from the consumption of resources (e.g. welfare or well-being). Other luck egalitarians, in contrast, support a different currency. G. A. Cohen (1989), for example, argues for the notion of *advantages*, which captures both resources and what people derive from the consumption of resources. Somewhat similarly, Richard Arneson (1989) argues for the notion of *opportunity for welfare* as the appropriate metric of brute-luck-neutralizing equality. In what follows, I will set aside the currency-of-justice issue. Instead, I will focus on a factor other than currency to discuss different versions of luck egalitarianism. The factor that I shall focus on is the nature of option luck. Focusing on different interpretations of the nature of option luck helps us to understand the substantive diversity within luck egalitarianism.

To begin with, what precisely does this "option luck" mean? As we saw earlier, Dworkin defines it as "a matter of how deliberate and calculated gambles turn out – whether someone gains or loses through accepting an isolated risk he or she should have anticipated and might have declined." In Dworkin's definition, there are two related elements that constitute the concept of option luck. The first is deliberative choice. In order for a certain case of misfortune to be the result of option luck, there must be some deliberative and calculated choice made by the relevant person. The second is the possibility of choosing among alternative actions after deliberation. If a person has no other option than to perform a particular act, he or she is not really choosing that act. If his or her situation turns out to be very bad as a result, he or she cannot be held responsible for the bad outcome. Luck egalitarianism assumes that, in order for a person to be responsible for the consequences of his or her choice, he or she must have had the option to act otherwise.

As Dworkin clearly notes in the passage quoted in section 2.1, it is difficult to draw a clear line between option luck and brute luck. The diversity within luck egalitarianism emerges partly from where the line is drawn. The first major division emerges when people's preferences are regarded as voluntary choices, whose bad consequences do not require compensation.

Dworkin implies that people should be held responsible for the bad effects of their preferences. This claim is derived from his argument that individuals with expensive tastes should be held responsible for the differential effects of their expensive tastes. Some people have expensive tastes, e.g. prefer to have pre-phylloxera claret and plovers' eggs, whereas other people have less expensive tastes, e.g. prefer to have beer and hens' eggs. Given that these two types of people possess the same amount of resources, those with expensive tastes are likely to end up worse off than those with less expensive tastes, because they must spend more resources to satisfy their expensive tastes. According to Dworkin, even if people with expensive tastes end up worse off than those with less expensive tastes, inequality between the two types of people does not require compensation for those with expensive tastes. For Dworkin, tastes and preferences are not a matter of brute luck, but factors for which people should be held responsible. Let us call Dworkin's understanding of option luck the crude choice view.

Cohen disagrees (G. A. Cohen 1989, 2004). He takes seriously the ways by which individuals come to possess particular tastes and preferences. In order to hold a person responsible for his or her preference, we must examine whether he or she had a genuine choice in developing a certain taste and preference. Cohen expresses his view through the following example:

Paul loves photography, while Fred loves fishing. Prices are such that Fred pursues his pastime with ease while Paul cannot afford to. Paul's life is a lot less pleasant as a result: it might even be true that it has less meaning than Fred's does. I think the egalitarian thing to do is to subsidize Paul's photography. ... Paul's problem is that he hates fishing and, so I am permissibly assuming, could not have helped hating it – it does not suit his natural inclinations. He has a genuinely involuntary expensive taste, and I think that a commitment to equality implies that he should be helped in the way that people like Paul are indeed helped by subsidized community leisure facilities.

No!

(G. A. Cohen 1989: 923)

In this example, Paul has relatively expensive tastes. Because of financial constraints, Paul cannot afford to satisfy his expensive tastes and thus may end up worse off than Fred. Cohen thinks that Paul's relatively expensive taste is not really his genuine choice: Paul could not have helped hating fishing. Cohen then claims that Paul cannot be held responsible for the differential effects of his expensive tastes. Cohen summarizes his view in the following way:

I distinguish among expensive tastes according to whether or not their bearer can reasonably be held responsible for them. There are those which he could not have helped forming and/or could not now unform, and then there are those for which, by contrast, he can be held responsible, because he could have forestalled them and/or because he could now unlearn them.

(G. A. Cohen 1989: 923)

According to Cohen, a person should be held responsible for the outcome of his or her choice if it reflects genuine choices he or she made. The genuineness of choices is determined by whether he or she had control over the formation of his or her preferences. Cohen does not claim that individuals can never be held responsible for their preferences. His contention is more modest. He merely contends that individuals should be held responsible for their preferences only if they had control over them, and that individuals cannot be held responsible for their preferences if they did not have control over them. Unlike Dworkin's resource egalitarianism, Cohen's version of luck egalitarianism does not necessarily hold individuals responsible for preferences. Let us call Cohen's understanding of option luck the *genuine choice view.*

Some luck egalitarians are satisfied with neither the crude choice view nor the genuine choice view. Imagine that a heavy smoker develops lung cancer and ends up very badly off. Suppose that the parents and friends of the heavy smoker are also heavy smokers. Under such circumstances, the heavy smoker probably takes it to be quite normal to smoke 40 cigarettes a day. According to one reading of the control view, the heavy smoker did not have control over his preferences and hence did not make a genuine choice about smoking. Therefore, on this reading of the control view, the heavy smoker cannot be held responsible even if he or she develops a serious disease and ends up in a bad state. Peter Vallentyne (2002) and Shlomi Segall (2010) find this result counterintuitive and propose the reasonable avoidability view. According to this view, a person is held responsible for an outcome if it would have been reasonable to expect him or her to avoid it. Similarly, a person is not held responsible for an outcome if it would have been unreasonable to expect him or her to avoid it. In the case of the heavy smoker, this view would claim that the heavy smoker should be held responsible for the bad outcomes resulting from smoking. This is because it is reasonable to expect that he or she should know the risk associated with heavy smoking and therefore refrain from smoking.

What is an outcome that one can reasonably avoid? This question is not easy to answer. More specifically, it is difficult to pin down the notion of reasonableness. One interpretation is that an outcome is reasonably avoidable for a person if he or she could foresee that the outcome might result from his or her choice. But this interpretation does not seem right. When I go to a supermarket, there is a very small risk of being hit by a car, struck by lightning, or stabbed by a psychopath. Although I can foresee these risks, I usually ignore them when I go to the supermarket. For practical purposes, I bracket out small risks. But now imagine that lightning strikes me on my way to the supermarket. The interpretation under consideration says that I am responsible for this outcome because I could foresee this possibility. However, lightning is naturally caused, and strikes some people randomly. It seems that nobody, including myself, is responsible for the bad outcome which I unluckily experience. Nonetheless, if option luck is understood as foreseeability, I should be held responsible for the bad outcome because I could foresee it. This does not sound right. So it seems that reasonableness is not foreseeability.

Most probably, reasonableness is meant to refer to justifiability. That is, ϕ-ing is an act that S is reasonably expected to avoid just in case S cannot justify ϕ-ing to other people. If something is reasonable, it must be intelligible. That means that there must be a reason, and that the reason must be understandable to other people. To say that a person is reasonably expected to avoid ϕ-ing is to say that ϕ-ing is not justifiable to other people. To say that he or she could not be reasonably expected to avoid ϕ-ing is to say that ϕ-ing is justifiable to other people. It is the justifiability of an act that the reasonable avoidability view takes to be the ground for the notion of responsibility. Yet, this interpretation does not sound right either. One of luck egalitarianism's job descriptions is to identify why some inequalities are justifiable. Why is a certain case of inequality justifiable? This is because the inequality is the result of unjustifiable choice. However, this explanation is uninformative because what luck egalitarianism is supposed to explain is explained by what it starts with. Thus, the reasonable avoidability view requires further theoretical development.

2.3 How much of luck is really option luck?

Although I have identified three different interpretations of option luck, there remains the question of how we draw the line between brute luck and option luck. It is difficult to draw a sharp line between the two. In theory, we can think of two extreme positions concerning where that line should be drawn. The first is what I call the no-luck view. According to the no-luck view, the line is drawn in a way that leaves little room for brute luck. This means that almost all inequalities reflect the differential effects of option luck, and hence that almost all people can be held responsible for bad outcomes. The no-luck view of luck egalitarianism gets closer to non-egalitarianism. There are few inequalities that require compensation, and many inequalities justifiably remain intact. To my knowledge, only Eric Rakowski (1991) takes this extreme view. The no-luck view is not awfully popular among advocates of luck egalitarianism.

Some philosophers are attracted to the other extreme, which I call the all-luck view, or views similar to this extreme view (N. Barry 2006, 2008; Fleurbaey 1995, 2001; Lippert-Rasmussen 2001; Otsuka 2001). The all-luck view draws the line in a way that leaves little room for option luck. This means that almost all inequalities reflect the differential effects of brute luck, and hence that very few people can be held responsible for bad outcomes. The all-luck view of luck egalitarianism gets closer, or extensionally almost equivalent, to simple egalitarianism in outcome, which I will discuss in chapter 3. On this view, almost all inequalities reflect the differential effects of luck that is beyond our control, and therefore, almost nobody can be held responsible for a bad outcome.

Ironically, the all-luck view emerges from the fact that it is difficult to draw a clear line between brute luck and option luck. More specifically, it emerges partly from the fact that many cases of option luck include some element of brute luck and there are few pure cases of option luck. On the one hand, it is easy to identify pure cases of brute luck. Differences in natural endowments and social circumstances are a matter of pure brute luck. Nobody intentionally chose any of these conditions. Nobody has any control over these conditions. No matter how we interpret the concept of option luck, it is fairly easy to agree on a wide range of instances of pure brute luck. On the other hand, it would be difficult to identify cases of pure option luck. After all, option luck is a form of luck. Even if option luck arises from deliberative and intentional choices, many morally arbitrary factors affect which state of affairs turns out to be the outcome. Thus, many results of intentional choices involve option luck and some degree of luck that the choosers cannot control. Almost all choices are affected by factors that are beyond a person's control, such as unforeseeable events, a lack of information, changes in society and technology, and the choices that other people make.

Consider a version of the prisoner's dilemma (table 2.1). Imagine that there are two persons, who each must choose to either *cooperate* or *not cooperate* simultaneously. The outcome is strictly better if both persons choose to cooperate than if they both choose not to cooperate. If one person chooses to cooperate and the other chooses not to cooperate, then the outcome for the one who chooses to cooperate is strictly worse than that resulting from each person's choosing not to cooperate. But the outcome for the person who chooses not to cooperate is strictly better than the outcome resulting from the cooperation of both persons. In this example, there are four possible states of affairs, and the pay-off for the two persons is as follows. The left-hand number in each bracket represents the pay-off for person 1, and the right-hand number the pay-off for person 2.

Table 2.1

		Person 2	
		Cooperate	Not cooperate
Person 1	Cooperate	(10, 10)	(0, 15)
	Not cooperate	(15, 0)	(5, 5)

Obviously, a person ends up better off if he or she chooses not to cooperate and the other chooses to cooperate. Now imagine that person 1 chooses to cooperate whereas person 2 chooses not to cooperate. The outcome is (0, 15). This means that person 1 is worse off than person 2. Presumably, person 1 chooses to cooperate after some deliberation. He or she considers how person 1 would decide and behave. However, as a result of deliberative choice, person 1 ends up worse off than person 2. In one sense, person 1 should be held responsible for the bad effect of his or her deliberative choice, and therefore inequality between these two persons does not require redistribution from person 2 to person 1. However, the choice of person 2 is beyond the control of person 1. Person 1 ends up worse off because it is his or her bad luck that person 2 chooses not to cooperate. Thus, according to the all-luck view, inequality between persons 1 and 2 requires redistribution from person 2 to person 1. Inequality in the prisoner's dilemma is a result of luck. The all-luck view then contends that, in this example, person 1 cannot be held responsible for the bad effects of luck and hence that the inequality between persons 1 and 2 requires redistribution from person 2 to person 1.

According to the all-luck view, almost all the differential effects of luck should be compensated, unless they are the result of pure option luck. Nicholas Barry (2006, 2008) seems to endorse this extreme position. He implies that a person can be held responsible for a bad outcome only if he or she deliberately and intentionally chooses that outcome. This means that Barry's version of the all-luck view does not hold any individuals responsible for a bad outcome if there is risk or uncertainty. On the all-luck view, the concept of brute luck absorbs almost all cases of option luck, and the distinction between brute luck and option luck evaporates. Since there are very few cases where people intentionally choose to end up worse off, the all-luck view is likely to support equality of outcome.

The all-luck view is problematic. The real problem with the all-luck view is that the view itself renders luck egalitarianism redundant and the notion of option luck unintelligible. What is the bad effect of pure option luck? It is the outcome that a person intentionally chooses to bring about, under no uncertainty or risk whatsoever. There is no element of luck here. If there is any element of luck, the outcome is said to be the result of luck that is beyond one's control. Thus, on the all-luck view, the bad effect of pure option luck really means the intended outcome, not the result of luck of any kind. What the all-luck view looks at is the contrast between intended and unintended outcomes, not between two kinds of luck. The all-luck view does not ground the notion of responsibility on the distinction between brute luck and option luck. Rather, it grounds the notion of responsibility on the distinction between intended and unintended outcomes. Thus, the all-luck view is really implying that inequality is bad or unjust if it is an unintended outcome, and that inequality is not bad or unjust if it is an intended outcome.

The all-luck view thus construed has three implausible features. First, few people would intend to become worse off than others. Even reckless gamblers do not intend to lose their money. Second, the notion of pure option luck does not make sense. Pure option luck is not a type of luck in any sense, because pure option luck includes no uncertainty or risk. Thus, the notion of option luck is unintelligible. Third, the all-luck view turns out to be something different from luck egalitarianism even though it is claimed to be an extreme version of luck egalitarianism, because it grounds the notion of responsibility on the distinction between intended and unintended outcomes, not the distinction between option luck and brute luck.

As I said at the beginning of this section, the no-luck view and the all-luck view are the two extremes. Most luck egalitarians would likely take the following pragmatic approach. The approach is to leave the brute/option luck distinction vague. There are definitely instances of pure brute luck and pure option luck. But these two types of luck are the two extreme ends of one continuous spectrum. As Dworkin clearly states, it is difficult to draw a sharp line. We may well draw an arbitrary line. Even if we cannot draw a non-arbitrary sharp line, this does not mean that there is no brute or option luck. It is just like the long-standing problem of vagueness. It does not follow from the fact that we cannot draw a clear line between hairy guys and bald guys that the concept of being hairy and the concept of being bald do not make sense. Most advocates of luck egalitarianism opt for a position between the no-luck and the all-luck views.

In the rest of this section, I will briefly introduce two other distinctive views that can be seen as versions of luck egalitarianism. The first is Peter Vallentyne's equal initial opportunities view (Vallentyne 2002). This view holds that people's initial opportunities or prospects at the early stages of their lives should be equalized. Some people have a genetic disorder, which is inherited from their parents and eventually restricts their future opportunities. Others do not. Nobody chooses to inherit a genetic disorder. Nonetheless, an inherited genetic disorder often constrains or diminishes the opportunities of people with the genetic disorder in their later life. The equal initial opportunities view claims that inequalities in initial opportunities, or prospects, should be equalized. However, it does not always require the neutralization of the differential effects of brute luck in later stages of people's lives even if a person becomes worse off than another through no fault of his or her own. This is the main difference from standard luck egalitarianism, which always requires neutralizing the differential effects of brute luck.

I said that the equal initial opportunities view does not *always* require compensation for the bad effects of brute luck in later stages of people's lives. However, it does *not* claim that such differential effects of brute luck should *never* be compensated. According to this view, if a certain condition holds, compensation is required. What is that condition? It is that this compensation improves everyone's initial prospects. This view requires compensation for the differential effects of brute luck when and only when such compensation increases the expected value of people's lifetime opportunities at the point of birth. Thus, whether or not the differential effects of brute luck should be compensated depends on the expected value of people's lifetime opportunities at the point of birth.

The second view is Marc Fleurbaey's fresh start view (Fleurbaey 2005, 2008). This view is similar to Vallentyne's view. The equal initial opportunities view requires the equalization of prospects only at the beginning of people's lives. In contrast, the fresh start view can demand the equalization of prospects multiple times over the course of people's lives, provided that they change their preferences. Some people make voluntary choices but end up with a bad state. They may well regret their past choices, change their life project, and hope to make a fresh start. That is, often, there are changes in people's preferences over the course of their lives. The fresh start view tries to be sensitive to changes in people's life projects and preferences over time. It attempts to support people's new life projects through the distribution of resources.

To understand the basic idea of the fresh start view, imagine the following situation. Anna dreamed of becoming a rock star and decided to drop out of school. However, she did not see any sign of success as a rock star and now lives in poverty. She regrets her past decision, gives up her dream of becoming a rock star, and decides to pursue a more realistic career and to go to college. However, she cannot afford to pay the college tuition fees because of her poverty. According to standard luck egalitarianism such as Cohen's and Arneson's, there is no need for a transfer of resources from better off people to Anna, because she should be held responsible for the bad outcome of her choice. In contrast, the fresh start view claims that some resource transfer should be made from better off people to Anna so that she can attend college. This is because the fresh start view respects the change in Anna's preferences. Insofar as Anna regrets her past decision and commits to a new life project, the fresh start view is willing to help the new Anna. It does not hold Anna responsible for the differential effect of her past decision.

good

The fresh start view is very forgiving, but not overly so. Many people make unwise choices at various stages of their lives. They often regret their past decisions and start pursuing a new life project. This is very common. Very few people commit to one life project throughout their lives. Thus, the fresh start view is commonsensical as well as realistic. Of course, if Anna stubbornly sticks to her dream of becoming a rock star, the fresh start view holds Anna responsible for the bad outcome of her choice and requires no transfer of resources from better off people to her. The fresh start view is equivalent to standard luck egalitarianism if and only if people never change their life projects (and underlying preferences) through their entire lives.

Some people would find the fresh start view unacceptable. They would claim that, on the fresh start view, prudent and cautious decision-makers must bear the cost of compensating for losses for which imprudent and careless decision-makers should be held responsible. Even if I make a stupid choice, which is highly likely to put me in a very bad state, I am guaranteed to possess equal opportunities insofar as I regret it. Do I then have any reason to make the prudent and cautious choice? Even if I drink and drive, there is nothing to worry about. The fresh start view would introduce the problem of moral hazard. Dworkin makes this point:

> [A view like the fresh start] seems an almost literal case of allowing people to eat cake and have it too. Why should the spendthrift be rewarded for hard work and frugality he never practiced, out of taxes raised from those who have in fact worked hard and been frugal?
>
> (Dworkin 2002: 113)

In putting forward the fresh start view, Fleurbaey attempts to challenge this sort of ethical intuition. He argues for a different ethical standard, which endorses the principle of forgiving past mistakes and welcoming changes of mind, and accepts the implication that the cost of such mistakes or changes has to be shared by the whole community.

2.4 Objections

I shall now examine the objections leveled against luck egalitarianism. I shall consider three objections among others.

The first objection contends that luck egalitarianism cannot justify equality. Susan Hurley (2003) poses this objection. According to her, for luck egalitarianism, the aim of egalitarianism is to neutralize the effects of brute luck on the distribution of resources or opportunity. If this is true, then it must be the case that, when a perfectly equal distribution is brought about through sheer brute luck, the aim of egalitarianism does not support such equality. This is because in this equal distribution, brute luck is not neutralized. If we attempt to achieve the aim of egalitarianism and neutralize the effects of brute luck, we must depart from this perfectly equal distribution. If equality by luck is claimed to be desirable, then luck-neutralization is not what luck egalitarianism aims at. Luck-neutralization does not tell us how we are to distribute resources or opportunity. It does not necessarily justify equal distribution. This is roughly what Hurley claims. According to this objection, luck egalitarianism simply takes a perfectly equal distribution to be a default state and treats unequal distributions as deviations from the perfectly equal distribution, which require correction if they result from brute luck. Equal distribution is a non-starter. This is a rough sketch of Hurley's objection.

Luck egalitarianism can avoid this objection if it is stated in a more precise way. What luck egalitarianism aims to neutralize is more specific than the general notion of luck. Luck egalitarianism aims to neutralize the effects of *differential* brute luck (Lippert-Rasmussen 2005). Differential brute luck means the luck that affects people differently and results in unequal distribution. The type of luck which happens to result in a perfectly equal distribution, as in Hurley's objection, is not differential brute luck. According to this reply, luck egalitarianism is not concerned with the effects of non-differential brute luck of the sort that Hurley has in mind.

The second objection is, once again, due to Hurley (2003). It is that there is a hidden assumption in luck egalitarianism, which makes it impossible to hold people responsible for anything. Luck egalitarianism is a responsibility-sensitive distributive principle. The notion of responsibility distinguishes morally relevant from morally irrelevant inequalities. According to Hurley, however, luck egalitarianism simply assumes but does not establish a particular notion of responsibility, even though it plays a central role. According to Hurley, the notion of luck employed in luck egalitarianism assumes the *regression requirement*. That is, luck egalitarianism assumes that if a person is responsible for something, it must be the case that he or she is responsible for its causes. This notion of responsibility, Hurley argues, is recursive. If a person is responsible for something, it must be the case that he or she is responsible for its causes, and the causes of its causes, and so on. Hurley thus points out that luck egalitarianism assumes a notion of responsibility that requires this recursive process. If the recursive process of the causal chain goes on, ultimately, nobody could be held responsible for anything. To avoid this, luck egalitarianism must establish a notion of responsibility that does not require such a recursive process. This is not an easy task. The relation between choice and responsibility is one of the major problems in the literature on free will. But luck egalitarianism dodges this important philosophical issue entirely. This is Hurley's second objection.

Admittedly, Hurley's objection is quite right. How to relate choice and responsibility is a big problem. Unless we settle this big problem that has been discussed in the literature on free will, luck egalitarianism will not be a complete moral theory. However, her objection is like throwing the baby out with the bath water. If determinism is true, luck egalitarianism collapses into simple outcome egalitarianism and turns out redundant. However, according to luck egalitarians, it is not the case that we cannot advance our theories about distributive justice unless we settle the free will debate. We can simply bracket out the free will debate and assume a certain notion of responsibility for the sake of discussing issues of distributive justice. We do similar things regarding other important and debatable notions. There is no settled view about the notion of well-being. Some people take pleasure to be well-being. Others take an objectively identifiable list of goods to be well-being. However, we can bracket out the debate about the notion of well-being and start discussing distributive principles. There is nothing wrong with such a strategy. Of course, no luck egalitarians claim that compatibilism is true simply because they support luck egalitarianism.

The third objection is what has become known as the *abandonment objection* or the *harshness objection.* Fleurbaey (1995) first addressed the issue, and then Anderson (1999) posed it as an objection to luck egalitarianism. Anderson considers the reckless driver case.

> Consider an uninsured driver who negligently makes an illegal turn that causes an accident with another car. Witnesses call the police, reporting who is at fault; the police transmit this information to emergency

> medical technicians. When they arrive at the scene and find that the driver at fault is uninsured, they leave him to die by the side of the road.
>
> (Anderson 1999: 295)

According to Anderson, luck egalitarianism must claim that the resulting inequality between the reckless driver and the other driver is not bad or unjust. That is, luck egalitarianism sees no problem in leaving the reckless driver unattended. This is because the reckless driver chose to drive recklessly (or, to put it in other terms, it would have been reasonable to expect this driver to drive more carefully) and therefore he or she should be held responsible for the differential effect of his or her option luck. Anderson, however, claims that this implication of luck egalitarianism is unjustifiable. Therefore, she claims that luck egalitarianism is hard to accept. This is the abandonment objection.

Originally, Anderson raised this objection to Dworkin's resource egalitarianism. But the objection applies equally to other forms of luck egalitarianism. How should advocates of luck egalitarianism respond to the abandonment objection? One thing they can say is "so what?" The reckless driver should be held responsible for his or her bad option luck. It looks harsh to abandon him or her. But, tough luck! It is justifiably harsh to abandon the reckless driver. However, to my knowledge, no luck egalitarians are willing to endorse such a response. Many advocates of luck egalitarianism believe that it is unjustifiably harsh to abandon the reckless driver. They take Anderson's counterexample very seriously.

Is there any way to give treatment to the reckless driver without giving up luck egalitarianism? Here is one way, which G. A. Cohen and Shlomi Segall adopt – one can appeal to a different distributive principle. Cohen (2006: 443) concedes that luck egalitarianism does not require rescuing the reckless driver. Yet, he thinks that fraternity-based egalitarianism requires rescuing the reckless driver. I will not attempt to explain what fraternity-based egalitarianism is, because I have no clear idea of it. For the present purposes, it suffices to assume that something other than luck egalitarianism requires rescuing the reckless driver. The point is that although luck egalitarianism leaves the reckless driver unattended, advocates of luck egalitarianism can appeal to something else in order to require the rescue of the reckless driver.

In a similar vein, Segall (2010: 64–66) appeals to the requirement of meeting basic needs. Segall adopts what he calls pluralism. By pluralism, he means that multiple principles of justice coexist simultaneously, and that each principle requires different things. According to Segall, luck egalitarianism is a distributive principle, and entails many things with regard to distributions. But it is not a comprehensive theory of justice. It is merely a part of such a theory. Another part of a comprehensive theory of justice, the requirement of meeting basic needs, requires rescuing the reckless driver. According to Segall, luck egalitarianism is perfectly consistent with the requirement of meeting basic needs, and the two principles can coexist. Thus, Segall concludes that "advocates of luck egalitarianism" (as distinguished from luck egalitarianism as such) do not need to abandon the reckless driver.

This pluralist response is not satisfactory, for three reasons. First, the idea of pluralism is not clear. Pluralism holds that two or more principles exist simultaneously. How many principles are there? Do these principles never conflict with each other? What is the relative priority among these principles? The idea of pluralism does more to invite such questions than to solve the problem of the abandonment objection.

Second, the response is not really directed to the abandonment objection. Both Cohen and Segall concede that luck egalitarianism abandons the reckless driver. They are free to support as many principles as they wish. But the bottom line is that luck egalitarianism abandons the reckless driver. The abandonment objection is not aimed at people who support luck egalitarianism, but at luck egalitarianism itself. Thus, the force of the abandonment objection to luck egalitarianism remains intact. The appeal to non-luck-egalitarian principles does not rescue luck egalitarianism.

Third, even if luck egalitarianism is confined to the domain of distributive justice, it cannot provide a satisfactory treatment of the most basic cases of distributive justice, such as the reckless driver case. The reckless driver case is a case of distributive justice. The question is whether we should allocate scarce resources to rescue the reckless driver even if he or she should be held responsible. This question is nothing if not one of distributive justice. However, luck egalitarianism itself cannot provide a justification for saving the reckless driver. Defenders of luck egalitarianism would claim that luck egalitarianism is far from a comprehensive theory of justice. That is true. Nonetheless, it also seems true that luck egalitarianism is far from a comprehensive distributive principle. If other parts of a comprehensive theory of justice can serve to answer questions of distributive justice, then we should probably let them solve those questions and assign more marginal tasks to luck egalitarianism.

There are at least two forms of luck egalitarianism that can avoid the abandonment objection: the all-luck view and the fresh start view. According to the all-luck view, almost all cases of luck are cases in which nobody can be held responsible for the differential effects of option luck. Unless the reckless driver intentionally chooses to have an accident and become very badly off, he or she cannot be held responsible for the differential effects of his or her reckless driving. This means that emergency medical technicians have every reason to give treatment to the reckless driver, even at the expense of other careful drivers. So the abandonment objection does not apply to the all-luck view.

The fresh start view can also avoid the abandonment objection if one condition is satisfied. The condition is that the reckless driver regrets his reckless driving and commits to driving carefully after this accident. If this condition is satisfied, the fresh start view does not hold the reckless driver responsible and demands that the reckless driver be rescued. If the reckless driver still insists on reckless driving, then the fresh start view leaves him or her unattended.

As I said earlier, many proponents of luck egalitarianism take Anderson's abandonment objection seriously. Although several advocates of standard luck egalitarianism attempt to respond to the abandonment objection, the force of the objection seems to remain intact. The all-luck and fresh start views can avoid the abandonment objection. However, as I pointed out in section 2.3, the all-luck view is problematic in itself. Probably the most successful reply to the abandonment objection comes from the fresh start view.

Chapter summary

Rawls's theory of distributive justice and luck egalitarianism agree that morally arbitrary factors such as natural and social endowments should be neutralized. Yet, these two theories disagree about how these factors should be neutralized. Rawls thinks that they should be neutralized to secure impartiality for the sake of choosing the basic structure of society. Luck egalitarianism holds that the differential effects of arbitrary factors should be neutralized by redistribution. If inequality reflects the differential effects of factors within the control of the worse off, luck egalitarianism does not require neutralizing those effects. If people are worse off than others through no fault of their own, luck egalitarianism requires neutralizing the differential effects of brute luck. There are three interpretations concerning the scope of choice. The crude choice view sees expensive tastes and other disadvantageous preferences as a matter of choice. The genuine choice view sees them as beyond one's control. The reasonable avoidability view takes irresponsible choices to be the acts that one is reasonably expected to avoid. The abandonment objection is the most serious one against luck egalitarianism. The objection points out that luck egalitarianism is unjustifiably harsh to anyone who becomes very badly off as a result of his or her voluntary choice. Some defenders of luck egalitarianism, e.g. Cohen and Segall, only hope that external factors rescue them from the abandonment objection, because there is no defense from the standpoint of luck egalitarianism itself. However, Fleurbaey's fresh start view can avoid the abandonment objection.

Further reading

The literature on luck egalitarianism is enormous. Although Lippert-Rasmussen (2009) provides an excellent overview of complicated literature on luck egalitarianism, it is always a good idea to start with, and frequently go back to, three seminal articles on luck egalitarianism: Arneson (1989), G. A. Cohen (1989), and Dworkin (1981). Then, move on to more comprehensive volumes such as G. A. Cohen (2008), Segall (2010), and Knight and Stemplowska (2011). The assessment of Dworkin's resource-egalitarianism and his option/brute luck distinction is one of the major issues, and is worth examining carefully (Clayton 2000; Lippert-Rasmussen 2001; Otsuka 2001; Sandbu 2004; Andrew Williams 2002). As I said, there is a huge variety of views within luck egalitarianism (Arneson 2000; N. Barry 2006; Fleurbaey 2001, 2005; Vallentyne 2002). For criticisms of luck egalitarian, see Anderson (1999), Hurley (2003), Scheffler (2003b, 2005), and Wolff (1998). For the responses to the objections raised by Anderson and Hurley, see Arneson (2004) and Lippert-Rasmussen (2005). The recent debate between Anderson (2010) and Lippert-Rasmussen (2012) may be useful to understand the (alleged) contrast between luck egalitarianism and democratic equality. Tan (2012) applies luck egalitarianism to global justice. Readers with an economics background may enjoy Fleurbaey (2008) and Roemer (1998a).

3

TELIC EGALITARIANISM

The Rawlsian and luck versions of egalitarianism are primarily concerned with its foundations. That is, they clarify why inequalities give rise to a moral concern. In chapters 3 through 5, we shall examine three evaluative principles. These evaluative principles are primarily concerned with the ranking of possible states of affairs, which exhibit different patterns of distribution of well-being. The three evaluative principles are *telic egalitarianism*, *prioritarianism*, and *sufficientarianism*.

The principle we shall examine in this chapter is one that takes equality to be a feature that makes the outcome *better*. I call this principle telic egalitarianism, following Derek Parfit's lecture "Equality or Priority?" (Parfit 1995, 2000). Parfit's paper is so influential that it has partly defined the way in which philosophers have discussed distributive justice in the past 15 years. In his paper, Parfit characterizes telic egalitarianism and raises at least two important problems with it. One is the *leveling down objection*. The other is the *scope problem*. As a result of these objections, few philosophers support telic egalitarianism. Many instead support Parfit's proposed view, prioritarianism, which we will examine in chapter 4.

This chapter begins with Parfit's characterization of telic egalitarianism. Some people have raised doubts about it. Nonetheless, many philosophers now accept and follow his characterization. Thus, I will begin with it. Section 3.1 explains Parfit's distinction between telic and deontic egalitarianism and his characterization of telic egalitarianism, which I call the intrinsic view. Section 3.2 explains the first of two challenges Parfit posed to telic egalitarianism: the leveling down objection. Section 3.3 examines three responses to the leveling down objection. Section 3.4 considers an alternative characterization of telic egalitarianism, which I call the aggregate view. Section 3.5 examines Parfit's second challenge to telic egalitarianism: the scope problem. Section 3.6 considers the significance (or insignificance) of the distinction between telic and deontic egalitarianism.

3.1 Telic egalitarianism: Parfit's intrinsic view

Parfit starts with a distinction between two types of egalitarianism and provides a rough definition of each type in the following way:

> There are two main ways in which we can believe in equality. We may believe that inequality is bad. On such a view, when we should aim for equality, that is because we shall thereby make the outcome better. We can then be called *Teleological* – or, for short, *Telic* – Egalitarians. Our view may instead be *Deontological* or, for short, *Deontic*. We may believe we should aim for equality, not to make the outcome better, but for some other moral reason. We may believe, for example, that people have rights to equal shares.
>
> (Parfit 2000: 84)

According to Parfit, telic egalitarianism is the view that takes equality to be something which makes the outcome better. That is, telic egalitarianism understands equality as a good-making feature. This is the most general definition of telic egalitarianism.

"Teleological" egalitarianism may be misleading. What Parfit means by teleological egalitarianism is *axiological* egalitarianism. If we say teleological egalitarianism, it sounds as if the version of egalitarianism that takes equality to make the outcome better is committed to teleology. This would imply that telic egalitarianism determines the rightness or wrongness of an act by the goodness of the outcome. But the definition above does not claim that much. It merely states that equality increases the goodness of an outcome. Even if an equal distribution is strictly better than an unequal distribution, it may well be wrong to bring it about if this act involves a violation of some deontic constraint. This means that what Parfit calls telic egalitarianism is not teleological but axiological. Therefore, it would be more accurate and precise to call it axiological egalitarianism. Nonetheless, as the term telic egalitarianism is widely used already, I will use this misleading name to refer to axiological egalitarianism.

Parfit's definition of deontic egalitarianism needs some qualification. In the quote above, Parfit defines deontic egalitarianism as the view that does not take equality to necessarily make the outcome better. However, this definition can include some non-deontic types of egalitarianism. For example, some people might claim that we should aim for equality because that is what a virtuous person would do. This sort of egalitarianism is based on virtue theory and therefore teleological. However, the above definition sees this type of egalitarianism as a version of deontic egalitarianism. I am fairly certain that this is not what Parfit has in mind. As I understand it, what Parfit really means is that, according to deontic egalitarianism, we should aim for equality because inequality involves a violation of some deontic constraint. Thus, the precise definition of deontic egalitarianism should be the following. According to deontic egalitarianism, we should aim for equality insofar as inequality involves the violation of rights, fairness, or justice.

Building on the above general definition of telic egalitarianism, Parfit offers a more specific characterization. According to Parfit, people who think that equality makes the outcome better accept, at least, the following principle:

> *The principle of equality*: It is in itself bad if some people are worse off than others.
>
> (Parfit 2000: 84)

According to the principle of equality, equality makes the outcome better because it reduces the badness or disvalue of inequality between individuals. On Parfit's interpretation, the principle of equality is a necessary and sufficient condition for characterizing telic egalitarianism. However, if telic egalitarianism consists solely in the principle of equality, it will have a counterintuitive implication. Think of two distributions where people could all be either (1) equally well off or (2) equally badly off. The principle of equality does not tell us that (1) would be better than (2), although it seems obvious that (1) is strictly better than (2). Parfit thinks that in order to explain why (2) is worse than (1), the principle of equality should be combined with:

> *The principle of utility*: It is in itself better if people are better off.
>
> (Parfit 2000: 84)

If we combine the two principles, then we can judge that (1) is strictly better than (2). According to Parfit, many advocates of telic egalitarianism support both principles. They are *value pluralists* in the sense that they think that there are two or more types of value.

Let us be more precise about value pluralism. On Parfit's understanding, telic egalitarianism is the view that the goodness of a distribution is a function of two types of value: the disvalue of inequality (the principle of equality) and the value of people's well-being (the principle of utility). This can be represented by the following equation:

$$G = f(I, W) \tag{1}$$

where I denotes some measure of inequality and W denotes the total or average amount of well-being. The function, $f()$, is decreasing in I and increasing in W. So if inequality increases (decreases), the goodness of the outcome decreases (increases). If the total or average amount of well-being increases (decreases), the goodness of the outcome increases (decreases).

How do we balance the disvalue of inequality and the value of people's well-being? Parfit thinks that there might be no principled way to determine the relative weight of these two types of value. He thinks that advocates of telic egalitarianism would appeal to intuition to determine the relative importance of these two types of value.

Equation (1) is very general. It merely conveys the general conceptual framework. A more specific formula can help us to understand the nature of telic egalitarianism. Consider the following application of telic egalitarianism in the simple two-person case:

$$G = \tfrac{1}{2}(W_1 + W_2) - \alpha \, |W_1 - W_2| \tag{2}$$

where W_1 denotes the well-being level of person 1 and W_2 that of person 2. In this formula, the goodness of the outcome is given by the average of two people's well-being and the absolute difference between their well-being. The average well-being is a positive value and represents the principle of utility. The absolute difference between their well-being is a negative value and represents the principle of equality. The value α is a weight given to the disvalue of inequality, and determines the relative importance of the two types of value. Parfit thinks that, to determine the size of α, we need to appeal to our intuition. If we take the disvalue of inequality very seriously, the size of α is greater. If we think that the relative importance of the disvalue of inequality is small, the size of α is smaller. The only restriction on α would be that $\alpha > 0$. This is because if α were negative, inequality would increase the goodness of the outcome. Obviously, if $\alpha = 0$, the formula becomes average utilitarianism, which is not concerned with equality. On the Parfitian characterization of telic egalitarianism, there is no upper limit on α in principle (in section 3.4, I will show that this cannot be the case).

I have a quick remark about the nature of the value of equality. Parfit states that the value of equality is *intrinsic*.

> If we claim that equality has value, we may only mean that it has good effects. Equality has many kinds of good effect, and inequality many kinds of bad effects. If people are unequal, for example, that can produce conflict, or envy, or put some people in the power of others. If we value equality because we are concerned with such effects, we believe that equality has *instrumental* value: we think it good as a means. But I am concerned with a different idea. For true egalitarians, equality has *intrinsic* value.
>
> (Parfit 2000: 86, original italics)

The intrinsic value of equality, or the intrinsic disvalue of inequality, may seem obvious enough from the principle of equality. It is *in itself* bad if some people are worse off than others. According to G. E. Moore's well-known analysis, intrinsic value "is a property which depends only on the intrinsic nature of the things which possess it" (Moore 1922: 22). That is, the intrinsic value of X supervenes exclusively on the intrinsic properties of X, independently of any other feature external to it. There is no restriction on the instances in which equality is valuable. Equality is always valuable. As we will see in section 3.3, some telic egalitarians disagree. Let us call Parfit's view about the value of equality the *intrinsic view*.

3.2 The leveling down objection

In "Equality or Priority?," Parfit poses two major problems with telic egalitarianism as he characterizes it. The first one is the *leveling down objection*. Many philosophers believe that this objection is devastating to telic egalitarianism. In this and the next section, I will examine the recent debate on the leveling down objection.

Parfit explains the leveling down objection in the following way:

> If inequality is bad, its disappearance must be in one way a change for
> the better, *however this change occurs*. Suppose that those who are better
> off suffer from some misfortune, so that they become as badly off as
> everyone else. Since these events would remove the inequality, they must
> be in one way welcome, on the Telic View [telic egalitarianism], even though
> they would be worse for some people, and better for no one. This implication
> seems to many to be quite absurd. I call this the *Levelling Down Objection*.
> (Parfit 2000: 98, original italics)

To begin with, let me define a leveling down. A leveling down occurs when
the well-being of a better off person is lowered to the level of a worse off
one *without benefiting any person*. For example, compare two distributions in the
two-person case, $X = (10, 5)$ and $Y = (5, 5)$. Moving from X to Y is an
instance of leveling down. It does not matter how Y is brought about.
The move from X to Y can be due to natural causes. Perhaps a hurricane
changes the outcome from X to Y: it injures person 1 and destroys his assets
while person 2 is fortunate enough to remain unaffected. The move can also be
man-made. Perhaps the government takes money from person 1 and burns
it so that person 1 ends up at the same level as person 2.

According to Parfit, telic egalitarianism judges that the distribution after
leveling down is, *at least in one respect*, better. Why? Because the leveling down
makes the outcome equal. By leveling down, we can remove inequality.
According to Parfit, telic egalitarianism judges the resulting distribution to
be better in terms of the reduced badness of inequality. However, Parfit
claims that the leveling down does not make the distribution better in any
respect. He thus concludes that telic egalitarianism is "quite absurd."

Notice that the leveling down objection is not concerned with our all-
things-considered judgment about leveling down. Telic egalitarianism may
well judge that leveling down makes things, all things considered, worse. For
example, if we move from $X = (10, 5)$ to $Y = (5, 5)$, the total or average
amount of well-being will be reduced. Even if the move makes things
better in one respect (i.e. in terms of the reduced badness of inequality), it
makes them worse in other respects (e.g. in terms of total or average
well-being). Telic egalitarianism may well judge that the badness of reduced
well-being outweighs the goodness of reduced inequality, and hence that X
is, all things considered, better than Y. But the objection is concerned with
the telic egalitarian judgment that the leveling down makes the state of

affairs better, at least in one respect. The outcome is strictly worse for person 1. It is not better for person 2. There is no person for whom the outcome is better. And yet, telic egalitarianism judges that it is better at least in one respect because it removes or reduces the inequality. The objection claims that such a judgment is quite absurd.

The alleged "quite absurd" implication of telic egalitarianism that the leveling down objection exposes is that an outcome is judged to be, in one respect, better even if it is better for no one. The force of the leveling down objection is derived from what has become known as the *person-affecting restriction* (Holtug 2010; Parfit 1984). There are different ways to state this restriction. Here is the version I opt for here:

> *The person-affecting restriction*: A state of affairs X cannot be better (or worse) than another state of affairs Y if there is no one for whom X is better (or worse) than Y.

This is equivalent to "a state of affairs X can be better (or worse) than another state of affairs Y only if there is some one for whom X is better (or worse) than Y."[1] In a nutshell, the person-affecting restriction holds that the better state must be better for someone, and that the worse state must be worse for someone. Some people object to this restriction (Temkin 1993). The person-affecting restriction is one of the most important and widely discussed topics in contemporary moral philosophy. So I will not go into it in much detail. It suffices to note that the person-affecting restriction underlies the leveling down objection.

What the person-affecting restriction serves to do is to eliminate the notion of good and bad that is not attributed to any person. According to Parfit's intrinsic view of telic egalitarianism, inequality is in itself bad, and equality is not a sort of good that can be attributed to particular people. This feature of the good of equality permits one respect in which the leveling down is better. Thus, Parfit's intrinsic view of telic egalitarianism violates the person-affecting restriction. If we adopt the person-affecting restriction and eliminate the concept of good or bad that cannot be attributed to particular people, we will not encounter problems like the leveling down objection. Whenever one believes in impersonal value like the intrinsic value of equality, objections like the leveling down objection can arise. At least, this is what many philosophers believe.

Of course, telic egalitarians can bite the bullet. They may reject the person-affecting restriction, and accept that leveling down makes the state of affairs better in one respect (Temkin 2000). Then, they can argue that the badness of reduced well-being outweighs the goodness of reduced inequality, and hence that the leveling down makes the state of affairs, all things considered, worse. What matters, these telic egalitarians would claim, is our all-things-considered judgment about states of affairs, not whether a state of affairs is better or worse in one respect.

Such a defiant attitude to the leveling down objection does not make the problems raised by the objection simply disappear. It is true that leveling down makes the state of affairs, all things considered, strictly worse in many cases. However, telic egalitarianism cannot rule out the possibility of judging that the leveling down makes the state of affairs, all things considered, strictly better. It all depends on how much relative weight telic egalitarianism assigns to the badness of inequality and the goodness of well-being. If a sufficiently large relative weight is assigned to the badness of inequality, there are some cases where the goodness of reduced inequality can outweigh the badness of reduced well-being. The fact that there is such a possibility might be absurd enough for those who are bothered by the leveling down objection. For them, it must be shown that leveling down *always*, all things considered, makes a state of affairs strictly worse. Otherwise, the force of the leveling down objection remains intact.

3.3 Three responses to the leveling down objection

I will examine three responses on behalf of telic egalitarianism. The first response is to impose a condition on the value of equality. As I mentioned in section 3.1, Parfit takes the value of equality to be intrinsic. According to this interpretation, the value of X is a property that depends only on the intrinsic nature of X. That is, the intrinsic value of X supervenes exclusively on the intrinsic properties of X, independently of any other feature external to it. As I said in the previous section, this interpretation is usually attributed to G. E. Moore. I believe that Parfit and many other philosophers view the value of equality as intrinsic in this Moorean sense. This means that telic egalitarianism takes equality to be always valuable, independently of any other feature external to equality.

Recently, some philosophers distinguish *final value* from intrinsic value. Instead of saying that X is valuable in itself, they say that X is valuable *for its own sake* or *as an end*, and they argue that the final value of X may well supervene on non-intrinsic properties of X. The category of final value is broader than that of intrinsic value. Intrinsic value is understood as a subcategory of final value (Korsgaard 1983; Olson 2004).

Here is an example from Rabinowicz and Rønnow-Rasmussen (2000). An evening dress is valuable for its own sake when and because Princess Diana wore it. The same dress might have little value if another random woman wore it. The intrinsic features of the dress remain the same, regardless of who wore it. Nonetheless, the dress that Princess Diana wore is valuable for its own sake, and is sold at an extremely high price at auction. The difference lies in a feature external to the dress. In this example, the relevant non-intrinsic feature is having been worn by Princess Diana. This feature is not an intrinsic property of the dress. Thus, the final value of something may well depend on its extrinsic properties.

If we take the value of equality to be the final value, we may well say that equality is valuable only given certain conditions that are external to equality. It is possible to say that equality is valuable under some conditions and not valuable under other conditions. Andrew Mason (2001) understands the value of equality in terms of final value and proposes *conditional egalitarianism*. According to conditional egalitarianism, equality is valuable for its own sake only if it benefits someone. Otherwise, equality is not valuable for its own sake. Conditional egalitarianism simply adds a condition, which identifies when equality is valuable for its own sake. In the case of leveling down, equality is valuable for its own sake because the leveling down does not benefit any person. Therefore, conditional egalitarianism judges that the leveling down is not better in any respect. This solution is simple but is well backed up by recent discussion on the foundations of axiology.

Conditional egalitarianism, however, encounters a problem. Nils Holtug (2010: 195–96) points out that conditional egalitarianism violates the transitivity of the betterness relation. Consider the following three outcomes:

$A = (5, 5, 5, 5)$
$B = (10, 10, 4, 6)$
$C = (30, 20, 10, 5).$

According to Holtug, A is better than B with respect to equality because A is more equal than B. Conditional egalitarianism agrees with this judgment because there is one person who benefits if A is chosen. Similarly, B is better than C with respect to equality because B is more equal than C. Conditional egalitarianism agrees with this judgment because there is one person who benefits if B is chosen. By transitivity of "better with respect to equality than," it must be the case that A is better than C with respect to equality. However, conditional egalitarianism claims that A is not better than C, because there is no person who benefits if A is chosen. More precisely, conditional egalitarianism claims that A is not better or worse than C with respect to equality, because there is no value of equality in this context. Thus, Holtug concludes that conditional egalitarianism violates the transitivity of the "better with respect to equality than" relation. A violation of transitivity is a deadly sin, or so Holtug (along with almost all analytical philosophers) claims. If Holtug's point is correct, conditional egalitarianism is not promising as a response to the leveling down objection.

That said, Holtug's point may not be devastating to conditional egalitarianism. Holtug is certainly right that conditional egalitarianism makes intransitive judgments in terms of the "better with respect to equality than" relation. However, conditional egalitarianism contends that the "better with respect to equality than" relation is conditional. It is not surprising that a conditional relation could be intransitive. Consider the following judgments:

(1)   If P, X is better than Y.
(2)   If Q, Y is better than Z.

From (1) and (2), can we appeal to transitivity and infer that X is better than Z? Obviously, we cannot. This is because there is a conditional in each comparative judgment, and we cannot appeal to transitivity by detaching " ... is better than ... " from the conditional. In contrast, consider the following:

(3)   X is better than Y.
(4)   Y is better than Z.

In this case, we can appeal to transitivity and infer that X is better than Z. This is because there is no conditional in either comparative judgment. In the context of distributive judgment, (3) and (4) are all-things-considered judgments, and the all-things-considered binary relation must be transitive. Advocates of conditional egalitarianism can concede Holtug's point about intransitivity in the "better with respect to equality than" relation, but argue that Holtug does not show a violation of the transitivity of the "better, all things considered" relation. They may claim that the violation of transitivity in the betterness relation with respect to equality is perfectly OK.

Does this mean that conditional egalitarianism can respond to Holtug's point successfully? No, it does not. There is no guarantee that conditional egalitarianism always yields a transitive all-things-considered ranking of states of affairs. As it stands, conditional egalitarianism only identifies the circumstances under which equality is valuable for its own sake. It does not identify how the value of equality and other values (e.g. the goodness of total or average well-being) should be combined. Conditional egalitarianism, as it stands, does not say anything about all-things-considered judgments about states of affairs. Thus, Holtug's point may be that conditional egalitarianism is an incomplete distributive principle, even if it may avoid the leveling down objection.

The second response to the leveling down objection is to understand the badness of inequality in a way different from Parfit. More specifically, it includes the badness of inequality as a negative part of personal good. John Broome (1991) adopts this strategy. He defines a person's good as everything that is good for that person. The notion of personal good is broader than well-being. According to Broome, if inequality is bad at all, it is bad for the worse off people. It is not good or bad for a better off person.

Consider a simple two-person case, where $W_1 < W_2$. In this case, there is inequality, and person 1 suffers from the badness of inequality. The personal good of person 1, in this simple case, is given by the value of his well-being, and the disvalue of inequality. That is, his personal good is $W_1 - \beta(W_2 - W_1)$, where β is some coefficient. On the other hand, the personal good of person 2 is just the value of his or her well-being because inequality is not good or bad for him or her (more precisely, the personal good of person 2 is a linear transform of the value of his well-being). Thus, the overall goodness of the outcome is given by the sum of the two people's personal good: $(W_1 - \beta(W_2 - W_1)) + W_2$. Within this analytical framework, leveling down could not occur. Remember that leveling down lowers the level of a better off person's well-being to the level of a worse off person *without benefiting any person*. Imagine that W_2 is lowered to the level of W_1. The lowering of W_2 reduces the badness of the inequality suffered by person 1, and consequently increases his personal good. Thus, it is not really a case of leveling down, because it benefits person 1. This interpretation of the badness of inequality dodges the leveling down objection.

This response is part of a broader theoretical issue. The issue is how we should understand the badness of inequality. According to Parfit's characterization of telic egalitarianism, the badness of inequality is not reducible to individual components of a state of affairs. That is, the badness of inequality is an impersonal, or communal, badness that is over and above personal goods. Parfit states that "[o]n their view [telic egalitarianism], inequality is *in itself* bad," and that "[t]his implies that inequality is bad *whether or not it is bad for people*" (Parfit 2000: 110, original italics). In contrast, Broome's analytical framework, which provides the second response to the leveling down objection, implies that inequality is in itself bad, but that the badness of inequality is reducible to a part of someone's personal good. Broome's interpretation of the badness of inequality is individualistic, as opposed to Parfit's impersonal interpretation. This is a substantive difference between Broome and Parfit concerning the very nature of the badness of inequality.

The third response is to doubt whether the leveling down making the state of affairs "better in one respect" can ground the absurdity of the telic egalitarian judgment. More generally, this response questions whether any substantive normative claim can be derived from talk about "respects" in which a state of affairs could be better or worse. The leveling down objection points out that telic egalitarianism is absurd because it judges that the leveling down makes things at least in one respect, better. Broome (2002) thinks that it does not make much sense to talk about "respects" in which a state of affairs could be better or worse. Consider a version of equation (2) as an example of telic egalitarianism:

$$G = \tfrac{1}{2}\,(W_1 + W_2) - \tfrac{1}{4}\,|W_1 - W_2| \tag{3}$$

Equation (3) is a particular version of (2) where $\alpha = \tfrac{1}{4}$. On Parfit's interpretation of telic egalitarianism, there are three respects with regard to which we evaluate the outcome. The first is with regard to person 1. The second is with regard to person 2. The third is with regard to inequality. Equation (3) partitions the outcome into three respects in which a state of affairs could be better or worse. The first respect is with regard to person 1. The second is with regard to person 2. And the third is with regard to inequality. To partition is to divide something into mutually exclusive and jointly exhaustive parts. On this interpretation, the leveling down makes the state of affairs better with regard to the third respect in which a state of affairs could be better or worse.

However, there is a different way to partition the outcome. Here is an example. We can rearrange equation (3) in the following way:

$$G = \tfrac{1}{4}\,W_1 + \tfrac{3}{4}\,W_2 \text{ if } W_1 > W_2$$

$$= \tfrac{3}{4}\,W_1 + \tfrac{1}{4}\,W_2 \text{ otherwise} \tag{4}$$

Equations (3) and (4) are mathematically equivalent. They calculate the same amount of good for every state of affairs. According to equation (4), however, the leveling down is not better in any respect. Equation (4) partitions the outcome into two respects in which a state of affairs could be better or worse. The first is with regard to person 1; the second, with regard to person 2. There is no other respect in which a state of affairs could be better or worse. Suppose that $W_1 > W_2$. The leveling down makes things worse for person 1, and not better or worse for person 2. There is no respect in regard to which the leveling down is an improvement. The third response, thus, claims that telic egalitarianism actually dodges the leveling down objection.

To this third response, two counterarguments might be raised on behalf of those who take the leveling down objection very seriously.

The first of these is the following. Telic egalitarianism as set out in equation (4) is in fact susceptible to the leveling down objection. Equations (3) and (4) are equivalent. Therefore, the counterargument concludes that telic egalitarianism as set out in (4) must also be susceptible to the leveling down objection. Advocates of the third reply can fight back in the following way. It is true that (4) is extensionally equivalent to (3). That is, (3) and (4) reach the same ranking of states of affairs. Although these different ways of mathematical representation refer to the same ranking of states of affairs, they represent different thoughts. Equation (3) represents the idea of Parfit's egalitarianism whereas (4) represents a different idea. The leveling down objection applies to the idea of Parfit's egalitarianism but not this different idea.

An analogy may be helpful. The morning star and the evening star refer to the same thing. But there are different senses attached to these stars. Suppose that the evening star is "hopeful." Does this mean that the morning star must also be hopeful? Obviously, not. Advocates of the third reply can claim that distributive principles are not only about the ranking of states of affairs, but also about the thought underlying that ranking. They can further claim that telic egalitarianism as set out in (4) represents a different thought from telic egalitarianism as set out in (3). What is that thought? One possibility is the aggregate view of telic egalitarianism that we will consider in the next section.

The second rejoinder to the third response is this. Why should the value of α be ¼? Is there any compelling reason to assume that $\alpha = $ ¼? If there is none, the choice of weight is arbitrary. If the choice of weight is arbitrary, the response based on such an arbitrary choice must also be arbitrary.

I believe that a concern along these lines is legitimate. However, there are two non-arbitrary reasons for assuming $\alpha = \frac{1}{4}$ in the two-person case. The first reason will be explained in the next section, so I shall merely mention it here. This reason is that, in (4), the weights given to people's well-being should add up to 1. For this reason, it must be the case that $\alpha = \frac{1}{4}$. I will come back to this point in the next section. The second reason comes from a requirement that economists call the *population invariance condition* on the size of inequality (Cowell 2011). Imagine a distribution of well-being in the two-person case: $X = (10, 20)$. Imagine that the population is duplicated while the distributional pattern remains unchanged. That is, $X' = (10, 10, 20, 20)$. Obviously, the average well-being remains unchanged. How should we measure the size of inequality? Does it increase or decrease if the population is duplicated? Almost all economists think that the size of inequality should be measured in such a way that the size of inequality remains unchanged. That is, the size of inequality in $(10, 20)$ should be the same as that in $(10, 10, 20, 20)$. In order to secure this, the total amount of inequality should be normalized by the number of people twice. Therefore, in the two-person case, it must be that $\alpha = \frac{1}{4}$. In the four-person case, $\alpha = \frac{1}{16}$. Thus, the choice of weight is not arbitrary.

The second and third responses invite a fundamental question that goes beyond the issue of the leveling down objection. Is Parfit's characterization of telic egalitarianism sound? In the next section, I will examine another characterization of telic egalitarianism.

3.4 An alternative interpretation: the aggregate view

In the beginning of section 3.1, I quoted Parfit's general definition of telic egalitarianism. He says that "[on telic egalitarianism] when we should aim for equality, that is because we shall thereby make the outcome better." On this general definition, telic egalitarianism holds that equality makes the outcome better. Parfit then proceeds to claim that telic egalitarianism is committed to the principle of equality, which basically creates the problem of the leveling down objection. This section considers an alternative characterization of telic egalitarianism, which is perfectly consistent with Parfit's general definition. I will call this alternative characterization the *aggregate view*. The aggregate view of telic egalitarianism understands equality as a feature of the process of aggregating people's well-being. Equality is essentially about the relation between different people's well-being, and telic egalitarianism estimates the goodness of a state of affairs with reference to the relative positions in a rank-order of different people's well-being.

The basic idea of the aggregate view is well represented in equation (4).[2] Equation (4) helps us to understand several interesting features of the aggregate view. I will first elucidate these four features.

The first feature is that telic egalitarianism is represented as the weighted sum of people's well-being. This is precisely why telic egalitarianism as set out in (4) seems to avoid the leveling down objection. It must be obvious enough what is going on when we rewrite (3) as (4). We reduce what Parfit's characterization calls the badness of inequality to the weight of individuals' well-being. Telic egalitarianism as set out in (4) does not commit its proponents to the claim that equality is an impersonal good. Rather, equality is a feature of a function that aggregates people's well-being. That is, in estimating the goodness of a state of affairs, telic egalitarianism adds up people's well-being in such a way that a more equal distribution is judged to be better than a less equal one, other things being constant.

The second feature is that telic egalitarianism as set out in (4) is not committed to value pluralism. Remember that Parfit's characterization of telic egalitarianism combines at least two different types of values: the goodness of people's well-being and the badness of inequality. To estimate the goodness of a state of affairs, it takes the form of $G = f(I, W)$, where W denotes the value of people's well-being, and I the disvalue of inequality. In contrast, telic egalitarianism as set out in (4) takes only one type of value into account. That is the value of people's well-being. It takes the form of $G = g(W)$. The disvalue of inequality does not appear as an argument of the function. Rather, the desirability of equality is incorporated into the shape of the aggregative function $g()$. Since equality is just a feature of the aggregative process, telic egalitarianism as set out in (4) is not committed to value pluralism. The only finally valuable thing is people's well-being. Equality plays an important role when we aggregate people's well-being. But it is not a good as such.

Let me move on to the third feature of (4). It is obvious that telic egalitarianism as set out in (4) gives priority to benefiting the worse off. A better off person receives a weight of ¼ for the value of his or her well-being, and a worse off person a weight of ¾. The weight assigned to a worse off person's well-being is strictly greater than that assigned to the well-being of a better off person. This means that an increase of one unit in the well-being of the better off person is less morally important than an increase of one unit in the well-being of the worse off. That is to say, given the total well-being remaining constant, a more equal distribution is strictly better than a less equal one. Telic egalitarianism as set out in (4) clearly shows that it gives priority to the worse off, whereas Parfit's characterization does not.

The fourth feature is that the weights given to people's well-being are determined by the rank-order position of each person in a ranking of well-being level. Telic egalitarianism as set out in (4) gives priority to benefiting the worse off by assigning a greater weight to the well-being of the worse off. The important point is what it is to be "worse off." According to (4), a person is worse off because his relative position is lower than another person. It does not matter whether he or she is worse off in absolute terms. Therefore, (4) shows that the relation between different people determines how much moral importance we attach to each person's well-being. Thus, the aggregate view of telic egalitarianism is relational. As telic egalitarianism is relational, it is not surprising that telic egalitarianism violates the condition of strong separability, which I introduced in order to characterize utilitarianism in section 1.1.

There are significant differences between the intrinsic view and the aggregate view. However, the two views are perfectly consistent with Parfit's initial definition of telic egalitarianism: "when we should aim for equality, that is because we shall thereby make the outcome better." Both views aim for equality because equality makes the outcome better. However, the two views drift away from each other. This is because although Parfit's most general definition of telic egalitarianism accomodates both the intrinsic view and the aggregate view, the aggregate view does not commit us to the principle of equality or value pluralism.

Once we establish the distinction between the two views, two distinct, but related, questions arise. First, which view best captures the idea of telic egalitarianism? I suspect that many people would think the intrinsic view better captures the essence of telic egalitarianism. Second, which view is more plausible? I shall not argue for or against either view here. However, as far as I can see, the aggregate view has one important advantage over the intrinsic view. Consider the size of α in (2). The sign α represents the relative weight of the value of people's well-being and the disvalue of inequality. The intrinsic view says nothing about restrictions on α. It can be any number insofar as it is greater than 0. Now suppose that $\alpha = 1$. This means that

$$G = -\tfrac{1}{2}W_1 + \tfrac{3}{2}W_2 \text{ if } W_1 > W_2$$
$$= \tfrac{3}{2}W_1 - \tfrac{1}{2}W_2 \text{ otherwise.}$$

When $\alpha = 1$, the well-being of a better off person counts negatively. An increase in the well-being of the better off decreases the overall goodness of the state of affairs. Clearly, this violates the principle of utility. The intrinsic view gives one the impression that the value of people's well-being and the disvalue of inequality stand or fall independently of each other and that we can determine the relative weight of the two types of values as we wish without undermining either type of value. However, this example clearly shows that this is not the case. If we assign a sufficiently large weight to the disvalue of inequality, we violate the principle of utility. Nonetheless, the intrinsic view obscures this important fact. The violation of the principle of utility is made clear if we adopt the aggregate view.

Those who favor the intrinsic view might accept that the value of the better off person's well being counts less, but claim that the principle of utility is not violated. They could argue that an increase in the better off person's well-being increases the value of people's well-being generally, but that this increase is outweighed by the overwhelming disvalue of inequality. Therefore, the principle of utility is not violated. But a response along these lines is not satisfactory. The response is simply deceptive in the sense that it would have us ignore the stone-solid fact that the well-being of the better off person counts negatively in estimating the overall goodness of a state of affairs. The function $f()$ in $f(I, W)$ is supposed to (a) be strictly increasing in W and decreasing in I, and (b) determine the relative importance of W and I. And yet (b) undermines (a) in some cases, like $\alpha = 1$ in equation (2). One of the basic ideas of the intrinsic view undermines another of its basic ideas and the above response obscures this internal inconsistency. This is a problem with the intrinsic view.

Here is a related problem for the intrinsic view. On the intrinsic view, it seems as though the goodness of people's well-being and the badness of inequality can be determined independently of each other. According to the intrinsic view, the goodness of a state of affairs is a function of the goodness of well-being, W, and the badness of inequality, I. We simply enter the value of W and I, and compute the overall goodness of the state of affairs. The value of W can be determined independently of the badness of inequality. Can the badness of inequality be determined independently of the goodness of well-being? Compare two states of affairs, (10, 20) and (110, 120). Is the badness of inequality the same? Many people would judge that the size of inequality in (10, 20) is greater than that in (110, 120), even though the absolute difference is the same in these two states of affairs. They would also judge that the badness of inequality in (10, 20) is greater than that in (110, 120). If these judgments are correct, the size and the badness of inequality depends partly on the goodness of well-being. Therefore it is not the case that W and I are determined independently of each other. But the intrinsic view obscures this important fact.

3.5 The scope problem

In "Equality or Priority?", Parfit posed two challenges to telic egalitarianism. We have already discussed the leveling down objection. We shall now examine the other problem: the scope problem. Parfit merely mentions this problem. It is not clear whether Parfit really believes this is a problem for telic egalitarianism. Needless to say, Parfit conceives of telic egalitarianism as the view that takes equality to be intrinsically valuable. Therefore, he poses the scope problem for the intrinsic view of telic egalitarianism, not the aggregate view.

Parfit starts with the following question: "who are the people who, ideally, should be equally well off?" (Parfit 2000: 88). Parfit speculates that telic egalitarianism would answer: "everyone who ever lives" (Parfit 2000: 88). According to Parfit's speculation, telic egalitarianism should not care where or when these people live.

However, there are at least two cases where such an answer appears counterintuitive. One is the *divided world case* (Parfit 2000: 87, 99–100). Imagine that two halves of the world population are each unaware of the other's existence. If one population is worse off than the other, is this in itself bad? According to Parfit, telic egalitarianism would say it is. But Parfit thinks that this might sound counterintuitive to some people. The other is the *Inca case* (Parfit 2000: 88). If Inca peasants, who ceased to exist a long time ago, were worse off than we are now, is this in itself bad? Parfit thinks that telic egalitarianism would say it is. But this might sound counterintuitive to some people.

Parfit then considers two responses on behalf of telic egalitarianism. First, telic egalitarians may still claim that inequality is in itself bad, but add that it is so only when it holds between related groups. To this possible response, Parfit points out that there is a "strange coincidence" (Parfit 2000: 88) between the disvalue of the inequality and the relation of the groups, and hence that the restriction on the scope of equality is not plausible. Second, telic egalitarians might concede that inequality is in itself bad only when it holds within one community. However, according to Parfit, these egalitarians are concerned with social injustice in a community instead of the intrinsic badness of inequality, and thus support deontic rather than telic egalitarianism. In sum, Parfit's scope problem is this: if the scope of equality is not limited, there are counterintuitive implications (the divided world case and the Inca case). If the scope is limited, telic egalitarianism is either strange, or it is no longer telic egalitarianism.

The scope problem does not seem particularly intriguing to proponents of telic egalitarianism. There is nothing counterintuitive about the unlimited scope of equality in telic egalitarianism. Telic egalitarians can simply assert that inequality is in itself bad, regardless of where or when people live. As for the divided world case, there are two things to mention. First, as I said in section 3.1, telic egalitarianism is about the goodness of states of affairs. That is, telic egalitarianism is axiological, not teleological. Telic egalitarianism judges that inequality between two divided halves makes the outcome worse. According to telic egalitarianism, if more coconuts wash up on the shore of the worse off half than on that of the better off half, the outcome gets better. As I said in section 3.1, what we ought to do about this inequality does not follow directly from the goodness of states of affairs unless we explicitly commit to consequentialism. There is nothing implausible or counterintuitive in simply asserting that equality between the two halves makes the outcome better even if there is nothing we can do about it. Second, it seems irrelevant to telic egalitarianism whether or not people know about other people's situations. Even within one community, people are not aware of the well-being level of every single other person. But this does not make it counterintuitive to support telic egalitarianism within one community. Likewise, the fact that two halves of the world population are not aware of each other's existence does not make it counterintuitive to support telic egalitarianism.

Next, consider how telic egalitarianism would respond to the Inca case. The state of deceased Inca people is rock solid, and there is nothing we can do about it. We cannot transfer any resources from ourselves to the Inca peasants. When distributive judgments are made at a period T, all possible states have a common history, regardless of distributive principles. All we can do is confined to present and future people, and the scope of our distributive judgments is also confined to present and future people.

The problem arising from the Inca case is not confined to telic egalitarianism. If the Inca case is a problem at all, it is a problem for any consequentialist theory. Given that the well-being of present-day people remains constant, if we increase the well-being of the Inca people, the outcome becomes better, and therefore it is right to increase the well-being of the Inca people. And yet, alas, we cannot increase their well-being. This is regrettable. But there is nothing we can do about it. Compare two states of affairs, which specify the history of the Inca people's well-being. For simplicity, there are two sets of people: Inca peasants and present-day people. Compare $X = (10, 20)$ and $Y = (20, 20)$. The number on the left-hand side represents the level of the Inca peasants' well-being, and the number on the right-hand side the level of present-day people's well-being. Telic egalitarianism judges that there is inequality in X and that this makes Y worse than X in one respect. Utilitarianism judges that the level of the Inca peasants' well-being is lower in X than Y, and that this makes Y worse than X. Both telic egalitarianism and utilitarianism make judgments about the relative goodness of X and Y (prioritarianism, which we will discuss in the next chapter, also judges that Y is better than X). If it were possible to choose to bring about X or Y, it would be the case that Y should be brought about. However, it is not possible. There is nothing we can do. But there is nothing peculiar to consequentialist theories in saying that Y is better than X.

The alleged problem from the Inca case is due to a misunderstanding about the notion of states of affairs. Usually, it is understood in the following way. A state of affairs is a complete description of the world, which includes the history of the world. Consequentialist theories establish an ordering defined over a set of states of affairs. The states of deceased people are taken into account. But we cannot do anything about what is past. Therefore, their states do not affect the rightness or wrongness of our present-day act. For example, Blackorby et al. (1995) make this point explicit and impose what they call the *independence of the utilities of the dead* on our evaluation of states of affairs.

Even if the unlimited scope of equality is seen as counterintuitive, there is nothing strange in claiming that there is a certain condition on the scope of equality. As we saw in section 3.4, a final value can be conditional. If the value of equality is understood as a final value rather than an intrinsic value, it is not strange to claim that equality is valuable for its own sake only under certain conditions. An evening dress is valuable for its own sake if it belonged to Princess Diana, whereas another evening dress with the same intrinsic properties is of little value for its own sake if it belonged to my mother. Likewise, telic egalitarianism can contend that equality is valuable for its own sake when it holds between related groups or when it holds between living people (which may include future people).

3.6 The telic-deontic distinction revisited

While not a serious threat to telic egalitarianism, the scope problem may illuminate a difference between telic and deontic egalitarianism concerning why inequality matters. Parfit, at least, who first introduced the distinction between telic and deontic egalitarianism, suggests that the scope of equality distinguishes telic egalitarianism and deontic egalitarianism. In section 3.1, following Parfit, I defined telic egalitarianism as the view that equality makes the outcome better, and deontic egalitarianism as the view that inequality involves a violation of some deontological constraint. In this section, I will consider why Parfit thinks that the scope of equality might distinguish the two views and whether his thought is correct.

Parfit suggests that the distinction between telic and deontic egalitarianism lies in the scope of equality. He points this out in the divided-world case (Parfit 2000: 88, 100). Two halves of the world population are each unaware of the other's existence. Suppose that one population is worse off than the other. Suppose further that this inequality was naturally caused, not the result of actions by any person, government, or social system. Telic egalitarianism claims that this inequality is a bad outcome. This is because, according to telic egalitarianism, inequality is a bad outcome, no matter how it is brought about. Deontic egalitarianism, on the other hand, claims that such inequality is not unjust. This is because the inequality was naturally caused, and nobody is held responsible for it. If this inequality was caused or maintained by some people or government, then deontic egalitarianism would find it unjust. In this particular example, where there is no interaction between the two halves, deontic egalitarianism does not find anything morally problematic. Whether inequality gives rise to moral concern depends on how it was brought about. This is Parfit's interpretation of the distinction of telic and deontic egalitarianism.

Parfit seems to think that telic egalitarianism and deontic egalitarianism are mutually exclusive. But they do not need to be so (Lippert-Rasmussen 2007). There is an alternative interpretation, which I will now turn to. Deontic egalitarianism sets limits to which cases of inequality are bad outcomes. Cases of inequality are not bad if nobody is responsible for them. Cases of inequality are bad if somebody can be held responsible for those unequal distributions. This means that deontic egalitarianism identifies the scope of telic egalitarianism. This is not a peculiar interpretation. Some proponents of telic egalitarianism support this interpretation in one way or another. For example, Larry Temkin takes telic egalitarianism to be the view that it is bad for some to be worse off than others through no fault or choice of their own (Temkin 1993: 13). This means that inequality is not bad for the worse off people if it results from a fault or choice of their own. By adding the "through no fault or choice of their own" clause, it is possible for telic egalitarianism to incorporate considerations to do with how inequality was brought about.

Temkin's characterization of telic egalitarianism has further implications. It can be seen as a form of luck egalitarianism. The "through no fault or choice of their own" clause gets at exactly what luck egalitarianism is concerned with. According to luck egalitarianism, some inequalities are morally relevant, and others are not. Luck egalitarianism offers grounds for explaining which inequalities are morally relevant and which inequalities are not. Some luck egalitarians understand the inequality resulting from intentional choice in deontic terms: it is unfair or unjust. Others understand it in teleological terms: it is bad. There is diversity among luck egalitarians concerning how they interpret the normative nature of inequalities arising from option luck. However, if it is understood as teleological, then telic egalitarianism is perfectly consistent with luck egalitarianism. This is one way to show that telic and deontic egalitarianism are consistent, not mutually exclusive.

Chapter summary

Telic egalitarianism contends that equality makes the outcome better. It is an axiological, not a teleological, principle. There are two interpretations concerning how we should characterize telic egalitarianism. The first is the intrinsic view, according to which equality is intrinsically good. The second is the aggregate view, which holds that equality is a feature of the aggregative process of people's well-being. It gives priority to benefiting people who are worse off than others. Although these views are extensionally equivalent, there are significant differences. We examined two major objections leveled against telic egalitarianism. The leveling down objection is often seen as a devastating objection. However, there are three responses in defense of telic egalitarianism. Furthermore, it could be argued that the aggregate view avoids the objection. The scope objection points to another alleged implausible implication of telic egalitarianism. According to this objection, telic egalitarianism must judge that inequality between two isolated worlds is bad for its own sake, and that inequality between deceased Inca people and present-day people is also bad for its own sake. The objection, however, points out that such a judgment is implausible. This is not an objection confined to telic egalitarianism, but extends to all axiological principles.

Further reading

The most comprehensive defense of telic egalitarianism is Temkin (1993), although he did not call it telic egalitarianism. Needless to say, the starting point of the current debate concerning telic egalitarianism is Parfit's lecture (2000), which must be read very carefully. Lippert-Rasmussen (2007) offers an original analysis of the distinction between telic and deontic egalitarianism. For the debate concerning the leveling down objection, see Broome (2002), Brown (2003), Christiano and Braynen (2008), Mason (2001), Raz (2009), and Temkin (2000). For the aggregate view of telic egalitarianism, see Hirose (2009). Peterson and Hansson (2005) argues that telic egalitarianism and prioritarianism are consistent. It is Atkinson (1970), who first introduced the notion of an equally distributed equivalent and attempted to measure inequality in terms of the good that could have been obtained under perfect equality. For the economic literature on inequality measurement, see Cowell (2011) and Sen and Foster (1997).

Notes

1 Notice that the person-affecting view is distinct from the Pareto principle. The Pareto principle holds that a state of affairs X is better than another state of affairs Y if (not "only if") there is some one for whom X is better than Y, and X is worse for no one than Y.

2 But equation (4) is for the two-person case. Equation (4) can easily be generalized to the n-person case. The formula in the n-person case is the following:

$$\frac{1}{n^2}\{w_i + 3w_j + 5w_k + \ldots + (2n-1)w_n\}, \text{ for } w_i \geq w_j \geq w_k \geq \ldots \geq w_n$$

This formula is known as the *Gini social welfare function* in economics.

4

PRIORITARIANISM

In chapter 3, we examined Parfit's view of telic egalitarianism and its alleged problems. In response to these problems, Parfit put forward his own distributive principle: the *priority view* or *prioritarianism* (Parfit 1995, 2000). In a relatively short period, prioritarianism has gained wide support. In this chapter, I will first present a precise formulation of prioritarianism. I will then compare prioritarianism with telic egalitarianism, because prioritarianism is presented as an alternative to telic egalitarianism. It is particularly important to understand the precise formulation of prioritarianism because some people might mistakenly think that it includes any principle that can be phrased as "giving priority to X." Nozick's side-constraint theory gives priority to individual rights over aggregate well-being, but is obviously not a version of prioritarianism. Thus, I will devote some space to elucidating what prioritarianism is and is not.

This chapter is organized in the following way. Section 4.1 first follows Parfit's characterization of prioritarianism and then presents a formal definition of it. Section 4.2 elucidates the formal structure of the doctrine and compares it with that of utilitarianism and telic egalitarianism. Section 4.3 clarifies that some distributive principles cannot be seen as a version of prioritarianism and explains why. Sections 4.4 and 4.5 examine three objections leveled against the theory. Section 4.6 examines the objections that advocates of prioritarianism raise against telic egalitarianism.

4.1 Prioritarianism: basic idea

As we saw, Parfit poses two problems to telic egalitarianism: the leveling down objection and the scope problem. These two problems motivate Parfit to propose an alternative principle. This is the priority view or prioritarianism. It rejects the idea that inequality is in itself bad. Instead, it contends that we should give priority to benefiting the worse off. Like egalitarianism, prioritarianism may be either telic or deontic. In this chapter, I will concentrate on the telic version. That is, I will examine a version of prioritarianism that concerns the relative goodness of states of affairs.

Parfit defines prioritarianism in the following way:

> *Prioritarianism* (informal definition): Benefiting people matters more the worse off those people are.
>
> (Parfit 2000: 19)

This definition needs explanation. Prioritarianism consists essentially in two basic features: non-relationality, and the law of diminishing marginal moral goodness. I will explain these two features in order.

I will start with non-relationality. According to Parfit's intrinsic view of telic egalitarianism, it commits us to the value of equality. Equality is essentially about the relation between different people's well-being. Because of the value associated with interpersonal relations, telic egalitarianism implies that leveling down makes a state of affairs better in one respect. To avoid this allegedly absurd implication, Parfit wants to eliminate the relational feature from his principle. His proposed prioritarianism is essentially non-relational.

Parfit maintains that the amount of good certain benefits do for a person should be determined only by the absolute level of his or her own well-being, independently of the well-being of other people. According to prioritarianism, if people are worse off it is because they are at a lower absolute level of well-being than they might have been: people are worse off in absolute, not relative, terms. Thus, according to prioritarianism, the goodness of a person's well-being depends only on the absolute level of his or her well-being. The goodness of his or her well-being constitutes the overall goodness of the state of affairs together with the goodness of other people's well-being. Therefore, Parfit's alternative principle takes the form $G = g(W_1) + g(W_2) + g(W_3) + \ldots + g(W_n)$, where $g()$ determines how good a person's well-being is.

Utilitarianism is also non-relational. However, Parfit does not commit to utilitarianism. Unlike the utilitarian, he thinks that the well-being of a worse off person "matters more" than the well-being of a better off person. This concern for the worse off is the second essential feature of prioritarianism. Parfit explains his idea with what he calls the law of diminishing moral goodness.

> We believe that, if benefits go to people who are better off, these benefits matter less. Just as *resources* have diminishing marginal *utility*, so *utility* has diminishing marginal *moral importance*. Given the similarity between these claims, there is a second similar argument in favour of equality: this time, not of resources, but of well-being. On this argument, whenever we transfer resources to people who are worse off, the resulting benefits will not merely be, in themselves, greater. They will also, on the moral scale, matter more. There are thus two ways in which the outcome will be better.
>
> (Parfit 2000: 24, original italics)

In section 1.1, I discussed the notion of diminishing marginal utility, and the way in which utilitarianism can be seen as egalitarian. We must distinguish Parfit's law of diminishing "moral goodness" from diminishing marginal "utility." The notion of diminishing marginal utility holds that the marginal increase in pleasure (or desire-satisfaction, or preference-satisfaction) from additional resources diminishes. On the other hand, Parfit's law of marginal moral goodness holds that the marginal moral importance of well-being diminishes as the absolute level of well-being gets higher. Utilitarianism does not accept the law of diminishing marginal moral goodness. According to utilitarianism, the moral importance of one unit of a person's well-being remains constant, regardless of the absolute level of his or her well-being. On the other hand, according to prioritarianism, the moral importance of one unit of well-being at a higher absolute level is smaller than that at a lower absolute level. The idea of the law of diminishing moral goodness is depicted in figure 4.1.

Figure 4.1 shows that the goodness of well-being, $g(W)$, diminishes as the absolute level of well-being, W, gets higher. The curve is strictly increasing, but bends downwards. The shape of this curve is called *strictly concave*.[1] That is, the goodness of a person's well-being is an increasing, strictly concave function of his or her well-being. Let us put it a bit more precisely. Consider some increase in a person's well-being, $e > 0$. An increasing, strictly concave function $g()$ is such that: $g(W + e) - g(W) < g(W' + e) - g(W')$, for $W > W'$. That is to say, the additional good derived

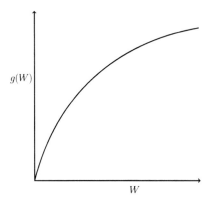

$g(W)$

W

Figure 4.1

from some increase, e, to the well-being of the worse off is greater than the additional good derived from the same increase e to the well-being of the better off. According to prioritarianism, giving some benefit to a worse off person yields more good than giving it to a better off person. For example, increasing the well-being level from 5 to 6 produces a greater amount of moral goodness than increasing the well-being level from 10 to 11, although the increase in well-being is the same.

I can now propose a slightly more precise formula for prioritarianism:

> *Prioritarianism* (formal definition): A state of affairs $(W_1, W_2, W_3, \ldots, W_n)$ is at least as good as $(W'_1, W'_2, W'_3, \ldots, W'_n)$ if and only if $(g(W_1) + g(W_2) + g(W_3) + \ldots + g(Wn)) \geq (g(W'_1) + g(W'_2) + g(W'_3) + \ldots + g(W'n))$, where $g()$ is an increasing, strictly concave function.

In this definition, the goodness of a state of affairs is given by the sum of weighted well-being where the weights are determined by an increasing, strictly concave function. One example of this formula is the sum of the square-root function of individual well-being ($\sqrt{2} = 1.414$, $\sqrt{3} = 1.732$, $\sqrt{4} = 2$, $\sqrt{5} = 2.436$, $\sqrt{6} = 2.449$, $\sqrt{7} = 2.645$, and so on): namely, that $(W_1, W_2, W_3, \ldots, W_n)$ is at least as good as $(W'_1, W'_2, W'_3, \ldots, W'_n)$ if and only if $(\sqrt{W_1} + \sqrt{W_2} + \sqrt{W_3} + \ldots + \sqrt{W_n}) \geq (\sqrt{W'_1} + \sqrt{W'_2} + \sqrt{W'_3} + \ldots + \sqrt{W'n})$.

4.2 The structure of prioritarianism

When we observe the formal definition, we immediately notice the following points. First, the goodness of each person's well-being is determined

human nature 2

independently of other people's well-being. The goodness of the well-being of person i is $g(W_i)$, and $g(W_i)$ is determined with no reference to the well-being of other people. The goodness of an increase in a person's well-being diminishes independently of other people's well-being. This reflects the non-relational aspect of prioritarianism.

Second, prioritarianism seems to avoid the leveling down objection. The leveling down of the better off is just bad for that person and not better in any respect. It is not entirely clear whether prioritarianism avoids the scope problem that Parfit posed for telic egalitarianism. Prioritarianism does not say that the inequality between the two disconnected halves of the world population is in itself bad. But it would certainly judge that the outcome is made better if some resources for increasing well-being washed up on the beach of the worse off half than if they washed up on the shore of the better off half. Now the scope problem may crop up for prioritarianism and indeed for any other consequentialist principle.

The formal definition of prioritarianism reveals another interesting fact. A seemingly non-prioritarian principle turns out to be a version of prioritarianism. Consider a principle that holds that the goodness of a state of affairs is given by the product of people's well-being. That is, $(W_1, W_2, W_3, \ldots , W_n)$ is at least as good as $(W'_1, W'_2, W'_3, \ldots , W'_n)$ if and only if $(W_1 \times W_2 \times W_3 \times \ldots \times W_n) \geq (W'_1 \times W'_2 \times W'_3 \times \ldots \times W'_n)$. On the face of it, it is not an additive function or a strictly concave function. Therefore, it is not clear whether this principle is a version of prioritarianism. However, if we take the logarithm, we have: $(W_1, W_2, W_3, \ldots , W_n)$ is at least as good as $(W'_1, W'_2, W'_3, \ldots , W'_n)$ if and only if $(\log W_1 + \log W_2 + \log W_3 + \ldots + \log W_n) \geq (\log W'_1 + \log W'_2 + \log W'_3 + \ldots + \log W'_n)$. Since the log function is strictly concave, this principle is an additive and strictly concave function. Thus, it is a version of prioritarianism.

Sometimes, it is said that prioritarianism is semi-utilitarianism or quasi-utilitarianism. This is not surprising because the formal definition of the doctrine is quite similar to that of classical utilitarianism. So let me consider whether the theory satisfies the basic features of utilitarianism. In section 1.1, I listed six features of utilitarianism. These are (1) consequentialism, (2) welfarism, (3) impartiality, (4) the Pareto principle, (5) strong separability, (6) the cardinal and fully comparable measure of well-being.

Let me start with consequentialism. The definition of prioritarianism I provided above is purely axiological. The definition identifies how the theory evaluates and ranks states of affairs. It does not say that the right act is the one that maximizes the sum of weighted well-being. Strictly

speaking, prioritarianism as set out in the above definition is not a version
of consequentialism, unless it is additionally stated that the right act is the
one which brings about the best state of affairs.

It is easy to verify that prioritarianism satisfies (2) welfarism, (3)
impartiality, and (4) the Pareto principle. When prioritarianism estimates
the goodness of a state of affairs, it only considers the well-being of people.
Therefore, it is a version of welfarism. According to prioritarianism, permutations of personal identities do not affect the distributive judgment.
Therefore, it satisfies impartiality. If a person's well-being is increased and
the well-being of other people is kept unchanged, the outcome becomes
strictly better. Therefore, prioritarianism satisfies the Pareto principle.

It is also easy to verify that the theory satisfies strong separability. Consider
the example of two binary comparisons in table 1.1 in section 1.1. I will
reproduce it as table 4.1 here. Strong separability holds that A is better than
B if and only if C is better than D, or that B is better than A if and only if D
is better than C. According to prioritarianism, the relative goodness of A
and B depends on the value of $g(2) + g(2)$ and $g(1) + g(4)$, and the
relative goodness of C and D also depends on the value of $g(2) + g(2)$ and
$g(1) + g(4)$. Therefore, prioritarianism makes consistent judgments in the
comparison of A and B and the comparison of C and D. Thus, it satisfies
strong separability. This is not surprising. Prioritarianism is supposed to be
non-relational, and strong separability captures the feature of non-relationality.

Prioritarianism requires a cardinal measure that is interpersonally comparable in terms of both the unit and level of well-being. In section 1.1, I
remarked that utilitarianism requires only the comparability of the unit of
well-being. That is, in order to determine the relative goodness of two
states of affairs, utilitarianism only requires comparing the gain and loss for
each person. However, prioritarianism requires knowledge of the level of
well-being, too. Utilitarianism holds that the increase of 1 unit in a person's
well-being has the same moral importance, no matter how well off he or
she is. In contrast, prioritarianism holds that the moral goodness of 1 unit

Table 4.1

	1	2	3	4	5	6
A	2	2	2	2	2	2
B	1	4	2	2	2	2
C	2	2	1	1	1	1
D	1	4	1	1	1	1

of a person's well-being depends on how well off he or she is. The moral goodness of an increase of 1 unit is smaller if the initial level of well-being is 20 than if it is 10. Thus, prioritarianism requires knowledge of both the level and unit of each person's well-being.

Prioritarianism satisfies five basic features of utilitarianism. Therefore, it is understandable to see prioritarianism as semi-utilitarianism or quasi-utilitarianism. But prioritarianism requires a stronger measure of well-being than utilitarianism. The most important difference is that in prioritarianism, the marginal moral goodness of an increase in well-being diminishes as the absolute level of well-being gets higher, whereas, on utilitarianism, it does not. This is a significant difference.

I want to examine the structure of prioritarianism by way of comparison with telic egalitarianism. It is particularly illuminating to compare prioritarianism with the aggregate view of telic egalitarianism. In section 3.4, I examined the theoretical structure of the aggregate view of telic egalitarianism, which takes the form of:

$$G = \frac{1}{4} W_1 + \frac{3}{4} W_2 \text{ if } W_1 > W_2$$

$$= \frac{3}{4} W_1 + \frac{1}{4} W_2 \text{ otherwise.}$$

According to this formula, it is clear that telic egalitarianism gives priority to benefits to the worse off. The well-being of the worse off receives a weight of ¾, and that of the better off receives a weight of ¼. This means that an increase of one unit of well-being for the worse off is more important than the same increase for the better off. Thus, telic egalitarianism implies that "benefiting people matters more the worse off those people are."

Certainly, that is strange. Prioritarianism is meant to be an alternative to telic egalitarianism. But these supposedly rival views both agree on giving priority to benefiting the worse off. What is going on? To answer this question, I must answer two separate questions. The first is: what is it to "give priority to benefiting the worse off"? The second is: is there any difference in the way that telic egalitarianism and prioritarianism give priority to benefiting the worse off?

I will answer the second question first. This is because it is easy to answer, and Parfit himself gives a clear answer:

The chief difference [between Prioritarianism and telic egalitarianism] can be introduced like this. I have said that, on the Priority View, we do not believe in equality. We do not think it in itself bad, or unjust, that some people are worse off than others. This claim can be misunderstood. We do of course think it bad that some people are worse off. But what is bad is not that these people are worse off than *others*. It is rather that they are worse off than *they* might have been. ... [O]n the Priority View, benefits to the worse off matter more, but this is only because these people are at a lower *absolute* level. It is irrelevant that these people are worse off *than others*. Benefits to them would matter just as much even if there *were* no others who were better off. ... The chief difference is, then, this. Egalitarians are concerned with *relativities*: with how people's level compares with the level of other people. On the Priority View, we are concerned only with people's absolute levels.

(Parfit 2000: 104, original italics)

The difference lies in what it is to be "worse off." According to telic egalitarianism, a person is worse off only in comparison with others. The well-being of the worse off person receives greater weight, but this weight is determined by his or her rank-order position in a ranking by well-being level. According to prioritarianism, a person is worse off in absolute terms, not in comparison with others. The weight of the well-being of the worse off depends only on the absolute level of his or her well-being. It does not matter how his or her well-being fares in comparison with others'.

Here is an interesting implication. Imagine a world in which only one person exists. In this world, on telic egalitarianism, this single person cannot be worse off, because there is no other person: there must be at least two people for it to be possible to say that a person is worse off. On the other hand, on prioritarianism, this person can be worse off even if there are no other people.

I will now move on to the first question. What is "giving priority to benefiting the worse off" all about? The answer is "egalitarianism in the broadest sense." By egalitarianism in the broadest sense, I mean a class of distributive principles that satisfy the Pigou-Dalton condition. The Pigou-Dalton condition holds the following:

> *The Pigou-Dalton condition*: A transfer of benefit from a better off person to a worse off person makes the outcome strictly better if (1) there is no net loss of well-being in this transfer, (2) the well-being of all other people remains constant, and (3) the relative position of the better off and the worse off is not altered.

According to the Pigou-Dalton condition, we can increase the goodness of a state of affairs by transferring some benefit from a better off person to a worse off one insofar as such a transfer does not affect the total well-being. This means that, provided the total well-being remains constant, the goodness of a state of affairs is maximized when people's well-being is equally distributed. The Pigou-Dalton condition, thus, seems to have an egalitarian implication.

In what follows, I will use PD-ism to refer to a class of distributive principles that satisfy the Pigou-Dalton condition. This is because I want to distinguish this broader notion of egalitarianism from telic egalitarianism. PD-ism includes any distributive principle that gives relatively greater weight to benefiting the worse off.

In the two-person case, the aggregate view of telic egalitarianism assigns a weight of ¾ to the well-being of the worse off and a weight of ¼ to the well-being of the better off. This implies that if some benefit is transferred from the better off to the worse off without a loss in the total amount of well-being, the goodness of the state of affairs increases. This equalizing transfer makes the outcome better up to the point where the level of well-being of the two persons becomes the same. Thus, telic egalitarianism satisfies the Pigou-Dalton condition, and hence is a version of PD-ism.[2]

Prioritarianism also satisfies the Pigou-Dalton condition and hence is a version of PD-ism. This may require some explanation. Prioritarianism gives greater weight to benefiting those with a lower absolute level of well-being. This implies that if some benefit is transferred from the better off to the worse off without a loss in total well-being, the goodness of a state of affairs increases. This equalizing transfer makes the outcome better up to the point where the absolute level of their well-being becomes the same. This means that, provided the total well-being remains constant, the goodness of a state of affairs is maximized when all people's well-being is at the same absolute level. More precisely, if $W_1 + W_2 = W'_1 + W'_2$ and $|W_1 - W_2| < |W'_1 - W'_2|$, it follows that $(g(W_1) + g(W_2)) > (g(W'_1) + g(W'_2))$, when $g()$ is some strictly concave function. As such, prioritarianism is not concerned with the inter-personal distribution of well-being. But it is certainly implied that the best outcome is the one in which people's well-being is distributed equally. Thus, equality plays an important role in prioritarianism. Parfit acknowledges this fact:

> On the definition with which I began, the Priority View is not Egalitarian. On this view, though we ought to give priority to the worse off, that is not because we shall be reducing inequality. We do not believe that inequality

is, in itself, either bad or unjust. But, since this view has a built-in bias towards equality, it could be called Egalitarian in a second, looser sense. We might say that, if we take this view, we are *Non-Relational Egalitarians*.

(Parfit 2000: 25, original italics)

Parfit admits that prioritarianism has a "built-in bias towards equality" although it is non-relational. By "[e]galitarian in a second, looser sense," Parfit refers to what I call PD-ism. PD-ism gives priority to the worse off, but is neutral with respect to whether judgments about well-being should be relational or non-relational. Parfit then says that the proponents of prioritarianism are "Non-Relational Egalitarians." That is, the doctrine is non-relational PD-ism.

Now we have a clear answer to the second question. "Giving priority to the worse off" is PD-ism, and entails both telic egalitarianism and prioritarianism. It is not synonymous with prioritarianism. Relational PD-ism is telic egalitarianism: "worse off" means worse off in comparison with others. Non-relational PD-ism is prioritarianism: "worse off" means being at a lower absolute level. Both telic egalitarianism and prioritarianism belong to the broad class of PD-ism. The difference is in the way "worse off" is understood.

4.3 What is not prioritarianism?

One might wonder if the formal definition of prioritarianism includes principles that give complete priority to the worse off or the worst off. I shall consider two distributive principles: the maximin rule and leximin. The maximin rule claims that we should give *absolute* priority to the worst off. Leximin claims that we should give *lexical* priority to the *worse off*. These principles seem to be a version of prioritarianism because each can be phrased as "giving priority to the worst/worse off." Let me examine each principle.

The maximin rule is defined as follows: a state of affairs $(W_1, W_2, W_3, \ldots, W_n)$ is at least as good as $(W'_1, W'_2, W'_3, \ldots, W'_n)$ if and only if $\min(W_1, W_2, W_3, \ldots, W_n) \geq \min(W'_1, W'_2, W'_3, \ldots, W'_n)$. Despite its popular characterization of "giving absolute priority to the worst off," the maximin rule is not a version of prioritarianism in light of this formal definition. The maximin rule does not satisfy strong separability or strict concavity. To see how the maximin rule violates strong separability, consider two comparisons: between X and Y, and between X' and Y'. Consider again the example of two binary comparisons (A and B, and C and D) in table 4.1 in section 4.2.

Strong separability claims that the relative goodness of two states of affairs is determined by the relative goodness for persons 1 and 2, independently of the well-being of other people. That is, A is better than B if and only if C is better than D, or B is better than A if and only if D is better than C. However, the maximin rule judges that A is strictly better than B while C is equally good as D. Thus, the maximin rule violates strong separability. It is not non-relational, because we cannot judge the relative goodness of distributions unless we compare the well-being of all people.

The maximin rule does not satisfy strict concavity, either. To see this, compare $X = (50, 20, 10)$ and $Y = (40, 30, 10)$. The well-being of person 1 is 10 units higher in X than in Y. The well-being of person 2 is 10 units lower in X than in Y. Person 2 is at a lower absolute level of well-being than person 1. The strictly concave function in prioritarianism implies that Y is strictly better than X because 10 units of well-being for a worse off individual is more important than the same amount of well-being for a better off person. However, the maximin rule judges that X and Y are equally good because the level of the worst off remains unchanged in X and Y (i.e. $\min(50, 20, 10) = \min(40, 30, 10)$).

The maximin function is not even increasing in its arguments. To see this, compare $(20, 10)$ and $(10, 10)$. The strictly increasing function says that the value of $(20, 10)$ must be greater than the value of $(10, 10)$. However, the maximin function says that $\min(20, 10) = \min(10, 10)$. Thus, the maximin function is not strictly increasing or strictly concave. This is not surprising at all. The maximin rule looks at only the worst off and ignores the others. Since the maximin rule violates the essential features of prioritarianism, it cannot be seen as a version of prioritarianism although it is often phrased as "giving priority to the worst off."

What about leximin? According to leximin, a state of affairs $X = (w_1, w_2, \ldots, w_n)$ is strictly better than another state of affairs $Y = (w'_1, w'_2, \ldots, w'_n)$ if there exists a position k in $N = \{1, 2, 3, \ldots, n\}$ such that (1) the well-being level of k is strictly higher in X than in Y and (2) the well-being level of every position $j < k$ is the same in X as in Y. Otherwise, X and Y are equally good. That is, we first compare the well-being level of the worst off across possible states of affairs. When the worst off is at the same level across states of affairs, we compare the second worst off. When the worst off and the second worst off are at the same level, we compare the third worst off across states of affairs. And so on. This process proceeds up to the best off person. It gives lexicographical priority (for short, lexical priority) to the worse off. It is called lexicographical because the distributions are ranked similarly to the way that words are organized in a dictionary: the order of the first letter of each word takes strict priority over the order of its second letter, and so on.

Leximin satisfies strong separability. I do not present a formal proof here. Instead, examine once again the two comparisons in table 4.1. Leximin judges that A is strictly better than B, and that C is strictly better than D. Leximin judges the relative goodness of states of affairs independently of the well-beings of unaffected people.

On the other hand, leximin does not satisfy strict concavity, and for a simple reason. Leximin disallows a trade-off between the worse off and the better off. It is a discontinuous ordering over possible states of affairs, and it cannot be represented in a functional form. Therefore, the goodness of a person's well-being does not diminish even if the absolute level of well-being increases. Leximin therefore does not support the law of diminishing marginal moral goodness.

However, leximin gives priority to the worse off in a limited sense. Compare again $X = (50, 20, 10)$ and $Y = (40, 30, 10)$. Leximin judges that Y is better than X. Leximin agrees with prioritarianism that the increase of 10 units is more important for the worse off than the better off. However, leximin makes a much stronger claim. It claims that *any* increase for the lexically worse off makes the outcome strictly better. For example, compare $X' = (50, 20, 10)$ and $Y' = (30, 21, 10)$, where the well-being of the second best off is increased at enormous cost to the well-being of the best off. This strong commitment to the lexically worse off is known as the *Hammond equity condition* (Hammond 1976). The Hammond equity condition holds that X is better than Y if there exists a j and k such that (1) the well-being level of j is strictly lower in X than Y, (2) the well-being level of k is strictly higher in X than Y, (3) j has a strictly higher well-being level than k in X, and (4) the utility of everyone else is the same in X and Y. Leximin is not concerned with the loss in the total well-being of the non-worse off people insofar as the well-being of the worse off is increased.

Given the Hammond equity condition, it could be asked whether leximin is really non-relational even if it satisfies strong separability. Wlodek Rabinowicz argues that leximin is not non-relational. He claims:

> [I]t is incorrect to interpret Rawls's difference principle as the extreme, lexical form of the Priority View. Rawls's principle gives absolute priority to those people who are worse off than all others. The priority given to the worse off is not, on that principle, due to the fact that these people

are 'worse off than they might have been'. If their welfare level were arbitrarily increased but they would still be worse off than others, improving their lot would still have the same (absolute) priority.

(Rabinowicz 2002: 13)

Supposedly, prioritarianism is non-relational in the sense that the goodness of a person's well-being is determined independently of other people's well-being. Whenever we give complete priority to benefiting the worst off (the second worst off, the third worst off, and so on), we must know who is the worst off (the second worst off, the third worst off, and so on). This means that we must compare the relative position of different people in order to identify whose position is worst, second-worst, and so on. The weight of a lexically worse off person's well-being does not depend on the absolute level of his or her well-being. It all depends on his or her rank-order position, which can only be identified through comparisons of people's well-being levels. Therefore, although leximin satisfies strong separability, from a practical standpoint it violates the two essential features of prioritarianism. For this reason, leximin cannot be seen as a version of prioritarianism.

4.4 Criticisms of prioritarianism: part I

Having identified what prioritarianism is, I shall now consider three criticisms of it in this and the next section. I will examine two criticisms in this section and one other in the next. I do not think any of these criticisms are devastating to prioritarianism. However, a close examination of these criticisms helps us to understand the theory better.

The first criticism is that prioritarianism may be susceptible to the leveling down objection. The leveling down objection is raised against telic egalitarianism. Supposedly, this objection does not apply to prioritarianism. Thus, the leveling down objection is meant to show that prioritarianism has an advantage over telic egalitarianism. In section 3.3, I examined three responses to the leveling down objection in defense of telic egalitarianism. If any of these responses are plausible, the leveling down objection proves too little. On the other hand, if it is shown that the leveling down objection also applies to prioritarianism, it proves too much. Either way, the leveling down objection cannot be seen as showing any advantage of prioritarianism over telic egalitarianism. This criticism is not an objection to prioritarianism. It merely points out that the leveling down objection does not establish a relative advantage of prioritarianism over telic egalitarianism.

There have been a few attempts to show that the leveling down objection applies to prioritarianism. I will concentrate on the argument of John Broome (2002). As Parfit admits, prioritarianism has a built-in bias towards equality, although it does not aim at equality itself. The goodness of a state of affairs is maximized when people's respective well-being is at the same absolute level. If individuals had varying levels of well-being, the goodness of the distribution could be improved by producing a more uniform distribution. Under conditions of inequality, there exists some wasted good thing that could be obtained under conditions of perfect equality. By leveling down, prioritarianism can reduce the wasted good. In the sense that this wasted good is reduced, the leveled down distribution is better. Thus, the leveling down objection actually applies to any principles of PD-ism. Broome appeals to A. B. Atkinson's concept of the *equally distributed equivalent* as a measure of the goodness of a distribution (Atkinson 1970).

What is the equally distributed equivalent? Consider a distribution of n people's well-being: $(w_1, w_2, \ldots, w_n)$. The total well-being of this distribution, W, is given by $W = w_1 + w_2 + \ldots + w_n$. The equally distributed equivalent, W_E, is the total well-being that would be equally as good as this distribution, if it were equally distributed across all people. That is, W_E is $(W_E/n, W_E/n, \ldots, W_E/n)$, which is equally as good as the distribution $(w_1, w_2, \ldots, w_n)$. One distribution has a greater W_E than another if and only if it is a better distribution. Therefore, the W_E of a distribution can serve as a measure of the goodness of the distribution.

PD-ism implies that a more equal distribution is better than a less equal one, other things being equal. Therefore, it is the case that $W \geq W_E$. $W = W_E$ only if the distribution is perfectly equal. When there is an inequality, the difference $(W - W_E)$ is a measure of the badness of inequality. $(W - W_E)$ measures how much less total well-being there could be in a distribution that still achieves the same overall goodness, if only it were equally distributed. In other words, $(W - W_E)$ is the amount of well-being wasted by inequality. Now, W_E can be represented by the following equation:

$$W_E = W - (W - W_E).$$

This equation shows that W_E, which measures the goodness of the distribution, is given by two components. The first is total well-being, represented by W. The second is the badness of inequality, represented by $(W - W_E)$. Leveling down reduces the badness of inequality $(W - W_E)$. Therefore, leveling down is good insofar as it reduces the badness of inequality $(W - W_E)$. This judgment applies to any principle which implies that a more equal distribution is better than a less equal one. Therefore, it applies to prioritarianism, too. Thus, prioritarianism is susceptible to the leveling down objection. By simply changing the measure of the goodness of a distribution, we can have a different perspective, according to which all PD-ist principles are susceptible to the leveling down objection.

It is not clear whether the leveling down objection proves too little or too much. And yet, it would be hasty to conclude that prioritarianism is more plausible than telic egalitarianism solely on the basis of the leveling down objection.

The second criticism is concerned with the measure of well-being and its effect on our distributive judgment. Prioritarianism claims that the goodness of each person's well-being is determined by the absolute level of his or her well-being. The choice of the measure of people's well-being, however, affects the distributive judgment of prioritarianism. To see this, consider a case where the numerical representation of the level of people's well-being is altered. We only alter the numerical representation of the level of well-being. This does not mean that people's actual levels of well-being are altered. Suppose now, that for some reason (say because of inflation), the numerical representation of the level of well-being is increased. Let us consider a simple two-person case, where the prioritarian function is a square-root function: a distribution $X = (W_1, W_2)$ is at least as good as $Y = (W'_1, W'_2)$ if and only if $\sqrt{W_1} + \sqrt{W_2} \geq \sqrt{W'_1} + \sqrt{W'_2}$.

Now, compare $X = (5, 20)$ and $Y = (12, 12)$. According to the square-root prioritarian function, Y is better than X (the goodness of X is $\sqrt{5} + \sqrt{20} = 2.24 + 4.47 = 6.71$, whereas the goodness of Y is $\sqrt{12} + \sqrt{12} = 3.46 + 3.46 = 6.92$). Next, suppose that the level of each person's well-being is numerically increased by 100. Notice that this alteration does not mean that people's actual levels of well-being are altered. The comparison we will consider is the one between $X' = (105, 120)$ and $Y' = (112, 112)$. In this new comparison, according to prioritarianism, X' is better than Y' (the goodness of X' is $\sqrt{105} + \sqrt{120} = 10.25 + 10.95 = 21.20$, whereas the goodness of Y' is $\sqrt{112} + \sqrt{112} = 10.58 + 10.58 = 21.16$). I have only changed the way of representing the level of well-being. This means that people's actual well-being remains the same. However, the distributive judgment of prioritarianism has changed. In this example, I used a square-root function for the prioritarian function. But this sort of change in the distributive judgment, due to the choice of numerical representation of well-being levels, always takes place so long as the prioritarian function is non-linear. We should ask why the distributive judgment changes when the numerical representation of well-being levels is altered, while the actual well-being of people remains the same. According to prioritarianism, the choice of the level of the measure alters the distributive judgment.

On the other hand, according to some distributive principles such as utilitarianism, the maximin rule, leximin, and telic egalitarianism, this sort of change in the distributive judgment, due to the choice of numerical representation of the level of well-being, does not take place. Take telic egalitarianism, for instance. According to telic egalitarianism, the goodness of a state of affairs is an increasing, linear combination of people's well-being. Apply equation (4) from section 3.3 to the two binary comparisons above. It is the case that $\frac{3}{4} \times 5 + \frac{1}{4} \times 20 < \frac{1}{2}(12 + 12)$ and that $\frac{3}{4} \times 105 + \frac{1}{4} \times 120 < \frac{1}{2}(112 + 112)$. This means that the distributive judgment of telic egalitarianism is not affected by the choice of the level of well-being. Nor is the distributive judgment of the maximin rule and leximin. Both the maximin rule and leximin judge that $(12, 12)$ is strictly better than $(5, 20)$ and that $(112, 112)$ is strictly better than $(105, 120)$.

The distributive judgment of prioritarianism is affected by the choice of the level of well-being. This sounds odd. But this criticism is not necessarily devastating to prioritarianism. Proponents of prioritarianism can claim the following: the shape of the prioritarian function is altered if the level of well-being is altered. That is, the shape of the prioritarian function depends on the measure of well-being. The plausibility of this claim hinges on how we see the measure of well-being. According to prioritarianism, the goodness of a person's well-being depends on the absolute level of his or her well-being. Does the absolute level of well-being make sense? Many natural properties such as height and weight can be measured in absolute terms. However, well-being is not like height or weight. In the literature on distributive justice, we often represent the level of people's well-being by a numerical scale. But usually we think that there is no independent meaning in the numerical representation of people's well-being. A higher numerical value of a person's well-being merely means a relatively higher level of well-being. Ten is higher than 1, and 0 is higher than -5. The measure of well-being is like the measure of temperature. When one state is hotter than another, we represent the relation of these two states by a numerical scale such as Celsius or Fahrenheit. These scales are not an absolute measure. Proponents of prioritarianism may well find an absolute measure of well-being in future. Until then, prioritarianism has been proved to have an odd implication, which telic egalitarianism and other principles do not have.

4.5 Criticisms of prioritarianism: part II

The third criticism is concerned with whether or not there exists a strict concave goodness function, independently of distributions. The prioritarian function determines how much a person's well-being counts in the overall goodness of a state of affairs. According to prioritarianism, a person's well-being counts less as the absolute level of his well-being becomes higher. How much each person's well-being counts is given by a strictly concave function, independently of distributions. This claim has an odd implication.

According to Parfit, there is a moral scale of how much a person's well-being counts, just like he claims that there is an absolute measure of well-being.

> It may help to use this analogy. People at higher altitudes find it harder to breath. Is this because they are higher up than other people? In one sense, yes. But they would find it just as hard to breath even if there were no other people who were lower down. In the same way, on the Priority View, benefits to the worse off matter more, but that is only because these people are at a lower absolute level.
>
> (Parfit 2000: 23)

Parfit thinks that the relation between a person's well-being and how much his or her well-being counts toward the overall goodness of a state of affairs is like the one between the altitude and how hard it is to breathe. He thinks that there is an absolute moral scale of how much each person's well-being counts. This is given as a fact. It is difficult to believe that there is no such moral scale. To see the implication of such an independent prioritarian function, imagine a situation, in which only one person exists. Call this person *Robinson*. Does the goodness of Robinson's well-being diminish as the absolute level of his well-being gets higher? Parfit's answer is "yes." He writes:

> It is irrelevant that these people are worse off *than others*. Benefits to them would matter just as much even if there *were* no others who were better off.
>
> (Parfit 2000: 23, original italics)

According to Parfit, benefits to Robinson matter more if he is at a lower absolute level. The goodness of his well-being diminishes as the absolute level of his well-being gets higher. This is counterintuitive, or so the objection says.

We should clearly distinguish three elements: a person's well-being, the goodness of his or her well-being, and the goodness of a state of affairs. What individual well-being means is clear, so there is no need to explain it. The goodness of each person's well-being is one individual component of the goodness of a state of affairs. It is concerned with how much each person's well-being contributes to the overall goodness of that state of affairs. The overall goodness of a state of affairs is the aggregated value of the goodness of each person's well-being. In the case of prioritarianism, the individual well-being of person i is W_i. The goodness of his individual well-being is $g(W_i)$, where $g()$ is a strictly concave function. And the goodness of the state of affairs is given by $g(W_1) + g(W_2) + \ldots + g(W_n)$.

In the one-person case, Robinson's well-being is W_R. The goodness of his well-being is $g(W_R)$. The goodness of the state of affairs is $g(W_R)$ because there are no other people. Thus, the goodness of Robinson's well-being is equal to the goodness of the state of affairs. It sounds odd that the goodness of Robinson's well-being diminishes as the absolute level of his well-being gets higher, even when there is no other person to be compared with him. Some people would think that the goodness of Robinson's well-being is exactly Robinson's well-being. This implication of prioritarianism is counterintuitive. And yet, such a counterintuitive implication cannot be seen as a knock-down argument against prioritarianism.

Several philosophers have pointed out this counterintuitive implication. However, there are different claims made based on this point. Rabinowicz (2002) made this point but does not see it as a knock-down argument against prioritarianism. It is not clear whether he supports prioritarianism or something else. McCarthy (2008) supports utilitarianism based on the fact that prioritarianism is committed to diminishing moral goodness even in the one-person case. This is because utilitarianism judges that the goodness of a person's well-being does not diminish in both the one-person and multiperson cases, thereby avoiding the above counterintuitive implication of prioritarianism.

On the aggregate view of telic egalitarianism, in the one-person case the goodness of Robinson's well-being is equal to his well-being. When there is only one person, there is no inequality. Therefore, according to telic egalitarianism, nothing can reduce or increase the moral importance of Robinson's well-being, and the goodness of the state of affairs is equal to Robinson's well-being. This contrast is not surprising. Prioritarianism contends that there is an absolute measure of the goodness of well-being, regardless of how people's well-being is spread out. This is the case even when there is only one person. The claim that the goodness of Robinson's well-being diminishes in the one-person case is the direct consequence of the claim that there exists a moral scale of the goodness of well-being independently of distributions.

It may strike some people as counterintuitive that the moral goodness of Robinson's well-being diminishes as the absolute level of his well-being gets higher. However, being counterintuitive is not a robust criticism. We may well change our intuition. Otsuka and Voorhoeve argue that prioritarianism's implication in the one-person case is more than counterintuitive (Otsuka and Voorhoeve 2009). They argue that it proves the implausibility of prioritarianism. They derive this argument by considering the relation between intra- and interpersonal distributive judgment.

Otsuka and Voorhoeve first invite us to consider the following case. Imagine a person who is now in perfect health but who will soon develop one of two health conditions, "slight impairment" or "very severe impairment," and has a 50 percent chance of developing either one or the other. Suppose there is a treatment that is available for each of these conditions, but, in order for it to be effective, it must be taken before it is known which impairment this person will suffer. Moreover, he or she cannot take both treatments. The treatment for the slight impairment would completely eliminate this mild disability. The treatment for the very severe impairment would be completely ineffective against the slight impairment but would move him or her up to the severe impairment, undoubtedly an improvement from the very severe impairment. Call this the *intrapersonal case*. According to Otsuka and Voorhoeve, many people are indifferent between these two types of treatment when they are asked to choose in this person's best interest. Imagine further that you are his or her morally motivated guardian. Otsuka and Voorhoeve stipulate that you are supposed to be indifferent between the two types of treatments.

Otsuka and Voorhoeve then invite us to consider a second case. There are two equally sized groups of people. Imagine that all of them are now in perfect health but the members of one group of individuals are already known to be about to develop the very severe impairment, and the members of the other group are already known to be about to develop the slight impairment. All members of this group have the same preferences regarding health states as in the intrapersonal case. It follows that they all regard a move from the very severe to the severe impairment as providing an increase in utility that is equal to the move from the slight impairment to perfect health. As before, you are the morally motivated guardian and supposed to choose the option that is in their best interest. Call this case the *interpersonal case*. According to Otsuka and Voorhoeve, many people would choose to give the treatment to the people whose condition could be improved from the very severe to the severe impairment.

People's intuitions are quite different in intra- and interpersonal cases. Their intuitions are such that we should be indifferent in the intrapersonal case, whereas in the interpersonal case, we should choose the option that improves the condition from the very severe impairment to the severe impairment. What would prioritarianism claim in these two cases? Otsuka and Voorhoeve rightly say that prioritarianism would choose, in both the intra- and interpersonal cases, the option that moves the patient(s) from the very severe to the severe impairment. Prioritarianism, therefore, goes against people's intuitions. Prioritarianism cannot distinguish the intra- and interpersonal cases, because the moral goodness of a person's well-being depends only on the absolute measure of his or her well-being, not other people's well-being. Otsuka and Voorhoeve assert that prioritarianism violates the separateness of persons because it cannot distinguish the intra- and interpersonal cases. They then conclude that prioritarianism is implausible because it violates the separateness of persons. For them, the separateness of persons is so important that if a principle fails to take the separateness of persons seriously, it is implausible. Otsuka and Voorhoeve take the notion of the separateness of persons very seriously.

Why is the separateness of persons so important? It is Rawls (1971) who first uses this notion. Rawls uses it to criticize classical utilitarianism and nothing else. He does not appeal to the separateness of persons to criticize average utilitarianism, although he is against average utilitarianism. According to Rawls, classical utilitarianism fails to respect the important fact that different people live different lives. What does he mean? On the one hand, it is perfectly legitimate for me to sacrifice 1 unit of my present well-being for the sake of 5 extra units of my well-being because 5 extra units of my future well-being offsets 1 unit of my present well-being. On the other hand, it is not legitimate to impose 1 unit of sacrifice on me for the sake of 5 units of benefit for another person, even though my sacrificing 1 unit of well-being makes the outcome strictly better, all things considered. The difference between the intra- and interpersonal cases is that, in the intrapersonal case, the same person experiences 1 unit of loss and 5 units of gain whereas, in the interpersonal case, there is no person who experiences the gain as well as the loss. Rawls thinks that there is an important difference between the intra- and interpersonal cases, and that utilitarianism fails to respect this difference. This is the objection to classical utilitarianism on the basis of the separateness of persons. As we saw in section 4.2, prioritarianism is a view close to that of classical utilitarianism. Therefore, it is not surprising that the same objection is raised against prioritarianism. As such, the success of the criticism put by Otsuka and Voorhoeve depends on whether the notion of the separateness of persons can serve as a ground for substantive moral argument.

4.6 Prioritarianism versus telic egalitarianism

One of the most hotly debated issues in the recent literature on distributive justice revolves around the relative plausibility of prioritarianism and telic egalitarianism. Therefore, I shall close this chapter by examining it.

In the two previous sections, we examined three objections to prioritarianism. The second and third objections contend that telic egalitarianism is more plausible than prioritarianism. So proponents of telic egalitarianism would claim that these are the relative advantages of telic egalitarianism over prioritarianism.

What are the relative advantages of prioritarianism over telic egalitarianism? Let me consider the intrinsic view and the aggregate view separately. Let me first consider what prioritarians would say about the intrinsic view? The answer is fairly obvious. There seems to be at least one advantage. That is, the intrinsic view is supposed to be susceptible to the leveling down objection whereas prioritarianism is not. By now, we know that this claim is not obviously true. As we saw in section 4.4, Broome claims that prioritarianism is susceptible to the leveling down objection. Broome's claim is perhaps debatable. Nonetheless, proponents of prioritarianism must do more in order to show that prioritarianism is more plausible than the intrinsic view.

I now turn to the aggregate view. Proponents of prioritarianism would make two criticisms. According to the aggregate view, the weight given to each person's well-being remains the same unless his or her relative position is altered. This implies (a) that this weight remains the same as long as his or her ranking is not altered, even if his well-being is increased or decreased, and (b) that this weight is altered when his or her ranking is altered, even when the absolute level is not altered. Proponents of prioritarianism would criticize these two implications of the aggregate view.

The first criticism proceeds as follows. Consider two states of affairs, X = (100, 200) and Y = (20, 200). In both states of affairs, person 1 is worse off than person 2. According to the aggregate view, the weight given to the well-being of person 1 is ¾ in both X and Y, and the weight given to the well-being of person 2 is ¼ in both X and Y. This is because, on the aggregate view, the weight of a person's well-being is determined by the rank-order position of the person in a ranking by well-being level. Proponents of prioritarianism would claim that it is implausible to give the same weight to the well-being of person 1 in X as to the well-being of person 1 in Y. They would claim that we should give *strictly greater* weight to the well-being of person 1 in Y than to the well-being of person 1 in X: we should register the change in the absolute level of person 1's well-being in terms of moral importance. The aggregate view of telic egalitarianism does not register the deterioration of person 1 in terms of moral importance. On the other hand, prioritarianism gives greater weight to benefiting a person with well-being at a lower absolute level. On the basis of this criticism, prioritarians would claim that prioritarianism is more acceptable than the aggregate view.

The second criticism is the following. Let us consider the three-person case. In the three-person case, the weight given to the well-being of the best off is ⅑, the weight given to that of the second best off is ⅓. Now, compare X = (100, 200, 10) and Y = (100, 200, 150), where the well-being levels of persons 1 and 2 remain the same, but the well-being of person 3 is altered in moving from X to Y. In X, the weight given to the well-being of person 1 is ⅓. In Y, it is ⅚. The weight of person 1's well-being is altered even though his or her well-being remains unchanged. What happened is that his or her relative position has been altered. More specifically, he or she has become the worst off in Y. Some proponents of prioritarianism would claim that it is counterintuitive. They might ask how it is possible that the weight of person 1's well-being can be altered without altering his or her well-being.

Defenders of the aggregate view can respond to these two criticisms in the following way. In both cases, the implications of the aggregate view are counterintuitive for prioritarians simply because they endorse non-relationality. The implications of the aggregate view appear to be counter-intuitive in the eyes of prioritarians because the aggregate view (and of course, telic egalitarianism in general) is relational. Prioritarianism holds that the moral goodness of a person's well-being should be determined independently of other people's well-being. The aggregate view rejects this claim and argues that the moral goodness of a person's well-being should depend on other people's well-being. This contrast is precisely what prioritarianism and the aggregate view disagree about. Therefore, it is not surprising that the implications of the aggregate view are counterintuitive for prioritarianism.

Given that proponents of telic egalitarianism can think of reasonable responses, prioritarianism's criticisms of telic egalitarianism do not establish the relative advantages of prioritarianism over telic egalitarianism. I will not attempt to make a final judgment about the relative plausibility of these two views. However, our understanding of both is improved by considering the debate between the two principles.

Finally, let me close this chapter by referring to one last possible criticism of telic egalitarianism that takes average well-being into account. This last criticism compares a one-person case and a multiperson case. Think of the two-person case where the goodness of a state of affairs is given by $\frac{1}{2}(W_1 + W_2) - \frac{1}{4}|W_1 - W_2|$. Suppose that $W_1 = 20$ and that $W_2 = 4$. The goodness of this state of affairs is $\frac{1}{2}(20 + 4) - \frac{1}{4}(20 - 4) = 8$. Imagine that the worse off person (i.e. person 2) is eliminated. In this case it will become a state of affairs where only one person exists. From our discussion in section 4.5, it follows that the goodness of a state of affairs where the well-being of person 1 remains at 20, is 20. This means that the goodness of a state of affairs is improved by eliminating the worse off person (i.e. person 2). Contrast this with a case where the better off person is eliminated. The goodness of this state, where the well-being of person 2 remains at 4, is 4. This is smaller than the goodness of (20, 4), i.e. 8. Eliminating the better off person decreases the goodness of a state of affairs. From these cases, we are tempted to conclude that telic egalitarianism would always recommend eliminating the worse off person because this would make the outcome strictly better. However, this sounds unacceptable.

In section 4.5, we contrasted prioritarianism and telic egalitarianism in the one-person case. Even if there is only one person, according to prioritarianism, the moral goodness of a person's well-being diminishes as the absolute level of his or her well-being gets higher. Critics of prioritarianism find this to be implausible. On the other hand, according to telic egalitarianism, the goodness of a state of affairs in the one-person case is the goodness of his or her well-being. Critics of prioritarianism would claim that telic egalitarianism is more plausible than prioritarianism in this respect. However, if telic egalitarianism judges that the outcome is made better by eliminating the worse off (but not the better off person) in the two-person case, defenders of prioritarianism would claim that telic egalitarianism is implausible.

Does telic egalitarianism really recommend eliminating the worse off person? The question is directly related to the issue we will discuss in chapter 6. There, we will discuss whether we can compare states of affairs with different population sizes. The alleged implausibility of telic egalitarianism is derived from the relative goodness of the one- and two-person states. As we will see later in chapter 6, it is not clear whether we can directly compare states of affairs with different population sizes. If we cannot compare these, the alleged implausible implication of telic egalitarianism turns out to make no sense, as it does not make sense to say that the outcome is made better by eliminating the worse off person. If we can compare such states of affairs, however, the alleged implausibility is a serious problem for telic egalitarianism.

Notice that this problem is not confined to the aggregate view of telic egalitarianism. It applies to almost all principles that take average well-being into account. Take average utilitarianism. The average of the two-person state $(20, 4)$ is 12. The average of the one-person state, where only person 1 exists, is 20. Thus, if the one-person state can be compared with the two-person state, average utilitarianism also judges that the outcome is made better by eliminating the worse off person. There is a general philosophical puzzle here, and I will come back to this problem in chapter 6.

Chapter summary

Prioritarianism is the view that the moral goodness of a person's well-being diminishes as the absolute level of his or her well-being gets higher, and that the goodness of a state of affairs is given by the sum of weighted well-being. It gives priority to benefiting the worse off people, like telic egalitarianism. The difference is that, by the "worse off," prioritarianism means a person at a lower absolute level whereas telic egalitarianism means a person at a lower level than others. Thus, the difference lies in whether the theory is relational or non-relational. Many people see the maximin rule as a version of prioritarianism. But it does not satisfy strong separability or strict concavity, and therefore fails to satisfy the condition of non-relationality. In contrast, leximin satisfies strong separability and other basic features of prioritarianism. We examined three types of objections to prioritarianism. The first is that it is susceptible to the leveling down objection, which Parfit raised against telic egalitarianism and used to motivate prioritarianism. The second is that it requires a tighter measure of well-being. The third is that it cannot distinguish the one- and multi-person cases, although many people believe in the importance of distinguishing the two cases and the notion of the separateness of persons requires this. Finally, in addition to the leveling down objection, we considered two objections that defenders of prioritarianism would put forward against telic egalitarianism. These objections turn out to be a simple restatement of their claim that distributive principles should be non-relational.

Further reading

Once again, Parfit's "Equality or Priority?" (2000) must be read very carefully in order to understand the far-reaching scope of prioritarianism. To my knowledge, it is Weirich (1983), who first proposed what has become known as prioritarianism. Most recently, a vigorous defense of the doctrine is put forward by Adler (2011) and Holtug (2010). For the relation between telic egalitarianism and prioritarianism, see Hirose (2009), Jensen (2003), McKerlie (1994, 2001a), Peterson and Hansson (2005), and Temkin (2000). For the formal structure of the doctrine, see McCarthy (2006, 2008, 2013) and Rabinowicz (2001, 2002). Fleurbaey et al. (2009) examine the possibility of non-aggregative versions of prioritarianism. The objection by Otsuka and Voorhoeve (2009) provoked a lot of discussion (Crisp 2011; Otsuka and Voorhoeve 2011). A recent issue of Utilitas (24(3), 2012) also contains useful papers on this debate, including Parfit's reply (Parfit 2012).

Notes

1 There are two different cases of the strictly concave curve. One is where the moral goodness of well-being increases infinitely. That is, the curve is not bounded above, and goes up infinitely. In this case, there is no limit to the value of the moral goodness of well-being. The other case is where the moral goodness of well-being strictly increases indefinitely but approaches a finite limit. In this case, the curve approaches the level of this limit indefinitely, but never goes above this limit. That is, the value of the moral goodness of well-being is bounded above. For present purposes, I assume that the moral goodness of well-being is not bounded above.

2 According to telic egalitarianism, the goodness of an outcome is a function of people's well-being. The function of telic egalitarianism is *strictly S-concave*, as opposed to strictly concave for prioritarianism. Strict S-concavity is defined as follows: $g()$ is strictly S-concave if for all bistochastic matrices Q, it is

the case that $g(Qx) > g(x)$, where Qx is not x or a permutation of x. A bistochastic matrix is a square matrix where all of the entries are non-negative and each of the rows and columns adds up to one. Suppose that there is a bistochastic matrix Q such that $y = Qx$, where y is not x or a permutation of x. Then, the goodness function is strictly S-concave if $g(y) > g(x)$. In other words, if there exists a bistochastic matrix such that $y = Qx$, there exists a vector of well-being such that a vector y can be obtained from x by a series of transfers from the better off to the worse off. Strict S-concavity claims that y, which is obtained from x by a series of transfers from the better off to the worse off, is better than x. This is exactly what the Pigou-Dalton condition contends, and actually it is as far as we can go with the Pigou-Dalton condition. The function is strictly S-concave if, whenever one distribution of well-being can be obtained from another distribution by a series of equalizing transfers, the goodness of the former is greater than that of the latter. See Dasgupta *et al.* (1973) and Sen and Foster (1997: 54–56).

There is a limit to what we owe others

5

SUFFICIENTARIANISM

Both telic egalitarianism and prioritarianism contend that we should give priority to benefiting the worse off. Should we really? This is the question raised by advocates of what has become known as *sufficientarianism*. Every person other than the best off is worse off to some extent. Should we give priority even to people who are very well off? Sufficientarianism contends that we should not. Instead, it contends that we should give priority to benefiting the badly off, i.e. people whose well-being is below a certain threshold level. Despite its awkward name, sufficientarianism has become a credible alternative to telic egalitarianism and prioritarianism.

In order to illustrate the intuitive attractiveness of sufficientarianism, section 5.1 introduces a result of experimental economics, which suggests that many subjects are attracted to a version of this doctrine. Section 5.2 explains Harry Frankfurt's version of the doctrine, which aims at minimizing the number of people below the sufficiency level. Section 5.3 then introduces Roger Crisp's version of sufficientarianism, which gives priority to benefiting the worse off among people below the sufficiency level and assigns equal weight to benefits to people above the sufficiency level. Capitalizing on Amartya Sen's analysis of the poverty measurement, section 5.4 sketches how the badness of sub-sufficiency well-being should be measured. Section 5.5 examines four objections to sufficientarianism.

5.1 Utilitarianism with a floor

In chapter 1, we compared Rawls's argument for the difference principle with Harsanyi's argument for average utilitarianism. Rawls claims that the rational and self-interested parties in the original position would unanimously choose his two principles of justice, one of which includes the difference principle. In contrast, according to Harsanyi, individuals deprived of information about their actual positions would rationally believe that they have an equal chance of occupying anyone's position. Harsanyi argues that this rational belief and his "representation theorem" jointly establish average utilitarianism. Both Rawls and Harsanyi appeal to rational choice in similar hypothetical situations, but they disagree about the chosen principles. A question arises – what will actual individuals choose when they are placed in a similar situation (as distinguished from the hypothetical question "what would individuals choose if they were placed in the original position?")? Some economists have attempted to answer this question by conducting experiments.

Frohlin and his colleagues conducted experiments at three universities in the US and Canada: the University of Manitoba, the University of Maryland, and Florida State University (Frohlich and Oppenheimer 1993). Students were told to choose one principle among (1) the principle of maximizing the floor, which maximizes the minimum level of income and supposedly corresponds to Rawls's difference principle, (2) the principle of maximizing the average, which maximizes the average income and supposedly corresponds to average utilitarianism, (3) the principle of maximizing the average with a floor constraint, which guarantees a rigid minimum level of income, and (4) the principle of maximizing the average with a range constraint, which guarantees a less rigid minimum level of income. I take (3) and (4) to be particular versions of sufficientarianism. Principles (3) and (4) guarantee a minimum level of income ($12,000 in (3) or around $12,000 in (4)), thus showing a serious concern for people below the floor level. However, if everyone is at or above the floor level, there is no concern for distribution of well-being.

The 220 subjects were grouped five by five. The experiment had three stages. First, subjects were made familiar with the four distributive principles. Second, subjects were given a chance to discuss and collectively choose one distributive principle. If the group reached consensus, payments for this experiment were made according to the principle they agreed upon. If they failed to achieve consensus, they were paid according to an income distribution that was randomly chosen from a set of possible income distributions.

Third, each subject was asked to rank the four principles at various stages of the experiment.

The result of collective choice was this. All groups reached consensus. Out of 44 groups, 35 groups chose the principle of maximizing the average with a floor constraint; 7 groups chose the principle of maximizing the average; 2 groups chose the principle of maximizing the average with a range constraint; and no group chose the principle of maximizing the floor.

The individual ranking of the four principles at the end of the experiment was the following. For the first-place ranking, out of 220 subjects, 150 chose the principle of maximizing the average with a floor constraint; 48 chose the principle of maximizing the average; 12 chose the principle of maximizing the average with a range constraint; and only 9 chose the principle of maximizing the floor. For the last-place ranking, 106 subjects chose the principle of maximizing the floor; 77 chose the principle of maximizing the average with a range constraint; 33 chose the principle of maximizing the average; and only 3 chose the principle of maximizing the average with a floor.

The results suggest the following. The principle of maximizing the floor is the least popular principle in both collective choice and individual choice. The principle of maximizing the average is more popular than the principle of maximizing the floor. But the principle of maximizing the average with a floor is the most popular principle by far (for more recent and comprehensive experimental research methods, see Gaertner and Schokkaert 2011).

Needless to say, we ought to be cautious about how we interpret these experimental results and what kind of normative conclusions we derive from them. It would be too hasty to conclude, for example, that Rawls's difference principle has been refuted. There are at least three reasons for caution. First, subjects were asked to consider distributions of income, not of primary social goods or well-being. According to Rawls, income is only one member of the list of primary social goods. We may not be able to equate distributive principles dealing with income and those dealing with primary social goods. Second, given that the difference principle is only a part of one of the two principles of justice, we should not consider the difference principle in isolation. Third, subjects were not in a situation remotely close to the original position that Rawls requires. In the original position, parties are deprived of information about their actual positions as well as their conceptions of goodness, their talents and endowments, their special attitudes towards risk, and so on. It is not clear whether the knowledge of the subjects in the experiment was constrained as much as Rawls demands. To borrow a neat line from Konow's critical survey of experimental economics, "[p]assing through the laboratory door is not necessarily equivalent to passing through a veil of ignorance, and previously formed knowledge and expectations might taint subjects' reasoning" (Konow 2003: 1196). There might be some subjects who have spent their entire lives in middle-class families and neighborhoods and have no first-hand knowledge of the challenges that people from disadvantaged socio-economic classes really encounter each day. It is hard to believe that such subjects would be able to bracket off their middle-class dispositions and be completely neutral with respect to different socioeconomic classes.

That said, the experimental results suggest that there is an undeniable intuitive attractiveness to the principle of maximizing the average with a floor. The principle does not allow people's income to remain below the "floor" level ($12,000 in this experiment). Unlike the principle of max-imizing the average, it is specially concerned about people with a very low income level. And yet, unlike the principle of maximizing the floor, it aims at the maximization of aggregate income in a society once the "floor" requirement is met. It is not concerned with equality or priority for people above the floor level. The distributive concern is confined to the badly off people. Thus, the principle of maximizing the average with a floor gives priority to benefits to the badly off, and no priority to benefits to the well off. I call sufficientarianism a class of principles that gives priority to benefits to the badly off. I take the principle of maximizing the average with a floor to be a version of sufficientarianism, but one that is concerned with the distribution of income, rather than of well-being.

Why do many subjects choose utilitarianism with a floor? What explains the intuitive appeal of sufficientarianism? I can think of three explanations. I think that these explanations capture the motivations for the doctrine.

The first explanation is that utilitarianism with a floor is not too extreme. In the eyes of many people, utilitarianism appears too extreme because it can permit indefinite losses to worse off people insofar as those losses are offset by sufficiently large gains of well-being of others. The difference principle also appears too extreme because it justifies any aggregated loss for the non-worst off, however large, for the sake of any gain for the worst off, however small. At first glance, utilitarianism with a floor seems to be a moderate distributive principle, which avoids these extreme implications. It is likely that the same explanation explains some of the appeal of sufficientarianism.

The second explanation is that we need not care about giving priority to people above a certain high level of well-being. As we saw in chapter 4, telic egalitarianism and prioritarianism are versions of PD-ism, and they both imply that, with total well-being kept constant, the transfer of benefits from a better off to a worse off person makes the outcome strictly better. This is the case for any pair of a better off and a worse off person. For example, take the best off and second-best-off person in a given outcome. PD-ism claims that we should give priority to benefiting the second best off over the first best off: if we transfer some benefit from the first best off to the second best off, the outcome will be better, even if there is no increase in the total well-being.

The third explanation is that the well-being of people below the sufficiency level brings forth a special moral concern in its own right. When people's basic needs are not met, their ability to think and act as moral agents may be constrained. Furthermore, people below the sufficiency level often experience suffering of some sort. The fulfillment of basic needs may be seen as a prerequisite for any workable ethical theory.

5.2 Frankfurt's headcount view of sufficientarianism

Utilitarianism with a floor is only one version of sufficientarianism. There are many different versions of sufficientarianism. Many versions of this doctrine seem to commit their proponents to two theses, which Paula Casal (2007: 297–98) calls the positive and negative theses:

> Positive thesis: Priority is given to benefits to those below the sufficiency level over those above the sufficiency level.
>
> Negative thesis: No priority is given to benefits to those above the sufficiency level.

These two theses are, as they stand, vague and open to interpretations. I need to clarify exactly what each thesis implies. Different versions of sufficientarianism emerge from different interpretations of these two theses. In sections 5.2 and 5.3, I will consider two of these versions.

To my knowledge, Harry Frankfurt is the first person who explicitly puts forward a version of sufficientarianism. At least, many people trace the origin of it back to Frankfurt. I believe that his version of the theory is pretty extreme. As such, it is a good idea to start with his sufficiency principle. Frankfurt explains his version of sufficientarianism in the following way:

what is important from the point of view of morality is not that everyone should have the same, but that each should have enough. If everyone had enough, it would be of no moral consequence whether one had more than others.

(Frankfurt 1987: 21)

Frankfurt further contends that resources should be allocated "in such a way that as many people as possible have enough or, in other words, to maximise the incidence of sufficiency" (Frankfurt 1987: 31). According to Frankfurt, the total amount or distribution of well-being above the sufficiency level has no moral importance. What matters morally is maximizing the number of people above the sufficiency level. This is equivalent to the minimization of the number of people below the sufficiency level when the total number of people is held constant. If the number of people is not held constant, Frankfurt's view becomes highly counterintuitive. This is because we can increase the number of people above the sufficiency level by adding new people to the group above the sufficiency level, while we leave the state of people below the sufficiency level unchanged. But I think this is not what Frankfurt has in mind. What Frankfurt means is that as many people below the sufficiency level as possible should be brought up to the sufficiency level, provided the total number of people remains constant. Let us call Frankfurt's version of sufficientarianism the headcount view.

Frankfurt's headcount view is consistent with both the positive and negative theses. But it implies the extreme end of the two theses. Let me start with the positive thesis. The positive thesis I presented earlier merely claims to give priority to benefits to those below the sufficiency level over those above that level. It does not identify what kind of priority is given to those below the sufficiency level. It might be relative, complete, or lexical priority. If priority is relative, then it will be possible to allow a trade-off between well-being below and above the sufficiency level. If it is complete, then such a trade-off will be ruled out. If it is lexical, then the well-being of people below the sufficiency level will first be compared across different states of affairs; and when the well-being of people below the sufficiency level is the same across states of affairs, the well-being of people above the sufficiency level will be compared.

Frankfurt's headcount view implies that complete priority should be given to benefits to those below the sufficiency level over those above that level. Consider the following simple four-person case, where the sufficiency level is assumed to be 10. The headcount view judges that X = (1, 10, 10, 10) is strictly better than Y = (9, 9, 30, 30) because X includes fewer people below the sufficiency level and more people above that level.

There are two important implications. First, all the headcount view is concerned with is the number of people below the sufficiency level. The view does not concern itself with the level of well-being below the sufficiency level. In X, there is one person whose well-being is far below the sufficiency level, whereas in Y there are two people just below that level. Simply because X includes fewer people below the sufficiency level, the headcount view ranks X above Y. Needless to say, the headcount view would judge that (1, 10, 10, 10) is equally as good as (9, 10, 10, 10). This means that the level of well-being below the sufficiency level does not affect our distributive judgment. This implication may appear counterintuitive. I will come back to this point in the next section.

Second, the headcount view does not concern itself with total (or average) well-being. The total well-being in X is strictly smaller than that in Y. Similarly, the average well-being in X is strictly smaller than that in Y. But simply because the number of people below the sufficiency level is smaller, X is judged to be better than Y.

Let us consider the negative thesis. The negative thesis contends that no priority is to be given to those above the sufficiency level. However, it is not clear what is meant by "no priority." According to Frankfurt's headcount view, "no priority" really means that the well-being of people above the sufficiency level does not count at all from the moral point of view. That is, well-being above the sufficiency level is morally irrelevant. For example, the headcount view judges that (9, 10, 10, 10) is equally as good as (9, 30, 30, 30). That is, well-being above the sufficiency level is not to be used even to play the role of a tie-breaker, when the number of people whose well-being is below the sufficiency level is the same. I call this extreme version of the negative thesis the *strong negative thesis*. Frankfurt's headcount view is committed to this strong negative thesis.

Some advocates of sufficientarianism would think that (9, 30, 30, 30) is strictly better than (9, 10, 10, 10), and that we should interpret the negative thesis in a weaker sense. Let us use the *weak negative thesis* to refer to the interpretation of the negative thesis according to which the badness of sub-sufficiency well-being remains constant, the well-being of all people above the sufficiency level has equal weight, and the total value of well-being above the sufficiency level determines the relative goodness of a state of affairs. According to the weak negative thesis, the well-being of each person above the sufficiency level has the same moral importance as the well-being of everyone else above this level. In this sense, no priority is given to benefits to people above the sufficiency level. However, their well-being has some moral significance.

According to Frankfurt's headcount view of sufficientarianism, the sufficiency level is morally privileged in a strong sense, and factors other than the number of those with well-being below the sufficiency level are ignored from the moral point of view. However, some other versions of sufficientarianism are not as extreme as Frankfurt's. Let me briefly refer to two such versions.

The first is David Wiggins's version (Wiggins 1998). Wiggins first establishes the absolute conception of needs. He then puts forward the limitation principle, according to which the public body should not intervene in a citizen's affairs in such a way that vital needs are sacrificed to mere desires, or that stronger vital needs are sacrificed to lesser ones. He thinks that the fulfillment of vital needs is a prerequisite for any workable social theory. Wiggins's version is different from, and more moderate than, Frankfurt's version for two reasons. The first is that Wiggins's version is more concerned with the level of well-being below the sufficiency level. According to Wiggins, stronger vital needs should not be sacrificed to lesser ones. Consider again the comparison between $X = (1, 10, 10, 10)$ and $Y = (9, 9, 30, 30)$. If X is judged to be strictly better than Y (as Frankfurt's version contends), Wiggins would argue that the vital needs of person 1 are sacrificed for the sake of bringing the well-being of person 2 to the sufficiency level by adding one unit of well-being. Wiggins's version would claim that Y is strictly better than X. Thus, it is sensitive to the size of the shortfall from the sufficiency level.

The second reason is that Wiggins's version is not committed to the strong negative thesis. The strong negative thesis in Frankfurt's version takes well-being above the sufficiency level to be morally irrelevant. Wiggins's version, in contrast, does not claim this. It is simply neutral between different distributive principles insofar as the distribution of well-being above the sufficiency level is concerned. The fulfillment of vital needs is a prerequisite for any workable social theory. However, once everyone's vital needs are fulfilled, Wiggins's version does not say anything about what principle is more desirable than others. Once everyone's needs are fulfilled, the distributive principle may be utilitarianism or libertarianism or anything else. Wiggins's version is unconcerned with the choice of principle above the sufficiency level. However, at the very least it does not claim that well-being above the sufficiency level is morally irrelevant. Wiggins is not committed to either the strong negative thesis or the weak negative thesis. I call Wiggin's version the *neutral negative thesis*.

The second version of sufficientarianism which is more moderate than Frankfurt's headcount view belongs to David Braybrooke (1987). Braybrooke first identifies the list of what he calls *matters of need* and the *minimum standards of provision* for these matters of need. He then put forward the *principle of precedence*, according to which satisfying the minimum standards of provision takes a lexicographical priority over other political concerns. That is, when and only when the minimum standards of provision are satisfied to the same degree, are we allowed to consider other political concerns. According to Braybrooke's principle of precedence, the concern for the well-being of those below the sufficiency level has almost complete priority over any other concerns such as total well-being above the sufficiency level.

All of these versions are committed to both the negative and positive theses. However, they are quite different from utilitarianism with a floor, which, according to the results of experimental economics, receives wide intuitive support. None of them are committed to utilitarianism. Are the negative and positive theses consistent with utilitarianism with a floor? In the next section, I will consider this question.

5.3 Utilitarianism with a floor: a philosophical approach

The versions of sufficientarianism we have examined seem to put greater emphasis on the positive than on the negative thesis. In other words, these versions emphasize that benefiting people below the sufficiency level has more or less complete priority over benefiting people above that level. But it is not clear what is meant by "no priority to people above the sufficiency level." There are some proponents of the doctrine who take the negative thesis to be utilitarian. That is, "no priority to people above the sufficiency level" really means equal weight should be given to the well-being of people above the sufficiency level. This is consistent with the weak negative thesis, but not the strong negative thesis.

John Skorupski proposes a version of sufficientarianism based on the weak negative thesis (Skorupski 1999). He calls his version *threshold justice*. According to Skorupski, threshold justice holds that "one should maximize aggregate utility subject to a threshold below which no individual is allowed to fall" (Skorupski 1999: 90). He believes that "our social ideas of social justice are much closer to the Threshold conception than to Utilitarianism or the Difference Principle and thus more easily rationalized by it than by them," because "[u]nlike leximin, Threshold Justice does not proscribe any improvement, however massive, to someone's position when it is offset by a deterioration, however small, in the well-being of someone less well-off. And unlike the principle of aggregate utility, it does not allow indefinite worsening of a person's position so long as that is offset by compensating gains of well-being to others" (Skorupski 1999: 91).

Skorupski's threshold justice is a version of sufficientarianism. It is committed to the positive thesis because bringing everyone up to the sufficiency level is a constraint on the maximization of aggregate utility above the threshold level. It is also committed to the negative thesis because equal weight is given to benefiting each person above the threshold, and hence no priority is given to people above the threshold. As the experimental results suggest, Skorupski is right in saying that threshold justice or a variant of it better captures people's intuitions about social justice than the difference principle or utilitarianism with no floor constraint. One relatively unsatisfactory feature of Skorupski's threshold justice is that it does not elucidate how we evaluate the distribution of well-being below the threshold level.

A more recent version of sufficientarianism based on the weak negative thesis is Roger Crisp's compassion principle (Crisp 2003). In the rest of this section, I shall concentrate on his compassion principle because he contrasts his version of the doctrine with telic egalitarianism and prioritarianism.

In searching for a plausible distributive principle, Crisp first thinks of telic egalitarianism. But he thinks that telic egalitarianism is untenable because it is susceptible to the leveling down objection. He then considers prioritarianism. But he thinks that prioritarianism is untenable, too. He invites us to imagine the *Beverley Hills case*, where we are to offer a fine wine to either of two very well-off groups, the "super-rich" and "rich." According to Crisp, prioritarianism claims that we should offer it to the rich rather than the super-rich. Crisp, however, believes this claim of prioritarianism to be implausible. He thinks that "when people reach a certain level, even if they are worse off than others, benefiting them does not, in itself, matter more" (Crisp 2003: 13). Thus, Crisp is not satisfied with telic egalitarianism or prioritarianism.

Crisp then considers how the truly virtuous impartial spectator would allocate people's well-being. The idea of an impartial spectator is usually used to justify classical utilitarianism (see Rawls 1971: 26–27). The job description of the impartial spectator is to sympathize with everyone's partial perspective, be neutral with respect to different individuals' self-interest, and treat everyone's interests equally. Consequently, the impartial spectator helps to justify classical utilitarianism, or so advocates of classical utilitarianism say. Needless to say, the impartial spectator has never and will never exist. It is supposed to be an analytical tool for justifying utilitarianism.

Crisp imagines that the spectator is not only impartial and sympathetic, but also truly virtuous. When everyone is above the sufficiency level, there might be no difference between the standard impartial spectator and the truly virtuous impartial spectator. In such a case, the truly virtuous impartial spectator would be simply neutral with respect to different individuals' interests. However, if some people are below the sufficiency level, according to Crisp's speculation, the truly virtuous impartial spectator would make a judgment different from the standard impartial spectator. Crisp claims that the truly virtuous impartial spectator would show compassion for those below the sufficiency level and thus assign priority to benefiting them over those above that level, while remaining neutral with respect to the latter.

Crisp then presents his version of sufficientarianism, the compassion principle, in the following way:

> Absolute priority is to be given to benefits to those below the threshold at which compassion enters. Below the threshold, benefitting people matters more the worse off those people are, the more of those people there are, and the greater the size of the benefit in question. Above the threshold, or in cases concerning only trivial benefits below the threshold, no priority is to be given.
>
> (Crisp 2003: 16)

Sufficientarianism, thus defined, gives (1) complete priority to benefits to people below the sufficiency level over those above, (2) relative priority to benefits to the worse off among those below the sufficiency level, and (3) no priority to those above that level.

Three remarks are in order. First, considering the historical role of the impartial spectator, it would be reasonable to believe that when there is no person below the sufficiency level, Crisp's version of sufficientarianism, like Skorupski's threshold justice, collapses into classical utilitarianism. Historically, the idea of the impartial spectator is used and required by those who support classical utilitarianism. In order to guarantee perfect impartiality with respect to different people's utility, proponents of classical utilitarianism assume an imagined perspective that is ideally sympathetic to every person and perfectly neutral. The idea of an impartial spectator is supposed to guarantee this perspective. Thus, it is reasonable to believe that Crisp's version of sufficientarianism is classical utilitarian above the sufficiency level.

Second, Crisp's version gives lexical priority to benefits to people below the sufficiency level over benefits to those above the threshold, like many other versions. Crisp rules out a trade-off between well-being above and below the sufficiency level. That is, any non-trivial gain for people below the sufficiency level, no matter how small, outweighs any loss for people above that level no matter how large (Crisp 2003: 16–17). Gains for people above the sufficiency level make a difference only when the well-being of people below the threshold is constant. Thus, Crisp's version of sufficientarianism gives lexical priority to the well-being of those below the sufficiency level over the well-being of those above.

Third, Crisp's version gives relative priority to benefits to the worse off below the sufficiency level. This is a feature that the other versions of sufficientarianism do not explicitly include. And I think he is right about it. Imagine a situation in which there are two people below the threshold level. We can increase the well-being of only one person by 1 unit. Suppose that one person is less badly off than the other, but that the increase of 1 unit is not enough for either person to reach the sufficiency level. Crisp's version contends that the truly virtuous impartial spectator would choose to increase the well-being of the more severely badly off rather than the well-being of the less badly off. Frankfurt's headcount view of sufficientarianism claims that we should be indifferent because, no matter who receives the benefit, both persons will remain below the sufficiency level. However, Crisp's version gives priority to benefits to the person far below the sufficiency level over benefits to the one just below.

Priority below the sufficiency level is not complete. As clearly stated in the above definition, Crisp's version also considers the number of people below the sufficiency level who receive benefits. It leaves open the possibility that a large loss for a small number of people below the sufficiency level can be outweighed by a small gain for a sufficiently large number of people below that level. For instance, compare X = (5, 8, 8, 8, 8, 20, ... , 20) and Y = (2, 9, 9, 9, 9, 20, ... , 20), where the sufficiency level is assumed to be 10. Choosing X gives a relatively large benefit to the worst off person whereas choosing Y gives a small benefit to four people below the sufficiency level. In this case, Crisp's version leaves room for judging that Y is better than X. Thus, Crisp's version gives relative (not complete or lexical) priority to benefits to the worse off.

This third feature is distinctive of Crisp's version of sufficientarianism. It is not captured by the negative or positive thesis. Let us call this the *sub-sufficiency priority thesis*.

> *Sub-sufficiency priority thesis*: Relative priority is to be given to benefits to the worse off below the sufficiency level.

This thesis opens up a new question. When there are two or more people below the sufficiency level, how should we evaluate different alternatives? In order to answer this question, we must consider how we estimate the aggregate badness associated with sub-sufficiency well-being.

5.4 The badness associated with sub-sufficiency well-being

What does sufficientarianism aim at below the sufficiency level? It aims at reducing the badness associated with well-being below that level. We must be careful here. Sufficientarianism should not say that we ought to maximize the amount of well-being below sufficiency. This is because we can increase the total well-being below the sufficiency level by bringing a person above the sufficiency level to a level below sufficiency. Sufficientarianism should not say that we ought to minimize well-being below the sufficiency level, either. This is because it is implausible to say that, in a case where there is only one person below sufficiency, we should make his or her well-being even lower, thus minimizing well-being below the sufficiency level. Any amount of well-being below that level is still a good. Higher levels of well-being are better than lower, even if the levels remain below the sufficiency level. But there is something bad about well-being below that level. It is the *badness associated with sub-sufficiency well-being* that sufficientarianism aims to minimize. eliminate

How do we measure the badness associated with well-being below sufficiency? To answer this question, the economic literature on poverty measurement is useful and insightful. Needless to say, it is concerned with poverty in terms of monetary value. But it is possible to interpret it in terms of well-being. In this section, I will introduce Amartya Sen's influential analysis of the poverty measurement (Sen 1976).

First, let us go back to the headcount method as a candidate for the measurement of the badness associated with well-being below the sufficiency level. According to Sen and other economists, the headcount method has two counterintuitive implications. Compare $A = (3, 10, 10, 10, 10)$ and $B = (9, 9, 10, 10, 10)$, where the sufficiency level is set at 10. The head-count method judges that the badness associated with sub-sufficiency well-being in A (where only one person is below the sufficiency level) is smaller than in B (where two people are below the sufficiency level), and therefore that A is better than B.

There are two counterintuitive implications of this judgment. First, the headcount view does not take stock of the total shortfall of sub-threshold well-being. The total shortfall from the sufficiency level is greater in A (7 units) than in B (2 units). Second and more importantly, in order to bring one person from just below the sufficiency level to that level, the headcount method justifies a large loss to a very badly off person (i.e. person 1). If B is brought about, person 1 is made significantly better off. If A is chosen, it seems that person 2 is brought to sufficiency at the cost of the well-being of person 1. Thus, the headcount method is insensitive to the deterioration of the badly off.

Now, consider the total shortfall method. The total shortfall method simply adds up the shortfall from the sufficiency level across people below that level, and takes the unweighted sum to be the badness associated with sub-sufficiency well-being. The total shortfall method, then, contends that we should minimize the total shortfall. This method, however, has a counterintuitive implication. Compare $A = (3, 10, 10, 10, 10)$ and $C = (8, 8, 8, 8, 10)$. The total shortfall in A (7 units) is smaller than that in C (8 units). The judgement of the total shortfall method is counterintuitive because, in A, the well-being of person 1 is significantly lowered. It seems as though three people just below the sufficiency level are brought to the sufficiency level by making a badly off person (i.e. person 1) even worse off. Yet, this appears counterintuitive. Like the headcount method, the total shortfall method is insensitive to the deterioration of the state of the worse off.

Both of the measures considered are therefore counterintuitive. The total shortfall method is insensitive to the state of the very badly off. The head-count method has two problems: (a) it does not capture the total shortfall of sub-sufficiency well-being, and (b) it is insensitive to the state of the very badly off. Even if we combine the two methods and take the average shortfall to be the measure of the badness associated with sub-threshold well-being, the problem of "insensitivity to the very badly off" remains intact. Unless we do something about this counterintuitive implication, we could be justified in reducing the amount of sub-sufficiency well-being by taking some benefit from a person living at far below the sufficiency level and giving it to the least badly off person just below this level. This, however, seems to be unacceptable to proponents of sufficientarianism because the state of people far below sufficiency should give rise to a greater moral concern than that of people just below.

How can sufficientarianism solve the problem of insensitivity to the very badly off? Crisp's version of the theory has already given a solution: the sub-sufficiency priority thesis. Sufficientarianism should give priority to benefits to those far below the sufficiency level over benefits to those just below that level. If we transfer some benefits from the worst off person to another person just below the sufficiency level, then neither the total shortfall nor the headcount view would record any change in the badness associated with sub-sufficiency well-being, even if the worst off would have been made even worse off. If this is unacceptable or counterintuitive, sufficientarianism should assign greater moral weight to benefits to a worse off person over those to a less badly off person below the sufficiency level. Thus, a plausible measure of the badness associated with sub-sufficiency well-being should give priority to benefiting the worse off, i.e. satisfying the Pigou-Dalton condition with regard to well-being below sufficiency. All this explains why Crisp's version of sufficientarianism gives priority to the worse off below the sufficiency level.

In his seminal paper on the measurement of poverty, Sen (1976) proposes six properties that a plausible poverty measure should satisfy. His proposal can be interpreted as providing a measure of the badness associated with sub-threshold well-being. The six properties are (1) symmetry, (2) monotonicity, (3) scale invariance, (4) the focus axiom, (5) replication invariance, and (6) the weak transfer condition. I shall explain these properties very briefly.

Symmetry corresponds to what I called impartiality in chapter 1. It holds that permutations of personal identities do not affect the measure of poverty. For example, when we compare two two-person cases, where the sufficiency level is set at 10, the measure of poverty is the same in (8, 9) and (9, 8). Monotonicity holds that an increase in a person's well-being below the poverty level decreases aggregate poverty. Scale invariance holds that multiplying the poverty level and all the well-being levels by the same positive number does not affect aggregate poverty. This ensures that the size of poverty does not depend on the chosen unit of measurement.[1] Imagine a situation (8, 15) with a poverty threshold of 10. If we double all the numerical values and represent the same situation as (16, 30) with a poverty threshold of 20, there will be no change in aggregate poverty. The focus axiom holds that aggregate poverty is not affected by changes in well-being above the poverty level insofar as no additional person goes below the poverty level. Where the poverty level is 10, aggregate poverty is the same in, for example, (8, 15) and (8, 13). Replication invariance holds that duplicating a given distributional pattern does not affect aggregate poverty. For example, aggregate poverty in (8, 15) is the same as that in (8, 8, 15, 15). This condition may appear counterintuitive to many people. I will set this issue aside. Finally, the weak transfer condition holds that aggregate poverty is reduced by a non-reversing transfer of benefits from a better off to a worse off person when both are below the poverty level. This is a weaker version of the Pigou-Dalton condition. The weak transfer condition is confined to the domain below the poverty level.

Sen proposes a poverty measure which incorporates headcount and total shortfall, and satisfies these six properties. It is quite simple: the poverty measure S is given by $S = H \times I + [H \times (1 - I)] \times Gp$, where H is the headcount ratio; I is the income-gap ratio; and Gp is the Gini coefficient, which is a measure of the distribution of well-being below the poverty level. The mathematical representation of the poverty measure is not so important for present purposes. The important point here is that, in order to measure the badness associated with sub-threshold well-being, we should consider (a) how many people are below the poverty threshold, (b) how large the total shortfall from the poverty threshold is, and should also ensure (c) that greater weight is given to the well-being of a worse off person than the well-being of a better off person below the poverty threshold. We can simply apply this formula to the badness associated with sub-sufficiency well-being, which sufficientarianism aims to minimize.

That is all I will say about how we measure the badness associated with sub-sufficiency well-being. Given a suitable measure of such badness, sufficientarianism seems to hold the following. First, we should minimize the overall badness associated with sub-sufficiency well-being, regardless of what happens to people above the sufficiency level. Second, only when the well-being of those below the sufficiency level remains the same, can the sum total or average of well-being above the sufficiency level be used to determine the relative goodness of overall outcomes.

5.5 Four objections to sufficientarianism

In this section, I shall examine four objections leveled against sufficientarianism. The first concerns the choice of the sufficiency level. This objection points out that the absolute level of sufficiency is always morally arbitrary. Critics of sufficientarianism claim that whatever sufficiency level we choose (high or low) must be more or less morally arbitrary, and hence that sufficientarianism rests on a morally arbitrary factor.

To this objection, some proponents of the theory have responded by offering an argument for a non-arbitrary sufficiency level. For example, Anderson (2007) and Satz (2007) have made the case recently for a level of sufficiency tied to the ability to participate in democratic society. If their case is plausible enough, then the sufficiency level is not arbitrary. Nonetheless, it is hard to identify a sharp absolute level of sufficiency. Does this imply that the sufficiency level is always arbitrary? No. The sufficiency level may be vague, but not necessarily arbitrary. Intuitively, it is obvious that the well-being of a homeless person with no health insurance is below the sufficiency level. It is also the case that some people are obviously above the sufficiency level. There is a range of well-being between being obviously well off and being obviously badly off, and the sufficiency level lies somewhere in that range. The borderline is just vague.

The following analogy may help to clarify this point. It makes perfect sense to say that "Kent is tall" or "Simon is short." It seems safe to say that a person who stands at 200 centimeters is tall, and that a person who stands at 150 centimeters is short. But it is difficult to draw a clear line between being tall and being short. From this, however, it does not follow that it makes no sense to speak of somebody's "being tall" or "being short." Even if we do not know exactly how tall a tall person has to be, it still makes sense to say that "Kent is tall." Likewise, it is hard to determine a clear line between being well off and badly off. A sufficiency level we set may be arbitrary to some extent. But it may be plausible within a limited range. Thus, the sufficiency level is not completely arbitrary (see Benbaji 2005).

Richard Arneson points out that the sufficiency level is arbitrary for a different reason. There are different constituent parts to well-being:

> Imagine a brilliant homeless mathematician who lives as a guest in the homes of one and then another of her mathematical colleagues, who offer hospitality in order to have the opportunity to collaborate on research projects with the guest. Not having the wherewithal to purchase anything at the supermarket does not make the itinerant mathematician a social outsider.
>
> (Arneson 2002: 190)

what kinds of well-being?

As I understand it, Arneson thinks that unless we select the sufficiency level in an arbitrary way, we cannot judge whether this mathematician is to be considered below that level. To put it more generally, the interaction of different constituent parts of well-being makes it difficult to select a sufficiency level in a non-arbitrary way. Arneson's concern is legitimate. However, it does not undermine sufficientarianism. It is really about the more general issue of interpersonal comparison of well-being. Is a billionaire with cancer worse off than someone who is homeless but in perfect health? This is a difficult question to answer. To answer this question, we must choose a relation between income and health. No matter how we rank these two people's overall well-being, the choice of substitution ratio is arbitrary. In the Introduction to this book, I acknowledged the difficulty of interpersonal comparison of well-being, and have simply assumed that one person's well-being can be compared with another's. Nothing meaningful can be said about distributive justice unless we assume some sort of interpersonal comparison. Assuming interpersonal comparison includes some arbitrariness. Likewise, selecting a sufficiency level includes some arbitrariness, as Arneson points out. However, if arbitrariness in selecting a sufficiency level is a problem in the way that Arneson describes, then any discussion of distributive justice, which always requires some sort of interpersonal comparison, is also arbitrary and problematic. Thus, arbitrariness is not a problem confined to sufficientarianism.

The second objection concerns the discontinuity between sub- and supra-sufficiency well-being (Arneson 2002). To my knowledge, all proponents of sufficientarianism rule out a trade-off between well-being below and above the sufficiency level. All versions of the doctrine give complete or lexical priority to the minimization of the badness associated with sub-sufficiency well-being, no matter how it is measured. That is, a non-trivial benefit to people below the sufficiency level outweighs any large loss for people above, no matter how large, insofar as none falls below sufficiency. Crisp states that the "smallest non-trivial benefit to any number of individuals below the threshold" outweighs "any benefits, no matter how large, to any number of individuals above the sufficiency level" (Crisp 2003: 758). Crisp admits that this implication seems implausible. But he claims that it is not as implausible as it seems. Why? The sufficiency level is the point at which compassion no longer applies. According to Crisp, there is something special about benefiting the worst off individuals, which cannot be said about benefiting people above the sufficiency level.

There are two problems with Crisp's claim. First, Crisp's argument is circular. Those who find sufficientarianism to be implausible want to know why we should give absolute priority to the well-being of those below the sufficiency level over those above it. Crisp's answer is that there is "something special." Presumably, "something special" is whatever would cause the truly virtuous impartial spectator to feel compassion. Then, those who find the implication of sufficientarianism to be implausible may in turn want to know why compassion is all or nothing. They would ask why no compassion whatsoever is given to those whose well-being is above the sufficiency level and why full compassion is given only to those whose well-being is below the sufficiency level. They would think that some people just above the sufficiency level should receive some compassion, rather than none. It makes perfect sense to say that compassion comes in degrees, and therefore that the level of compassion is not discontinuous between those above and those below the sufficiency level. Consequently, it makes perfect sense to say that there are cases where there should be a trade-off between the badness of sub-sufficiency and the goodness of supra-sufficiency well-being. What Crisp must establish in this context is that compassion does not come in degrees. However, he fails to do so. Thus, it seems that Crisp's claim about the plausibility of discontinuity is simply a direct consequence of his concept of the truly virtuous impartial spectator.

Second, Crisp's claim about the plausibility of discontinuity is in conflict with his argument against what he calls the absolute priority view. Crisp takes this to be the view that gives absolute priority to benefits to the worst off. I interpret Crisp's "absolute priority view" to be equivalent to the maximin rule or leximin. According to Crisp, the absolute priority view allows "the smallest benefit to the smallest number of worst off to trump any benefit, however large, to any but the worst off, even the next worst off." And yet, this implication is "almost as absurd as levelling down" (Crisp 2003: 752). The same argument can be made against his own claim about the absolute priority of the badness of sub-sufficiency well-being over the goodness of supra-sufficiency well-being. Crisp might claim that the case of sufficientarianism is different from that of the absolute priority view. If so, he must offer an argument to show why these two cases are different. Admittedly, this implication of the absolute priority view seems implausible. But it "may not be as implausible as it seems." Thus, Crisp's version of the doctrine and the absolute priority view stand and fall together. Crisp cannot endorse discontinuity if he rejects the absolute priority view on the basis that it is discontinuous. More generally, advocates of sufficientarianism must, in a non-circular way, show why the sufficiency level has such a morally privileged cutting-power.

3

The third objection is this. It is not clear whether Crisp's version commits one to the strong or to the weak negative thesis. Consider the Beverley Hills case again. There are three possible scenarios in this case.

(A) Neither the rich nor the super-rich receive the bottle of wine (e.g. the bottle is destroyed).
(B) The super-rich receives the bottle of wine.
(C) The rich receives the bottle of wine.

Utilitarianism would be indifferent between (B) and (C), but rank (B) and (C) above (A). Prioritarianism would rank (C), (B), and (A) in descending order. Frankfurt's version of sufficientarianism, which commits to the strong negative thesis, is indifferent between the three scenarios. How does Crisp's version rank these scenarios? It is not clear from his definition of sufficientarianism above. If his version is committed to the strong negative thesis, then it is indifferent between all three scenarios. If it is committed to the weak negative thesis, Crisp's sufficientarianism is indifferent between (B) and (C), but ranks (B) and (C) above (A). The only thing we know from what Crisp has said is that (C) is not ranked above (B). To this point, Larry Temkin offers the following criticism:

> I rail at the prospect of the Rich or the Super-rich getting yet more bottles of fine wine. My thought is: "A pox on both alternatives!" I'd rather see neither group get the bottles of wine than one group get them, one group get them rather than both, and if one group must get wine, I'd rather see 10 Rich get bottles than 10,000 Super-rich. Moreover, in the latter case, I wouldn't regard the 10 Rich getting the wine as a particularly desirable outcome but, rather, as the best of two bad outcomes.
> (Temkin 2003a: 771)

Temkin would rank (A) above (B) and (C), but thinks that if the choice is, for some reason, between (B) and (C) and it is not possible to choose (A), the benefits should go to the rich rather than the super-rich. However, benefiting the rich leads us to an undesirable outcome because it does not benefit people at a lower absolute level. Benefiting the super-rich (or neither) also leads us to a bad outcome for the same reason. Even if prioritarianism judges that we should give the benefits to the rich, such a judgment does not mean that it is less concerned with people at a lower absolute level.

Prioritarianism would claim that even if fine wine does benefit only well-off people, some other benefits should be transferred from the rich and super-rich that would truly improve the well-being of people at a lower absolute level. Thus, nothing is embarrassing about prioritarianism's claim that benefits should be offered to the rich rather than the super-rich if there is no other alternative.

The fourth objection is directly related to the third. It is a more direct criticism of the negative thesis. This objection claims that we should give priority to benefits to the worse off even above the sufficiency level. Imagine a situation where we can transfer some benefits from some person above the sufficiency level to another below. If the same moral weight is given to every person's well-being above the sufficiency level, sufficientarianism is indifferent between taking benefits from a person just above sufficiency, and taking the same size of benefits from another person far above the sufficiency level, unless the one above sufficiency would fall below it as a result of the transfer. However, this may not be something the proponents of sufficientarianism are willing to commit to.

To illustrate the point, suppose that the present distribution is (5, 15, 100), and that the sufficiency level is set at 10. Compare two possible distributions, X = (9, 11, 100) and Y = (9, 15, 96). Moving to X, we take 4 units of benefit from the person just above the sufficiency level. On the other hand, moving to Y, we take the same size of benefit from the person far above the sufficiency level. Given that the badness of sub-threshold well-being is the same in X and Y, sufficientarianism must be indifferent between X and Y. However, some proponents of the theory would not be willing to accept this judgment. They may well judge that Y is strictly better than X. The reason is as simple as this: whenever we improve the well-being of a person below the sufficiency level, we should take the benefits from someone far above rather than someone just above the sufficiency level. In other words, we should give priority to benefits to the worse off above the sufficiency level as well as to those below that level. This, then, means that sufficientarianism should satisfy the Pigou-Dalton condition above the sufficiency level as well as below.

Critics of sufficientarianism may thus claim that it should give priority to benefits to the worse off even above the sufficiency level. More specifically, sufficientarianism should (1) first minimize the badness associated with sub-sufficiency well-being with greater weight to benefits to the worse off, and (2) then maximize the goodness of well-being above the sufficiency level with greater weight to benefits to the worse off, where the badness of sub-sufficiency well-being is constant. That is, this revision of sufficientarianism makes it give up the negative thesis and give priority all the way down. It is closer to prioritarianism. The only difference lies in the lexical priority of the minimization of the badness associated with sub-sufficiency well-being over the maximization of the goodness of supra-sufficiency well-being.

Proponents of sufficientarianism can attempt to defend the negative view in two ways. The first is to bite the bullet in the case of X and Y above. Proponents can simply claim that the theory is indifferent between transferring benefits from a person far above the sufficiency level or a person just above it. This may appear counterintuitive to critics of the negative thesis, but proponents of sufficientarianism can say that they simply experience a different intuition.

The second way is to opt for multiple thresholds. Admittedly, the well-being of a homeless person and that of a plumber belong to different categories: any improvement for the homeless person, no matter how small, is more important than any for the plumber, no matter how large. Now, it seems equally clear that the well-being of a plumber and the well-being of a multibillionaire belong to different categories as well. If multilevel thresholds are introduced, proponents of sufficientarianism can claim that benefiting people below the lowest threshold matters more than benefiting people above that threshold, yet below the second lowest threshold, and that benefiting people below the second lowest threshold matters more than benefiting people above the second lowest threshold, and so on. They can claim that, in order to bring a person to the level of the lowest threshold, we should transfer the benefit from the person far above the lowest threshold rather than the one just above it. It is therefore tempting to set multiple categories of well-being and multiple threshold levels. This makes sufficientarianism more complicated. The cost of multilevel sufficiency is simplicity. The loss in simplicity, however, is not a serious theoretical problem.

I am not sure how many proponents of sufficientarianism would be willing to accept the complexity of multiple thresholds for the sake of making this theory a gimmicky version of quasi-prioritarianism. This second way of revising sufficientarianism makes it closer to prioritarianism. Presumably, within each threshold category, benefiting the worse off matters more than benefiting the better off. This means that benefiting the worse off matters more than benefiting the better off all the way down, except for those above the highest threshold.

I have examined four objections to sufficientarianism and considered possible responses to these objections. I believe it can be defended against three of these objections. However, the second remains a serious threat. Proponents of sufficientarianism must show why the morally privileged absolute level of well-being has such strong cutting power – not simply assume it.

Chapter summary

Sufficientarianism contends that priority should be given to benefiting those below the sufficiency level over those above it (the positive thesis) and that no priority is to be given to benefits to those above the sufficiency level (the negative thesis). As for the positive thesis, all proponents of sufficientarianism support complete priority that disallows a trade-off between sub- and supra-sufficiency well-being. There are different interpretations of the negative thesis. Some people, e.g. Frankfurt, take well-being above the sufficiency level to be morally irrelevant whereas others, e.g. Skorupski and Crisp, endorse the equal weight of well-being above the sufficiency level. An appropriate measure of the badness associated with sub-sufficiency well-being should combine three factors: (a) the number of people below the sufficiency level, (b) the total shortfall from the sufficiency level, and (c) a greater weight to the well-being of a worse off person than that of a better off person below the sufficiency level. The theoretical problem with sufficientarianism is not how the sufficiency level is determined, but why the sufficiency level is so morally privileged as to disallow a trade-off between sub- and supra-sufficiency well-being.

Further reading

Frankfurt (1987, 1997, 2000) and Crisp (2003) are the most important works that put forward sufficientarianism. The most philosophically sophisticated analyses of the theory would be Benbaji (2005, 2006) and Brown (2005). For criticisms of Crisp's compassion principle, see Arneson (2006, 2002), Casal (2007), Holtug (2007), and Temkin (2003a, 2003b). Huseby (2010) and Shields (2012) are useful surveys of this debate. Some versions of democratic equality are seen to ground sufficientarianism (Anderson 1999, 2007; Nussbaum 2009; Satz 2007). To understand how we measure the badness associated with sub-sufficiency well-being, the economic literature on poverty is directly relevant. For the measurement of poverty, see Sen (1976, 1982).

Note

1 If we opt for prioritarianism below the sufficiency level, the scale invariance condition may be violated. This is partly why Sen uses the Gini coefficient in his proposed poverty measure.

6

EQUALITY AND TIME

In this chapter, I shall examine two recent theoretical issues concerning egalitarian distributive judgment across time. The first issue has to do with the temporal unit of distributive judgment. It asks whether we should consider the distribution of lifetime well-being or the distribution of people's well-being at specific times. The second issue is concerned with the distribution of future people's well-being. It asks how we should compare future states of affairs with variable population sizes. To my knowledge, there is no widely accepted solution to the second issue. I shall not attempt to give a solution to it but merely elucidate the nature of the issue and illustrate how egalitarianism and prioritarianism come apart with regard to it. The two issues are primarily theoretical. As such, I shall present them as abstract theoretical issues. But they are related to many practical and pressing problems that our society encounters. The first issue has direct implications for the philosophical foundations of distributive justice between the young and the old (e.g. the pension system and the health care system). The second issue has direct implications for global environmental policies in general and population policy in particular.

Sections 6.1 through 6.3 discuss the first issue. Section 6.1 introduces an objection to principles that take people's well-being over their entire lives as the temporal unit of distributive judgment. Section 6.2 introduces an objection to principles that focus on the distribution of people's well-being at specific periods. Section 6.3 examines whether telic egalitarianism and prioritarianism can consider both the distribution of well-being at specific periods, as well as the distribution of lifetime well-being. Section 6.4 considers what egalitarianism and prioritarianism have to say in cases where population size varies.

I need to state one terminological qualification. So far, I have examined the relative goodness of states of affairs, where a state of affairs is defined as a vector of people's well-being. In sections 6.1 through 6.3, I shall compare something else. In these sections, I shall compare *alternatives*. An alternative includes information concerning both the distribution of people's well-being at specific times, and the distribution of different people's well-being over their entire lives.

6.1 The lifetime view

I have examined the distribution of people's well-being without asking about the temporal unit of distributive judgment. Should we evaluate the distribution of people's well-being over their entire lifespan? Or should we evaluate the distribution of a temporal part of their well-being at specific periods? Many critics of utilitarianism think that the temporal unit of distributive judgment should be people's complete lives, not part of their lives. I will introduce three representative cases of the lifetime view.

The first example is Rawls. He maintains that the parties in the original position consider the life prospects and long-term life plans of representative people in different social groups when they choose the basic structure of society (Rawls 1971: 78). The second example is Ronald Dworkin. In explaining the envy test in the hypothetical auction, Dworkin (1981: 304–5) claims that each person considers whether he or she envies another person's resources over an entire life. The third example is Thomas Nagel. He states that "the subject of an egalitarian principle is not the distribution of particular rewards to individuals at some time, but the prospective quality of their lives as a whole, from birth to death (a point stressed by Rawls)" (Nagel 1991: 69; see also 1979: 124n). Let us call their view of the temporal unit of distributive judgment the *lifetime view*.

The lifetime view is popular among critics of utilitarianism. Why? It is difficult to answer because none of them offer a clear explanation. They simply endorse the lifetime view, rather than argue for it. Here is my speculation. Many critics of utilitarianism take the lifetime view because they want to take the separateness of persons seriously. I introduced the notion of the separateness of persons in section 4.5 (see also Rawls 1971: 27–28). Many critics of utilitarianism object to it on the basis that it does not take the separateness of persons seriously.

To recap, according to this objection, it is perfectly legitimate to sacrifice some of my present well-being for the sake of a sufficiently large gain in my future well-being. However, it is not legitimate to demand that I sacrifice some part of my present well-being for the sake of other people's gain, no matter how large the net gain would be. Utilitarianism, however, demands that I must make such sacrifices for the sake of others. Utilitarianism thus cannot distinguish intra- and interpersonal trade-offs. Different people live different lives, and each person has his or her own projects and life plan to pursue. This important fact should be respected. But utilitarianism does not respect it. To differentiate their own position from utilitarianism, critics emphasize the contrast between intra- and interpersonal trade-offs. And, to emphasize the contrast, they reject interpersonal aggregation (as we saw in chapter 1) and take the distribution of lifetime benefits as the appropriate temporal unit of distributive judgment. This partly explains why the lifetime view is popular among critics of classical utilitarianism.[1]

Despite its popularity, the lifetime view may appear counterintuitive to some, if not many, proponents of egalitarianism broadly construed, and may not adequately capture the basic egalitarian concern. This is simply because the lifetime view does not consider the distribution of people's well-being at specific periods. Consider the following two-person case (table 6.1), where an 80-year-long life consists of two 40-year periods, T_1 and T_2 (McKerlie 1989).

For simplicity, let us assume that the value of a person's lifetime well-being is given by the sum of the value of his or her well-being at T_1 and T_2. In alternatives 1 and 2, in terms of lifetime well-being, persons 1 and 2 are equally well off because the value of each person's lifetime well-being is 20 in both alternatives. The lifetime view of telic egalitarianism finds no inequality between alternatives 1 and 2. Likewise, the lifetime view of prioritarianism finds no worse off or better off person in alternatives 1 and 2.

Table 6.1

	T_1	T_2		T_1	T_2
Person 1	16	4	Person 1	10	10
Person 2	4	16	Person 2	10	10
Alternative 1			Alternative 2		

Therefore, the lifetime view, be it in the context of telic egalitarianism or of prioritarianism, judges that alternative 1 is equally as good as alternative 2.

Some advocates of telic egalitarianism and prioritarianism would disagree. Some telic egalitarians would claim that alternative 2 is strictly better than alternative 1 because, in alternative 1, there is inequality between persons 1 and 2 at both T_1 and T_2, whereas, in alternative 2, there is no inequality at T_1 or T_2. They would claim that inequality at each of these periods gives rise to a normative concern and should be taken into account when we judge the relative goodness of these two alternatives.

Here is another way to understand why some supporters of telic egalitarianism might find the lifetime view implausible. Imagine that you are an egalitarian distributive policy planner and are at the end of T_1 in alternative 1. You are motivated to realize an egalitarian distribution between persons 1 and 2, and are planning how you will distribute resources during T_2 after you observed inequality at T_1. If you take the lifetime view, you would distribute benefits as at T_2 in alternative 1. This means that you would intentionally create inequality at T_2 because this would make the distribution of lifetime well-being equal. However, according to some telic egalitarians, this is not what egalitarianism should say.

Some proponents of prioritarianism would also claim that alternative 2 is strictly better than alternative 1. This is because, in alternative 1, person 2 at T_1 and person 1 at T_2 are worse off in absolute terms. If alternative 2 is brought about, persons 1 and 2 could avoid the lower absolute level of well-being that they would endure in alternative 1. Thus, some prioritarians would rank alternative 2 above alternative 1, and claim that the lifetime view does not capture the concern of prioritarianism.

6.2 The time-slice view

If inequality, or a lower absolute level of well-being, at specific periods is taken to be a morally relevant consideration, then lifetime well-being is not the most plausible temporal unit for distributive judgment. For the sake of argument, let us agree that the lifetime view does not capture the egalitarian or prioritarian concern. If that is true, there seems to be a case for the time-slice view. The time-slice view holds that the distribution of people's well-being at specific periods is morally relevant, whereas the distribution of people's lifetime well-being is not. Consequently, it contends that the relative goodness of alternatives should be assessed on the basis of the distribution of people's well-being at specific periods.

As I understand it, the time-slice view involves a two-step process. The first step is to determine the goodness of a distribution at each period, independently of the distribution at other periods. The second step is to add up the goodness of the distribution at all the relevant temporal periods and determine the overall goodness of any given alternative. This means that the overall goodness of an alternative is a function of the goodness of the distribution at each period.

One quick remark is needed. The time-slice view must assume each period to be sufficiently long. If each period is taken to be very short, the time-slice view has the following counterintuitive implication (McKerlie 1989: 483). Imagine that two people, who each have a toothache, will see a dentist tomorrow. Suppose one accepts a version of time-slice egalitarianism that considers the distribution of well-being again each hour. What does it have to say? It has to say that the two patients should schedule simultaneous appointments so that they may suffer and receive treatment simultaneously. Are there serious egalitarian reasons for preferring (a) two appointments at 10:00 to (b) an appointment at 10:00 and an appointment at 11:00? Intuitively, the answer is "no." In order to avoid this sort of counterintuitive implication, the time-slice view must assume each period to be long enough.

Let us turn to an examination of how egalitarianism and prioritarianism operate within the framework of the time-slice view. I shall start with time-slice egalitarianism and show how it works with regard to the comparison of alternatives 1 and 2. For simplicity, I will use the formula for the aggregate view which I presented in chapter 3. Time-slice egalitarianism first estimates the goodness of a distribution at each period. The goodness of the distribution at T_1 in alternative 1 is $\frac{1}{4} \times 16 + \frac{3}{4} \times 4 = 7$. The goodness of the distribution at T_2 in alternative 1 is also 7. As the overall goodness of an alternative is given by the sum of the goodness of the distribution at each period, the overall goodness of alternative 1 is 14. I now estimate the overall goodness of alternative 2. The goodness of the distribution at T_1 and T_2 in alternative 2 is $\frac{1}{4} \times 10 + \frac{3}{4} \times 10 = 10$ at each period. Thus, the overall goodness of alternative 2 is 20. Therefore, time-slice egalitarianism judges that alternative 2 is strictly better than alternative 1. Time-slice egalitarianism certainly registers inequality at each period in judging the relative goodness of the two alternatives.

Time-slice prioritarianism is also based on a two-step aggregation process. In the first step, it assigns a greater weight to well-being at a lower absolute level and adds up the weighted well-being of different people at each time period. By doing this, we can estimate the goodness of a distribution at each time. In the second step, time-slice prioritarianism adds up the goodness of the distribution at each period across time and estimates the overall goodness of an alternative. Compare alternatives 1 and 2 again. The goodness of the distribution at T_1 and T_2 in alternative 1 is $f(16) + f(4)$ and $f(4) + f(16)$ respectively. The overall goodness of alternative 1 is thus $2 \times (f(16) + f(4))$. On the other hand, the overall goodness of alternative 2 is $2 \times (f(10) + f(10))$. Given that $f()$ is some increasing, strictly concave function, $f(16) + f(4) < f(10) + f(10)$. Therefore, alternative 2 is strictly better than alternative 1. Time-slice prioritarianism certainly registers the fact that the well-being of person 2 at T_1 and the well-being of person 1 at T_2 are at a lower absolute level.

There is an interesting feature of the time-slice view that comes from its two-step process. According to the time-slice view, the goodness of a distribution at a period is determined independently of the distributions at other periods. Following Broome (2004), I call this feature the *separability of time*. The separability of time has the following implication: the unity of a person's well-being across time does not matter. In other words, it does not matter who has how much well-being across time. As the goodness of a distribution at a period is determined independently of the distributions at other periods, how much well-being a person has through his or her lifetime does not affect our overall assessment of alternatives.

The separability of time may be challenged. The goodness of a distribution at a period may well depend on the distributions at other periods. Compare alternatives 1 and 3 (table 6.2).

Both time-slice egalitarianism and time-slice prioritarianism judge that alternative 1 is equally as good as alternative 3. Why? The distribution at T_1 in alternative 1 is equally as good as that in alternative 3. The distribution at T_2 in alternative 1 is equally as good as that in alternative 3. Therefore, alternative 1 must be equally as good as alternative 3.

Some people would disagree. They would judge that alternative 1 is strictly better than alternative 3. This is because, in alternative 3, person 2 endures a low level of well-being throughout his or her entire life, whereas

Table 6.2

	T_1	T_2		T_1	T_2
Person 1	16	4	Person 1	16	16
Person 2	4	16	Person 2	4	4
Alternative 1			Alternative 3		

person 1 enjoys a high level of well-being throughout his or her entire life. In contrast, in alternative 1, both persons 1 and 2 endure the same low level of well-being at some time, and enjoy the same high level of well-being at another time. Few egalitarians would find a normatively compelling reason to judge that alternative 1 is equally as good as alternative 3. There is an important normative difference between the two alternatives. This difference is not captured by any version of the time-slice view. Arguably, this is a drawback of the view. The source of this drawback is the separability of time, which is an essential feature of the time-slice view. The distributive judgment at each period is not separable from the distributive judgment at other periods, and the time-slice view is therefore not a good alternative to the lifetime view.

I said that few people would find a normatively compelling reason to judge alternative 1 to be equally as good as alternative 3. Some people may really think that alternative 1 is equally as good as alternative 3. A particular view about personal identity can support such a judgment, although it does not necessarily entail it. Some people claim that personal identity as such does not matter rationally and morally. On the basis of his metaphysical argument, Derek Parfit (1984: Part III) reaches such a conclusion. The view that personal identity does not matter can support the time-slice view. Parfit does not necessarily claim that the goodness of a distribution at a time can be determined independently of distributions at other times. Therefore, Parfit's view of personal identity does not commit him to the time-slice view. However, Parfit's view is perfectly consistent with the time-slice view. Proponents of the time-slice view might appeal to Parfit's view of personal identity. They would claim that it does not matter who endures the lower absolute level of well-being across time, but that we should attempt to improve the lower absolute level of well-being at each time, no matter whose well-being we find ourselves concerned with. Thus, insofar as we acknowledge the moral relevance of the lower absolute level of well-being at T_1 and T_2, there is no normatively relevant difference between alternatives 1 and 3 because each distribution contains the same low level of well-being at T_1 and T_2.

That said, it is true that few people support the time-slice view. Here is another argument against it. It is John Broome's argument against the separability of time (Broome 2004: 106–9). Consider alternatives 4 and 5 (table 6.3).

The omega (Ω) indicates the non-existence of a person. In alternative 4, person 1 lives through T_1 and T_2 and person 2 never lives. In alternative 5,

Table 6.3

	T_1	T_2		T_1	T_2
Person 1	10	10	Person 1	Ω	10
Person 2	Ω	Ω	Person 2	10	Ω
Alternative 4			Alternative 5		

person 2 lives at T_1 and then dies, and person 1 lives at T_2. In this comparison, the time-slice view judges that alternative 4 is equally as good as alternative 5. Yet, according to Broome, this is an intuitively implausible judgment. Alternative 4 has an advantage over alternative 5. Alternative 4 contains one long life rather than two short lives. Many people believe it is better that a person live for a longer rather than a shorter time. That is, longevity is good for its own sake. Thus, intuitively, alternative 4 is better than alternative 5. This judgment goes against the time-slice view.

Broome's argument may be challenged (Arrhenius 2008). Although many people intuitively value longevity, it might be argued that longevity is not necessarily valuable for its own sake. Suppose that each period consists of 100 years. Is it really better that one person live for 200 years than that two people live for 100 years in different periods? Some people would claim that it is not. I have no intuition about it, because I cannot imagine what it would be like to live for 200 years. However, if each period consists of 40 years, I am pretty sure that many people would think it better that one person live for 80 years than that two people live for 40 years in different periods. As such, the intuition to which Broome appeals is understandable. If Broome's point is correct, then the time-slice view (and the separability of time in particular) is implausible.

6.3 The hybrid view

Both the lifetime view and the time-slice view may be challenged. What about combining these two views? That is, why don't we consider both the distribution of well-being at specific periods and the distribution of lifetime well-being? I call this combined view the *hybrid view*. The hybrid view might be an attractive alternative for those who are not satisfied with the lifetime view or the time-slice view (Hirose 2005; McKerlie 2001a). However, the hybrid view does not provide a perfect solution.

Let us start with prioritarianism. The hybrid view of prioritarianism would claim that we should give greater weight both to well-being at a lower absolute level at each period and to lifetime well-being at a lower absolute level. More specifically, it adds the result from the lifetime view and that from the time-slice view, and then divides the overall value by two in order to avoid double-counting each person's well-being. Assume now that we use the square-root function as the prioritarian function.

First, consider alternative 1 in table 6.2. The goodness with respect to the time-slice distribution is $2 \times (\sqrt{16} + \sqrt{4}) = 12$. The goodness with respect to the distribution of lifetime well-being is $\sqrt{20} + \sqrt{20} = 2\sqrt{20}$. Thus, the overall goodness of alternative 1 is $\frac{1}{2}(12 + 2\sqrt{20}) = 6 + \sqrt{20} = 10.47$. Next consider alternative 3. The goodness with respect to the time-slice distribution of well-being is $2 \times (\sqrt{16} + \sqrt{4}) = 12$. The goodness with respect to the distribution of lifetime well-being is $\sqrt{32} + \sqrt{8} = 4\sqrt{2} + 2\sqrt{2} = 6\sqrt{2}$. Thus, the overall goodness of alternative 3 is $\frac{1}{2}(12 + 6\sqrt{2}) = 6 + 3\sqrt{2} = 10.24$. Therefore, hybrid prioritarianism concludes that alternative 1 is strictly better than alternative 3. If we follow the same process, hybrid prioritarianism judges that alternative 2 is strictly better than alternative 1. Thus, hybrid prioritarianism avoids the alleged problems that lifetime and time-slice prioritarianism encounter.

However, there is something strange about hybrid prioritarianism thus construed. It discounts the moral importance of well-being twice. It discounts the absolute level of well-being at each period, and also the absolute level of lifetime well-being, whose temporal parts have already been discounted. That is, hybrid prioritarianism includes a double-discounting of each person's well-being. In the previous paragraph, I used the square-root function for the purpose of discounting both temporal and lifetime well-being. Yet, there is no reason to believe that the same function applies to both temporal and to lifetime well-being. The discounting functions may well be different. That is, the goodness of the absolute level of temporal well-being may well diminish in a way different from that of the absolute level of lifetime well-being. Thus, if supporters of prioritarianism opt for the hybrid view, they must show (a) how marginal temporal well-being and lifetime well-being diminish in value, and (b) how the double-discounting is justified.

Let me move on to the hybrid view of egalitarianism. The aggregation procedure would be like the following. First, we estimate the goodness of the distribution at each period separately in an axiological egalitarian way. Second, we estimate the goodness of the distribution of lifetime well-being. We then add up the goodness of the distribution at each period across time, and the goodness of the distribution of lifetime well-being. Third, in order to avoid double-counting well-being, the value of the second step is divided by two.

For example, take the formula for the aggregate view in the two-person case which I presented in chapter 3. Compare alternatives 1 and 3 in table 6.2. The goodness of alternative 1 is $\frac{1}{2}((16 \times \frac{1}{4} + 4 \times \frac{3}{4} + 4 \times \frac{3}{4} + 16 \times \frac{1}{4}) + (20 \times \frac{1}{4} + 20 \times \frac{3}{4})) = 17$. The goodness of alternative 2 is $\frac{1}{2}((16 \times \frac{1}{4} + 4 \times \frac{3}{4} + 16 \times \frac{1}{4} + 4 \times \frac{3}{4}) + (36 \times \frac{1}{4} + 8 \times \frac{3}{4})) = 14.5$. Therefore, according to hybrid egalitarianism, alternative 1 is strictly better than alternative 3. Hybrid egalitarianism also judges that alternative 2 is strictly better than alternative 1. This is a satisfactory result for those who are concerned with both equality at specific times and equality of lifetime well-being.

Hybrid egalitarianism, however, has a strange implication. This strange implication actually suggests an important difference between hybrid egalitarianism and hybrid prioritarianism. Compare alternatives 1 and 6 in table 6.4.

In both alternatives, there is no inequality of lifetime well-being, or no worse off person with respect to lifetime well-being. In alternative 1, there is inequality at each time and one person is worse off during each period. In alternative 6, there is no inequality during any period. Persons 1 and 2 are equally well off at T_1 and equally badly off at T_2. According to hybrid prioritarianism, alternatives 1 and 6 are equally good. In contrast, hybrid egalitarianism judges that alternative 6 is better than alternative 1.[2] This is because, in alternative 1, there is inequality during each period whereas, in alternative 6, there is no inequality at any period. Hybrid egalitarianism and hybrid prioritarianism disagree in this example.

Proponents of hybrid prioritarianism would say that it does not matter at what time a person has a lower level of well-being within his or her life, given that the absolute level of lifetime well-being is constant. In contrast, hybrid egalitarianism implies that it is better if people have low and high levels of well-being simultaneously, other things being equal. Is it really better if people have low and high levels of well-being simultaneously?

Table 6.4

	T_1	T_2		T_1	T_2
Person 1	16	4	Person 1	16	4
Person 2	4	16	Person 2	16	4
Alternative 1			Alternative 6		

I cannot think of a good argument for judging that alternative 6 is better than alternative 1. Here is a bad argument, which egalitarians should not endorse. In alternative 1, the worse off person at each time envies the position of the better off. Envy is a bad thing. In alternative 6, there is no person who envies the other. Therefore, alternative 6 is better than alternative 1. This is not a good argument. If envy is thought to be a disvalue for the worse off (this is a highly debatable assumption), it should have been built into the measure of well-being. If such a disvalue had been built in, however, then egalitarianism could not explain why we should prefer alternative 6 over alternative 1. Probably, the only thing egalitarianism can do is simply repeat its main claim, that inequality during each period makes the distribution strictly worse. But this would not persuade supporters of hybrid prioritarianism or those of the lifetime view.

With this last example, I wanted to stress two points. The first is that there is an important difference between hybrid egalitarianism and hybrid prioritarianism. The second is that, if hybrid egalitarianism disagrees with hybrid prioritarianism concerning the comparison between alternatives 1 and 6, the burden of explanation is on the side of egalitarianism, not on the side of prioritarianism.

6.4 Distributive judgments about future people's well-being

I have discussed the issues surrounding the temporal unit of distributive judgment. In this section, I will point to another topic. This is the distribution of future people's well-being. This issue includes one additional variable, which makes our analysis complicated – the size of the population. Up to this point, I have assumed that every distribution or alternative contains the same number of people. However, when we consider the distribution of future people's well-being, each distribution may well contain a different number of people. In this section, we will consider the distribution of well-being among differing numbers of people.

Future people do not exist yet. A future person may or may not come into existence, depending on which population we choose to bring into existence. There are no properties that instantiate the well-being of any person in the future. We are going to talk about an abstract people and their abstract well-being. Our philosophical analysis in this book has been abstract enough. But our analysis in this section will be even more so. Furthermore, we are going to compare the well-being of two mutually exclusive sets of future people. That means that we will have to deal with cases where there is no overlap between sets of future people whose well-being is considered. This sort of case is called the (complete) *non-identity case*. That is, there are no individuals who have the same identity across future outcomes. A person who exists in one future outcome does not exist in another future outcome.

The non-identity case makes our distributive judgment very difficult. Why? To begin, it does not make much sense to say that a person has a gain or loss. Compare two future states of the two person non-identity case: X = (8 [Annie], 5 [Betty]) and Y = (5 [Cathy], 5 [Diane]). Each future state consists of two persons, and they do not exist in the other state. In this case, there is no one who gains 3 units of well-being by choosing X.

Here is a general philosophical problem that has become known as the *repugnant conclusion*. Imagine that we have to choose between one of two populations. Population A contains a small number of people each with an extremely high level of well-being. Population B contains an extremely large number of people each with a very low level of well-being. For the sake of argument, let us assume that the well-being of people in population B is still at the level worth living, and that there are no morally relevant differences between the two populations except the number of people and the level of their well-being.

Which population should we choose? Classical utilitarianism claims that we should choose population B insofar as the number of people is large enough to render the sum total of population B's well-being greater than that of population A. Many philosophers find this judgment to be counterintuitive, and think that we should choose population A. Parfit (1984) calls the judgment of classical utilitarianism the repugnant conclusion.

The issue of the repugnant conclusion is very difficult and complicated. So I shall merely outline one unsuccessful attempt to avoid it. You may think that average utilitarianism would avoid the repugnant conclusion. It is true that average utilitarianism would judge population A to be better off than population B. But it is not clear whether it is plausible as a general principle in cases where the population size varies. Imagine the following two populations. Population C consists of a large number of people with a very high level of well-being. Population D consists of just two people leading a life at a slightly higher level of well-being. Average utilitarianism judges that population D is strictly better than population C. Parfit (1984: 420–22) claims, and I concur with him, that such a judgment is counterintuitive.

I shall not go any further concerning how to avoid the repugnant conclusion. However, let me make two points that are relevant for understanding the nature of distributive principles.

First, one of the main objections leveled against leximin loses its force in the non-identity case. As we saw in chapter 1, leximin justifies any loss for people in the non-worst off groups, no matter how large, for the sake of any gain for the worst off, no matter how small. Many people find this implication to be objectionable. However, this objection does not apply to leximin in the non-identity case. When we compare the well-being of two mutually exclusive sets of future people, it does not make sense to talk about gains or losses for those people.

For example, compare two distributions in the two-future-person case: $X = (10, 20)$ and $Y = (11, 13)$. Leximin judges that Y is strictly better than X. If this comparison were a same-identity case, it would be argued that such a judgment is objectionable because there is a large loss for person 2 for the sake of a small gain for person 1. However, in the non-identity case, talk of gain and loss does not make sense. Person 1 in X does not exist in Y. Person 1 in Y does not exist in X. Likewise, person 2 in X does not exist in Y, and person 2 in Y does not exist in X. The correct representation of this comparison is actually a comparison between $X = (10, 20, \Omega, \Omega)$ and $Y = (\Omega, \Omega, 11, 13)$, where Ω denotes the non-existence of a person. Unless we are able to assign a numerical scale to Ω, there is no way to talk about gains or losses for people in the non-identity case.[3] Thus, one of the major objections to leximin does not make sense in the non-identity case.

Second, prioritarianism may be hopeless. Gustaf Arrhenius (2009: 335–36) shows precisely how hopeless it might be. Suppose that population E consists of n people with well-being level of 100 and that population F consists of 20n people with well-being level of 1. Population E is far better off than F in terms of both total and average well-being. Assume now that we use the square-root function for the prioritarian function. According to this version of prioritarianism, the goodness of population E is $n \times \sqrt{100} = 10n$ and the goodness of population F is $20n \times \sqrt{1} = 20n$. Thus, prioritarianism judges that population F is better off than E. Analogous results can be obtained for any increasing, strictly concave function. Therefore, prioritarianism implies that a population with lower total and average well-being can be better off. This implication is hard, if not impossible, to accept. Based on this implication, Arrhenius concludes that prioritarianism is a principle mainly about how to distribute well-being among a fixed number of people.

On the other hand, axiological egalitarianism judges that population E is strictly better than F. Remember that axiological egalitarianism coincides with average utilitarianism if people's well-being is distributed equally.

Obviously, the average well-being of population E is much higher than that of population F. Thus, egalitarianism can obtain an intuitively plausible result when it comes to the comparison of populations E and F, and egalitarianism is more acceptable than prioritarianism when it comes to this particular comparison.

However, this does not mean that egalitarianism is a plausible distributive principle in cases of variable population size. Consider what egalitarianism has to say about populations C and D. In this case, like average utilitarianism, egalitarianism judges that population D is better than C, because people's well-being is assumed to be equally distributed in both populations C and D and the average well-being in population D is higher than that in C. Nevertheless, such a judgment is intuitively implausible. Therefore, egalitarianism itself is not a plausible distributive principle in cases of variable population size.

It is not surprising that egalitarianism turns out to be implausible in cases of variable population size. The implausibility of egalitarianism comes from the repugnant conclusion. The issue of the repugnant conclusion is deeper and broader than those arising from the choice of distributive principles. Given that there is no widely accepted solution to the repugnant conclusion, we cannot count on the plausibility of any distributive principle in cases of variable population size. I have shown one particular instance where egalitarianism and prioritarianism come apart. This instance suggests that the two principles differ in scope. Prioritarianism is confined to cases of the same population size, whereas egalitarianism may be a plausible distributive principle in cases of variable population size if a solution to the repugnant conclusion is given. But this is a big "if." Unfortunately, as I have not come up with a solution to the repugnant conclusion, I have nothing more to say with regard to egalitarian distributions in variable populations.

Chapter summary

Should egalitarians evaluate the distribution of lifetime well-being (the lifetime view) or the distribution of well-being at a given temporal period (the time-slice view)? Many contemporary egalitarians (John Rawls, Thomas Nagel, Ronald Dworkin, and so on) endorse the lifetime view. However, the lifetime view permits temporal inequality, no matter how large, so long as an equal distribution of lifetime well-being is achieved. Proponents of the time-slice view might find this implication to be counterintuitive. Such a seemingly counterintuitive implication, however, is not a knock-down argument against the lifetime view. The time-slice view, on the other hand, implies the separability of time, which entails a more counterintuitive implication (e.g. it cannot capture the value of longevity). Unless one commits to a particular metaphysical position about personal identity such as reductionism, it is likely that the time-slice view is hard to support. One may adopt the hybrid view. It is easy to say that we should consider both the distribution of lifetime well-being and the distribution of well-being at each temporal period. But it is a very complicated task to combine the two views. We also considered how egalitarian theories of distributive justice would operate in cases where the population size varies. Any distributive principle, be it egalitarian or prioritarian, encounters the problem of the repugnant conclusion. There is no easy solution to this difficult problem.

Further reading

The contemporary issue of the temporal unit of distributive judgment stems from a series of McKerlie's seminal works (McKerlie 1989, 1997, 2013). Read also Adler (2011), Daniels (1988, 2008b), Hirose (2005), Kappel (1997), and Temkin (1993). For the issue of the separability of time, see Arrhenius (2008) and Broome (2004). The challenge of variable population size is one of the most difficult in contemporary moral philosophy. One cannot afford to avoid reading Parfit (1984) carefully. Fortunately, there are some excellent comprehensive studies on the issue (Blackorby et al. 2005; Broome 2004; Holtug 2010). Arrhenius (2009, 2000), Brown (2007), and Vallentyne and Tungodden (2007) discuss how egalitarianism or prioritarianism operates in cases of variable population size. Ryberg and Torbjörn (2004) and Roberts and Wasserman (2009) contain useful discussions on the repugnant conclusion.

Notes

1 Note that Rawls (1971) uses the notion of the separateness of persons when he criticizes classical utilitarianism. He thinks that there is a surprising contrast between classical and average utilitarianism, and puts forward a different set of objections to average utilitarianism. I shall not discuss whether this objection is sensible or plausible here since I have already discussed it elsewhere (Hirose 2014). My purpose here is to explain the motivation for the lifetime view.

2 The goodness of alternative 1 is 17, as we saw earlier in this section. The goodness of alternative 6 is $\frac{1}{2}((16 \times \frac{1}{4} + 16 \times \frac{3}{4} + 4 \times \frac{3}{4} + 4 \times \frac{1}{4}) + (20 \times \frac{1}{4} + 20 \times \frac{3}{4})) = 20$. Therefore, alternative 6 is strictly better than alternative 1.

3 Some philosophers argue that the non-existence of a person has the well-being level of zero (Bradley 2009).

7

EQUALITY IN HEALTH AND HEALTH CARE

In chapters 1 through 6, I examined egalitarianism at a very abstract level. The study of distributive justice is one of the areas of philosophy that can have a direct impact on pressing practical and policy problems. However, it is not easy to articulate abstract theories of distributive justice with reference to how we ought to go about things in real-life contexts. This final chapter will attempt to bridge the gap between the abstract analysis of theories of distributive justice and the substantive analysis of distributive judgment in a particular context. I have chosen the context of health. Distribution of health and health care is an area in which many philosophers have made significant contributions recently. This chapter is not meant to be a comprehensive survey of the literature but an overview of selected arguments in that literature.

The reason I chose the distribution of health and health care is very simple. Nobody would deny that health is important for every one of us. As a matter of fact, societies pour an enormous amount of resources into health and health care. In 2009, Germany spent 11.7 percent of its GDP on health, Japan 9.5 percent, the United Kingdom 9.8 percent, and the USA 17.6 percent (World Health Organization 2012). As health is one of the most important parts of human life, many societies are willing, or forced, to devote and distribute sizable resources to ensure their populations' health and health care. The issues of health and health care have been, and will continue to be, a major topic in political and public discussion. It is one of the areas to which philosophical theories of distributive justice should be able to contribute. I think that philosophers ought to be prepared to say something about this big issue. Hare (1996: 1) opens his book by saying that "[i]f the moral philosopher cannot help with the problems of medical ethics, he ought to shut up shop." Likewise, if the scholar of egalitarianism cannot help with the problems of the distribution of health and health care, he ought to shut up shop.

Sections 7.1 through 7.3 deal with the distribution of health, and sections 7.4 through 7.7 with the distribution of scarce health care resources. Section 7.1 considers the way in which the Rawlsian theory of justice takes the distribution of health into account. Section 7.2 looks at the luck egalitarian challenge to the Rawlsian theory of the distribution of health. Section 7.3 considers how egalitarian theories of distributive justice should approach the issue of the social gradient in health. Sections 7.4 and 7.5 focus on how egalitarian theories of distributive justice can be used in the area of health care distribution. Sections 7.6 and 7.7 examine the temporal unit of distributive judgment in the distribution of health care resources.

In this chapter, I understand the concept of health to refer to the absence of pathology. That is, health is the normal level of functioning for a member of the human species. Of course, the concept of health itself is not purely scientific, and is subject to philosophical analysis. Until quite recently, in some countries, homosexuality was believed to be a type of mental illness, and to require medical intervention. But it is now believed to be a matter of sexual orientation, not a matter of health. Philosophical thinking is needed to determine the "normal" level of functioning and whether the idea of a "normal" level makes sense at all. That being said, I will set aside this issue here.

Second, we must distinguish health and health care. Health care contributes to health. But it is not the only thing that contributes to health. Other factors such as public safety, clean water, vaccination, better nutrition, education, income, wealth, housing conditions, workplace safety, the degree of stress, and so on, affect people's health. We must also distinguish equality of health and equal access to health care. As we see in section 7.3, equal access to health care does not imply equality of health. Countries with universal health care systems (e.g. Canada, the United Kingdom, and Japan) exhibit health inequalities among different social groups.

7.1 The Rawlsian approach to health

John Rawls (1971) does not talk about health at all. But let us recall what he said about distributive justice in general. His theory of justice requires satisfying the first principle (the priority of liberty), and one part of the second principle (fair equality of opportunity) before considering the distribution of goods. Once the requirements of these two principles are met, we are allowed to apply the difference principle as a distributive principle. Rawls's difference principle holds that socioeconomic inequalities are justified only when, and only because, these inequalities maximize the expectation of a representative member of the least advantaged group in society. The relative level of different social groups is determined by their bundle of social primary goods – the goods that every rational person is presumed to want. Social primary goods include liberties, income and wealth, the social basis of self-respect, and so on. The list is not meant to be exhaustive. However, Rawls does not include health. Rawls (1971: 62) claims that health is not one of the social primary goods, but a natural primary good. Other natural primary goods include vigor, intelligence, and imagination. According to Rawls, health is influenced by the basic structure of society, but it is not directly under its control. This is why Rawls eliminates health from the list of social primary goods and does not see health or health care as a consideration for distributive judgments.

Immediately after the publication of *A Theory of Justice*, Kenneth J. Arrow (1973) pointed out that Rawls should add health to the list of social primary goods. Arrow invited us to imagine a group of individuals with hemophilia, who need a lot of money for coagulant therapy. When we compare a representative person in this group with a representative person in the group of individuals with no health problems, equality of social primary goods does not secure equality between these two groups. Obviously, individuals with hemophilia seem to be worse off than those with perfect health. However, Rawls's idea of the difference principle would say that these two groups are equally well off. Thus, Arrow speculated that Rawls would have to add health to the list of social primary goods. Arrow's motivation behind this example is to show that if there are two or more social primary goods, the index-number problem (i.e. the difficulty of determining the relative importance of different primary goods) arises, and therefore, the problem of interpersonal comparability remains intact, although the notion of social primary goods is meant to solve this problem. However, in this section, we understand Arrow's point rather as the claim that Rawls and his followers should add health to the list of social primary goods.

This simple point by Arrow strikes me as reasonable. As I said at the very beginning of this chapter, health is one of the fundamental parts of human life, and this is why many countries spend an enormous amount of their resources on their populations' health and health care each year. Of course, we cannot transfer health from one person to another. However, it is possible to improve the health status of specific groups, and reduce health inequalities, by investing resources in promoting healthy lifestyles and diets, providing vaccinations, improving hygiene and housing conditions, implementing better access to health care, and, more controversially, modifying people's genetic make-up (Buchanan et al. 2001). Quite contrary to what Rawls thinks, people's health can be controlled by the basic structure of society, and is thus a matter of distributive justice. Arrow's speculations about social primary goods also make perfect sense. It is reasonable to think that health and health care are things that every rational person would want, and therefore that it should be considered as one of the social primary goods. Adding health to the list of social primary goods is one way, and the most straightforward way, to bring health into the framework of the Rawlsian theory of justice.

Norman Daniels (2008a) proposes that we include health in the Rawlsian theory of justice in a different way. Daniels does not add health to the list of social primary goods. He thinks that health has a special moral importance that social primary goods lack. According to him, good health protects people's opportunity to pursue their life plan, and meeting health care needs thus has important effects on the distribution of such opportunity. Admittedly, it is unfair if some people have less opportunity to pursue their life plan than others due to factors over which they have little control. To eliminate this inequality and guarantee fair treatment for everyone, Daniels argues that people's health should be regulated by the principle of fair equality of opportunity instead of the difference principle.

On the standard interpretation of Rawls's theory of justice, the principle of fair equality of opportunity is seen as a procedural, rather than distributive, principle that ensures equal opportunity for everyone, regardless of social class, race, ethnicity, sex, religion, or sexual orientation. Usually, it is interpreted as a principle of non-discrimination. However, Daniels interprets health as a safeguard to protect people's opportunity, and argues that the principle of fair equality of opportunity better accommodates the importance of health than the difference principle. In a nutshell, health has a special moral importance which social primary goods lack. Daniels' claim is now called the *specialness thesis* about health.

On Daniels' interpretation of the Rawlsian theory of justice, fair equality of health is required as part of fair equality of opportunity. This means that Daniels does not aim at complete equality of health. He aims at *fair* equality of health. What kind of situation gives rise to the concern for fair equality of health? Here is an example. Consider the difference in the life expectancy at birth, which is usually understood as one of the major health indicators. In the United States in 2008, life expectancy at birth was 76.2 years among non-Hispanic white men, and 70.2 years among non-Hispanic black men, yet it was 81.2 years among non-Hispanic white women, and 77.5 years among non-Hispanic black women (Harper et al. 2012). There are significant inequalities in life expectancy at birth between white and black people, and therefore inequalities in opportunity in their lifetime. Daniels thinks that such inequalities in health are unfair, like racial discrimination in hiring and promotion, and therefore should be regulated by the principle of fair equality of opportunity.

Shlomi Segall (2007, 2010) objects to Daniels' specialness thesis. According to Segall, fair equality of opportunity in health cannot be achieved in isolation from social primary goods, especially income and wealth. The principle of fair equality of opportunity has lexical priority over the difference principle. People's health cannot be divided and transferred from one person to another. Health care alone cannot meet the demands of fair equality of opportunity in health, because other factors such as income, wealth, housing, employment, and so on, affect people's health status. In order to achieve fair equality of opportunity in health, it is necessary to redistribute the socially controllable determinants of health. However, at least some of these socially controllable determinants of health are also social primary goods. How can the distribution of social primary goods be required in order to meet the demands of the principle of fair equality of opportunity, which has lexical priority over the difference principle? According to Segall, health cannot be special in Daniels' sense, because fair equality of opportunity in health requires the redistribution of some social primary goods through the difference principle, which must come into play only when fair equality of opportunity is satisfied.

To an objection along these lines, Daniels could respond in the following way (Daniels 2008a: 53). It is true that Rawls gives lexical priority to fair equality of opportunity over the difference principle. But this does not mean that the difference principle cannot come into play before the requirements of fair equality of opportunity are all satisfied. What Rawls really means by lexical priority is that the difference principle is constrained by fair equality of opportunity when these two principles conflict with each other. As we saw in chapter 1, Rawls's difference principle can tolerate inequalities of social primary goods insofar as such inequalities work to make those who are worst off as well off as possible, compared with alternative arrangements. However, according to Daniels' interpretation, what Rawls means is that "inequalities allowed by the difference principle must not undercut fair equality of opportunity" (Daniels 2008a: 53). On Daniels' interpretation, the difference principle can come into play even before the requirements of fair equality of opportunity are met, unless the difference principle undercuts fair equality of opportunity. Therefore, according to Daniels, there is nothing wrong in cases where fair equality of opportunity requires redistribution of some social primary goods.

7.2 Luck egalitarianism in health

The motivation for luck egalitarianism is to bring the notions of luck and responsibility to bear in distributive judgment. That is to say, luck egalitarianism attempts to neutralize the differential effects of brute luck and hold individuals responsible for bad effects that reflect their choices. The distribution of health seems to be an ideal area for luck egalitarians to test their theory. Nobody chooses to be ill, injured, or disabled. But some people become ill, injured, or disabled, whereas others do not. Becoming ill is a bad effect of brute luck. However, the risk of certain types of illness and injury can be affected by the choices one makes. Heavy smokers have a high risk of developing cardiovascular diseases and cancer. But some heavy smokers never develop cardiovascular diseases or cancer. This is a clear case of option luck. Intuitively, when a non-smoking heart-disease patient is compared with a heavy smoker with heart disease, few people have the same degree of sympathy for these two patients. Many people would think that a socialized health care system or private insurance should fully fund the health care resources needed to treat the non-smoking heart-disease patient, but not the heavy-smoking heart-disease patient. Luck egalitarianism attempts to capture this intuition and appears to be promising particularly in the context of the distribution of health and health care resources.

Luck egalitarianism in health contends that inequality in health is bad or unjust if it reflects the differential effects of brute luck, and that inequality in health is not bad or unjust if it reflects the differential effects of option luck. If you are a heavy-smoker and develop lung cancer, luck egalitarianism in health holds you responsible for being in a worse health condition than others. Your worse health condition does not give rise to a concern for justice. However, if you are in a worse health condition than others due to the differential effects of sheer brute luck, then luck egalitarianism demands some compensation for these differential effects. This is a direct application of luck egalitarianism to the context of health.

The major contrast between the Rawlsian theory of distributive justice and luck egalitarianism is that luck egalitarianism in health is responsibility-sensitive whereas the Rawlsian theory is not. As we saw in the previous section, the Rawlsian theory of justice can take the distribution of health into account in two ways. If health is added to the list of social primary goods (as Arrow speculates), the difference principle requires maximizing the expectation of a representative individual in the worst off group, regardless of their choices, thus being responsibility-insensitive. If health is regulated by the principle of fair equality of opportunity (as Daniels contends), the normal range of opportunity for pursuing a life plan would be guaranteed as part of fair equality of opportunity, regardless of whether people are imprudent or reckless, thus being responsibility-insensitive. Either way, the Rawlsian theory of distributive justice in health is responsibility-insensitive. But luck egalitarianism is responsibility-sensitive. For proponents of luck egalitarianism, this fact appears to show an advantage of luck egalitarianism in health over the Rawlsian theory of distributive justice. This claim is not surprising, because it is a supposed advantage of the general form of luck egalitarianism over the general Rawlsian theory of distributive justice. Nor is it controversial, for many people intuitively think that the notion of responsibility should play an important role in the distribution of health and health care.

You can probably imagine that the objection we discussed in chapter 2 to the general form of luck egalitarianism may also be raised against luck egalitarianism in health. That was Elizabeth Anderson's abandonment objection, which we discussed in section 2.4. Recall her reckless driver case. The case is such that the reckless driver is left unattended and consequently worse off than the careful driver, who is rescued by paramedics. According to luck egalitarianism, there is nothing unjust in such a situation. This is because the reckless driver is reasonably expected to drive carefully enough and purchase insurance and therefore should be held responsible for the bad consequences of his or her choice. The purported objection contends that it is unjustifiably harsh to leave the reckless driver unattended. Not surprisingly, the same abandonment objection applies to luck egalitarianism in health. According to the objection, luck egalitarianism in health can happily leave the reckless driver unattended, but this is unjustifiably harsh.

As we saw in section 2.4, Segall (2010) attempts to respond to the abandonment objection by appealing to pluralism of distributive principles. He concedes that luck egalitarianism itself abandons the reckless driver. Yet, he claims that proponents of luck egalitarianism can be pluralist in the sense that they can support two or more distributive principles simultaneously. That is, they can support luck egalitarianism and other distributive principles, such as the principle of meeting people's basic needs. The principle of meeting people's basic needs can offer grounds for providing treatment to the reckless driver. In other words, luck egalitarianism in health requires, and must coexist with, the principle of meeting people's basic needs. Thus, Segall concludes that proponents of luck egalitarianism do not necessarily require abandoning the reckless driver. Now you can easily imagine that the two criticisms of Segall's response considered in that section could be applied in the case of luck egalitarianism in health. The abandonment objection is a serious challenge to luck egalitarianism in health.

As we saw in section 2.4, the all-luck view and the fresh start view of luck egalitarianism avoid the abandonment objection. The all-luck view claims that almost all differential effects of luck are the results of luck that is beyond the control of the worse off people. According to the all-luck view, unless the reckless driver intentionally gets injured, he or she cannot be held responsible. Insofar as the reckless driver did not intend to get injured, he or she can demand compensation for the bad effects of reckless driving. As I said in section 2.3, however, it is highly dubious that the all-luck view is plausible.

The fresh start view may also avoid the objection insofar as this reckless driver truly regrets his or her reckless driving and commits to careful driving after this accident. If the reckless driver changes his or her pre-ference about how he or she drives, the fresh start view respects such a change and supports securing a fresh start for this person by providing the necessary treatment.

Here is another interesting proposal, which concerns the scope of luck egalitarianism in health. Cappelen and Norheim (2005) claim that a dis-tributive principle should be responsibility-sensitive, but that responsibility does not need to play a significant role at the point of health care delivery, as long as it does so somewhere else. For example, heavy smokers pay a high tax on tobacco products. Heavy smokers pay more tax than occasional smokers. Insofar as their tax payment is sufficiently large, smokers compensate for the increased cost of health care through taxes, and thus should not be treated differently from non-smokers at the point of health care delivery. Thus, Cappelen and Norheim suggest that we should treat smokers and non-smokers equally at the point of health care delivery, but that smokers should pay the cost of their irresponsible behavior in other ways, such as paying a higher tax. Their proposal avoids the abandonment objection, yet holds smokers responsible.

7.3 Social gradient in health

Many people share the intuition that heavy smokers should be held responsible for the bad effects of their behavior in one way or another. Should they really? The situation is a bit more complicated if we look at the larger picture. It is easy to notice the following fact: people with lower socioeconomic status (e.g. lower incomes, lower level of education, poorer neighborhood, lower rank in professional ladder) are more likely to smoke, and therefore to be less healthy, than people with higher socioeconomic status. The same thing can be said about obesity, alcohol abuse, and other risky behaviors that determine health status. There is some correlation between socioeconomic status and risky behavior.

Typically, epidemiologists call the socioeconomic factors the *upstream factors*, and the risky behavior and lifestyle the *downstream factors*. The distinction between downstream and upstream merely reflects the relative position between two ranges of factors. The lifestyle of eating a cheeseburger every day is more upstream compared with a high level of cholesterol. Lower socioeconomic status is more upstream compared with the lifestyle of eating a cheeseburger every day. The upstream/downstream distinction is relative. It is used to capture how close to a given health status the determinants of health are. It is not possible to draw an absolute line between the downstream and upstream factors. For present purposes, by upstream factors, I mean socioeconomic status, and I refer to people's behavior as downstream factors.

The upstream factors predict the downstream factors, and the downstream factors predict the health status. Thus, roughly, individuals with lower socioeconomic status are more likely to be less healthy than individuals with higher socioeconomic status. If this is taken seriously, should we hold smokers responsible for the bad effects of their behavior? Heavy smokers tend to be of lower socioeconomic status. They did not choose to be born into a lower socioeconomic group. However, by sheer brute luck, they happened to be born into a lower socioeconomic class. As a consequence, they are more likely to have lower health status.

Is smoking really a matter of choice? This is a question for the crude choice view and the genuine choice view of luck egalitarianism. The answer to this question partly depends on the answer to the long-standing problem of free will. Proponents of determinism would claim that heavy smokers cannot be held responsible. Proponents of compatibilism can claim that they should be held responsible. The answer also depends on whether one takes the crude choice or the genuine choice view. Recall what these views claim about the issue of expensive tastes. The crude choice view (e.g. Ronald Dworkin) claims that a person should be held responsible for the bad effects resulting from having expensive tastes. In contrast, the genuine choice view (e.g. G. A. Cohen) claims that a person should not be held responsible for the bad effects resulting from having expensive tastes, because he or she did not choose to develop expensive tastes. If there were a sufficiently strong similarly between expensive tastes and the smoking habit, then the crude choice view of luck egalitarianism would claim that heavy smokers should be held responsible for the bad effects of smoking, whereas the genuine choice view would claim that they should not.

There is another way to ask the question. Is it reasonable to expect people with lower socioeconomic status either not to start smoking or to stop smoking? Needless to say, this is a question for the reasonable avoidability view (e.g. Peter Vallentyne and Shlomi Segall). This view would claim the following. Heavy smokers did not choose to develop the smoking habit. But, given that the health risk associated with smoking is widely advertised and recognized, it would be reasonable to expect anyone, including people with a lower socioeconomic status, to refrain from smoking, and hence smokers should be held responsible for the bad effects of smoking. Thus, the reasonable avoidability view of luck egalitarianism can hold individuals with a lower socioeconomic status responsible for the bad effects of smoking without getting into the free will debate.

The issue of socioeconomic status, however, leads us to a more general normative question, and this question is for all those who care about equality. The question is this: how should we deal with the *social gradient in health*? Let me explain the social gradient in health very briefly. The social gradient in health means that there exists a correlation between health inequalities and socioeconomic inequalities: that is, there exist health inequalities between different socioeconomic groups within society. As I mentioned in the previous section, there is a noticeable inequality in life expectancy at birth between white US citizens and black US citizens. Health inequalities are not confined to those between black and white, or rich and poor, however. Similar inequality is also found among many other social groups, such as those defined by income level, education level, residential area, sex, and so on.

The social gradient in health goes further. Health inequalities exhibit a fine gradation from the top socioeconomic status through to the bottom. That is, the highest socioeconomic group is healthier than the second highest socioeconomic group; the second highest group is healthier than the third highest group; and so on. This gradient is found not only in life expectancy at birth, but also in many major causes of death such as obesity, high blood pressure, high cholesterol, heart disease, and so on. Individuals with higher income, higher wealth, higher education, or otherwise higher social status live longer and healthier lives. This is the social *gradient* in health. The implication of the social gradient in health is that, statistically, socioeconomic status predicts health status.

One of the most famous sets of studies regarding this relationship is the *Whitehall studies* (Marmot *et al.* 1984). The Whitehall studies derived from observational research that analyzed the major causes of mortality within the British civil service.[1] Before the Whitehall studies, many people believed that civil servants with a higher rank would have a higher risk of, for example, heart attack than civil servants with lower rank. However, the studies found that civil servants with a lower rank were at higher risk than civil servants with a higher rank. In England, everyone is entitled to use the universal health care system, and civil servants all engage in non-industrial, office-based work. However, the Whitehall studies found a striking health gradient in the hierarchy of British civil servants. That is, the rate of disease and mortality increases progressively as grade level goes down. The first Whitehall study (which surveyed 18,000 male civil servants from 1967 onward) reported that the men at the bottom grade level (e.g. messengers, doorkeepers, etc.) displayed a risk of death four times greater than the men at the top grade level (e.g. administrators). Individuals with lower rank were more likely to smoke and therefore to have cardiovascular disease. But even if we control for this risk factor, the gradient still exists. Downstream factors such as smoking, blood pressure, cholesterol, being overweight, and so on, account for only some of the gradient in mortality. This means that smokers with lower rank are more likely to become ill than smokers with higher rank.

Many people find the social gradient in health ethically problematic. As we saw in section 7.1, Daniels (2008a) thinks that health directly protects people's opportunity to pursue their life plans, and therefore that fair equality of health should be guaranteed, regardless of race, sex, income level, social class, and so on. Some governments and international organizations, including the World Health Organization, also take this issue very seriously and claim that the social gradient in health, and health inequality, is a matter of justice (World Health Organization 2008). Those who are concerned with the social gradient in health tend to claim that health equality itself is desirable and can be achieved by manipulating the socially controllable determinants of health. That is, by reducing the socioeconomic inequalities, we could work toward the reduction of health inequalities.

There are two issues to be clarified. The first is whether equality of health should (or can) be achieved by redistribution of socially controllable determinants of health. The second is whether we should really aim at health equality.

Let me start with the first issue. Many people, including Norman Daniels and the Commission on Social Determinants of Health at the World Health Organization, imply that health equality should, and can, be achieved by redistributing the socially controllable determinants of health. This view implicitly assumes the following: the relation between health inequalities and socioeconomic inequalities is *causal*. More specifically, the thought is that socioeconomic inequalities cause health inequalities, and so reduced socioeconomic inequalities imply reduced health inequalities. This causal claim is a debated issue in the literature on public health: there is no consensus regarding a one-way causal relation from socioeconomic status to health status. Deaton (2002), for example, claims that lower health status can cause a lower economic condition (imagine a fifty-year-old who retires due to illness but must pay the medical bills even though she or he has no source of income). If this observation is correct, the causal direction is also from health status to socioeconomic status, at least in some cases.

The cause may also be something other than socioeconomic status or health status. For example, substance abuse tends to cause both a lower economic status (i.e. poverty) and a lower health status (infectious diseases and malnutrition). It is hopelessly difficult to identify how we should intervene to reduce health inequalities. Furthermore, it is not clear what socioeconomic status amounts to. Is it income, housing, education, race, gender, or all of these? These factors are intricately interconnected, and it is not clear what really should be equalized. It is easy to say that we should equalize socioeconomic conditions in order to equalize health between social groups. But it is not easy to identify what we should redistribute in order to equalize socioeconomic conditions.

Let us move on to the second issue. Is it health equality that we should aim at? To say that health inequalities between social groups are problematic is one thing. To say that we should aim at health equality is quite another. At least, there must be philosophical arguments to establish that health equality is what we are to aim at. Fortunately, we have already looked at one such argument. This is Norman Daniels' specialness thesis. However, some people may not be persuaded by the specialness thesis. Those who care about equality of overall well-being (e.g. proponents of telic egalitarianism) would think that health is just one part of overall well-being and that health equality does not necessarily track equality of well-being. For them, what we should aim at is equality of overall well-being, not health equality. The implication of this claim is that health inequalities may be tolerated insofar as there are no inequalities in overall well-being. Obviously, Daniels would object to this because it violates the requirements of fair equality of opportunity. Nonetheless, for those who are not committed to the specialness thesis, health equality may not be a goal.

These two issues come down to the following fundamental question: How do we understand the relation between health and overall well-being? If health is of distinct importance, then it makes sense to aim at health equality and equalize socioeconomic conditions as a means to equalize health. If health is just one aspect of overall well-being among others, and equality of well-being is what we aim at, then health equality is not in itself a goal.

7.4 Distribution of health care: QALY maximization

In what follows, I shall focus on the distribution of health care. Health care is just one of many contributors to health. But it is an important one. Furthermore, health care is the biggest expenditure in most countries. Health care is also an issue of distributive justice. Health care resources are always scarce. There are many patients who require health care. However, the budget, time, beds, physicians, organ donors, and other resources are always limited. We cannot treat all patients, and hence must decide who will receive treatment and who will not. The scarcity of health care resources is expected to become more acute in the future because newer medical technologies are more costly than older ones and many countries are in transition to ageing societies. Thus, the issue of health care distribution will become even more pressing.

How should we decide how to distribute scarce health care resources? This is a horrible question. Essentially, we must decide who will receive treatment and who will not. Many people want to avoid answering such a question. Should we leave it to civil servants or politicians or administrators in private health insurance companies? I do not know. At the very least, ethics must offer certain arguments for public discussion. As a result, ethicists must face the difficult question and come up with principles that are justifiable.

There is one principle that has been adopted by several governments such as those of the United Kingdom, New Zealand, Oregon, etc. That is the maximization of health benefits from health interventions. Its basic idea is to choose an allocation that yields the "best value for money." But how is the *value* of health benefits estimated? In many cases, it is measured by *quality-adjusted life years* (QALYs).

The idea of QALY considers and combines two factors: health-related quality of life and years of life. Health-related quality of life is assigned a number between 0 and 1 where 1 represents the state of full health, and 0 represents the state of death. One year with full health is 1 QALY. If a person has an illness or injury, his/her health-related quality of life should be strictly smaller than 1. The health-related quality of life is then multiplied by the years of life a person continues to live. So 1 QALY can represent 1 year of life in full health; or it can represent 2 years at health-related quality of life level 0.5; or it can represent 4 years at 0.25. For example, suppose that one treatment for cancer patients provides 5 years of remission at 0.4, while another treatment provides 3 years of remission at 0.7. The outcome of the first treatment is 2 QALYs; the outcome of the second treatment is 2.1 QALYs. The second treatment, taking into account both health-related quality of life and quantity of life, produces more health benefits. It results in more QALYs. QALYs enable us to compare all sorts of resource uses in health care. They can represent the value of the health outcomes of different treatments and interventions.

Given a fixed amount of resources, we can identify an allocation that provides the best value for resources and hence is most cost-effective.

Whether or not health care is provided to patients with a particular type of condition is often a matter of life and death. Do we decide on the basis of cost and benefit? It seems as if we are saying that some people's lives are cheaper than others'. For example, in England and Wales, the National Institute for Health and Care Excellence (formerly the National Institutes for Health and Clinical Excellence, and ironically, abbreviated as NICE) recommends whether new medical technologies should be provided through the National Health Service on the basis of cost-effectiveness analysis. Their initial policy was not to approve a new technology that would cost more than £30,000 per 1 QALY although this criterion was somewhat relaxed later. This sounds horrible. It sounds like a patient's life has a price tag. However, health care resource distribution on the basis of QALY maximization does not imply that the life of any person has a price tag. Furthermore, everyone's life has the same moral worth. However, it is perfectly sensible to say that resources for health care have a price.

It is obvious that the principle of QALY maximization is utilitarian in spirit. It adds up different people's good, and claims that we should choose the allocation that maximizes the total good. In the context of health care resource allocation, the good is QALY, which measures health benefit. QALY is added up across individuals to estimate the goodness of different outcomes. Then, the alternative that maximizes the goodness of outcome is chosen. It is not surprising that, according to QALY maximization, it does not matter how QALYs are distributed across individuals. Needless to say, all sorts of objections leveled against utilitarianism are raised against QALY maximization.

Here is one example in which the principle of maximizing QALYs appears to be counterintuitive. As part of the Oregon Plan, the Oregon Health Services Commission released a list of treatment-condition pairs ranked by a cost-benefit calculation. However, some parts of the rankings appear counterintuitive, or at least, it is unclear how we could justify them from the ethical point of view. For example, tooth capping was ranked higher than appendectomy. This is counterintuitive because many people think that an appendectomy is far more urgent and important and therefore should be ranked higher. An appendectomy is a matter of life and death, whereas tooth capping is just a matter of pain and dental function. In light of QALY maximization, the reason behind this counterintuitive ranking is quite simple. An appendectomy costs many times more than a tooth capping, and we can offer tooth capping to many more people for the cost of an appendectomy. Even though one appendectomy is more urgent and important than one tooth capping, the aggregated net health benefit of tooth capping is strictly greater than that of appendectomy. This is why appendectomy is ranked lower than tooth capping.

Many people, however, find this counterintuitive. I can think of two reasons. The first is a worry about aggregation. An appendectomy is so important that it might seem that a tooth capping, no matter how many patients would require it, cannot outweigh an appendectomy. This is a reason to reject the aggregation of health benefits. Those who agree with this first line of reasoning would support principles such as the maximin rule, leximin, and Nagel's pairwise comparison. As we saw in chapter 1, these principles are non-aggregative. That is, according to these principles, a small increase in well-being for a large number of people does not outweigh a large decrease in well-being for a small number of people. If these principles were applied to the distribution of health care resources, appendectomy would be ranked higher than tooth capping, no matter how many people would benefit from tooth capping. If Oregon's ranking of appendectomy and tooth capping is taken to be implausible, then there is a good reason to adopt a non-aggregative principle.

However, non-aggregative principles would encounter the same kind of objection as that leveled against aggregative principles. The objection directly follows from the rejection of aggregation. It is known as the *bottomless pit objection*. The maximin rule and leximin give complete priority to the worst off over others. These principles imply that any gain for the worst off, however small, outweighs any loss for other people, however large. For example, patients with severe chronic obstructive pulmonary disease or with severe chronic schizophrenia are largely resistant to standard pharmacological treatments. The severity of their respective disorders makes them significantly worse off. However, in order to make a small improvement for the worst off patients, so much of the health care resources would be spent for them and so little would be left for other patients that not many could see this as an acceptable way of allocating resources.

The second reason to find the priority of tooth capping over appendectomy counterintuitive is based on the claim that we should give priority to benefiting the worse off. This is not a reason opposed to aggregation. However, the claim is that we should aggregate QALY in a way that gives greater moral weight to benefiting the worse off. Patients in need of an appendectomy are worse off than those who require only a tooth capping. Their state should therefore receive greater weight than patients who require tooth capping. This does not rule out aggregation. Ultimately, appendectomy may still be ranked below tooth capping. However, by giving greater moral weight to benefits to the worse off, things will become more difficult. The general concern for the state of the worse off in health care distribution has been widely recognized among health economists since Alan Williams (1997) claimed that QALY maximization should take the notion of equity into account.

As we saw in section 4.3, the idea of giving priority to the worse off is captured by PD-ism. PD-ism is a class of distributive principles that satisfy the Pigou-Dalton condition. The Pigou-Dalton condition claims that, given that total well-being remains constant, a transfer of benefit from a better off to a worse off person makes the outcome strictly better. This claim is formulated by assigning a strictly greater weight to benefits to the worse off. Both telic egalitarianism and prioritarianism satisfy the Pigou-Dalton condition. Thus, these principles give priority to benefiting the worse off. In the context of health care resource allocation, telic egalitarianism and prioritarianism each give greater weight to benefits to patients suffering from a more severe health condition. The difference is that telic egalitarianism determines the weight by the rank-order position of each respective patient's condition in a ranking of severity level, whereas prioritarianism determines the weight by the absolute level of severity. Among health economists and health policymakers, the issue of how we determine the weight of the worse off is increasingly known as the issue of *equity weights*.

Some people have proposed using aggregative methods that satisfy the Pigou-Dalton condition. For example, Bleichrodt et al. (2004) and Norheim (2009) each propose a variant of telic egalitarianism for QALY aggregation. Their models assign rank-dependent equity weights to QALYs, i.e. equity weights are determined by the rank-order position of a disease in a ranking of severity level. Likewise, Nord et al. (1999) propose a variant of prioritarianism. In their model, the absolute level of QALYs determines equity weights.

Usually, QALY maximization is understood as the unweighted sum of QALYs. However, it does not need to be so. We can make it a weighted sum and give priority to the worse off. If we give priority to the worse off, then it is possible to bring egalitarian concerns to bear on the allocation of health care resources.

7.5 What is it to be worse off?

It is easy to say we should give priority to benefiting the worse off. However, it is not easy to determine what it is to be worse off. There are two difficult questions. The first is whether "worse off" should be understood in terms of the severity of health condition or QALYs. In the comparison between appendectomy and tooth capping, it is clear that patients needing an appendectomy are worse off than those who require tooth capping, other things being equal. In this case, by worse off, we mean patients at a lower level of health-related quality of life. However, the notion of QALY combines two considerations: health-related quality of life and number of years. By worse off, do we usually mean patients with fewer QALYs or patients with lower health-related quality of life? Probably, by worse off, we mean patients with lower health-related quality of life, not fewer QALYs.

Imagine the following case. There are two patients with the same type of disease. Assume that their health-related quality of life is 0.5. With a certain health intervention, we can restore the two patients to full health (this means that we can improve one of the two patients from 0.5 to 1.0). There are no morally relevant differences between the two patients. The only difference is the number of life years after the treatment: patient A will continue to live for 20 years, and patient B for 10 years. The severity of the disease is the same. The only difference is number of years. If we give priority to patients with more severely depleted health-related quality of life, then A and B are equally worse off. However, if we give priority to patients with fewer QALYs, B is worse off than A. Thus, there are at least two possible points of view on how we identify the worse off patients.

The second question concerns how we take into account the non-health-related quality of life. One of the attractive features of QALY maximization is that it ignores features of non-health-related quality of life for the sake of distributive judgment. Imagine two patients with the same health condition and the same expected QALY from the same health intervention. There are no morally relevant differences between the two patients. The only difference is that one patient is a billionaire and the other is a homeless person. But we can treat only one patient. If we focus on the health benefit from the intervention and ignore other features, we will be indifferent between these two patients, regardless of their economic status or their contribution to the national economy. The primary task of the health care system is to restore patients' health and to protect the population's health, not to promote the national economy. Thus, it makes perfect sense to ignore features of non-health-related quality of life for the sake of deciding how we should distribute scarce health care resources. QALY maximization has this positive property.

However, it is not clear whether ignoring features of non-health-related quality of life is really a desirable property. For example, imagine a professional pianist who injured a finger. The finger injury is not a serious health condition, nor does it necessarily entail that the pianist would be particularly worse off in terms of health. However, its impact on his or her overall quality of life might be enormous. It may end his or her career as a professional pianist. Some people would claim that we should consider the impact on the overall quality of life, in addition to the health-related quality of life, when we decide how to distribute scarce health care resources. However, it is precisely this claim that QALY max-imization would reject, and furthermore, it is because of its rejection of this claim that QALY maximization is seen as attractive. Thus, there are both advantages and disadvantages in ignoring non-health-related quality of life. This point leads us back to the general issue we discussed in section 7.3. That is, how should we relate health and overall well-being? I do not attempt to provide an answer to this question here. But the question is fundamental.

It seems that sufficientarianism makes sense only when we consider both the health-related quality of life and the non-health-related quality of life. If sufficientarianism focuses on the health-related quality of life, then it does not play a distinctive role, and collapses into PD-ism. Sufficiency level would be the normal level of functioning. Anyone below this level is below the sufficiency level. If people are at or above the normal level of functioning, then the health care system does not need to be concerned with them. In the distribution of health care resources, all patients are below the normal level of functioning and therefore below the sufficiency level. As we saw in chapter 5, sufficientarianism gives priority to the worse off below the sufficiency level. The state of people at or above the normal level of functioning will not affect our distributive judgments. Thus, sufficientar-ianism is likely to collapse into PD-ism if health-related quality of life is at stake. However, certain types of disease or injury restrict one or more major life activities that are required to attain the sufficiency level with respect to the overall quality of life. For example, let us say some illness would make a patient paralysed. Mobility is required for many basic life activities. Paralysis would therefore put the patient below the sufficiency level when it comes to overall quality of life. If this is correct, sufficientar-ianism in health care allots special moral importance to treatments designed to prevent patients from suffering paralysis. However, other minor diseases or injuries do not put patients below the sufficiency level with respect to overall quality of life, and therefore, do not warrant any special moral concern. Thus, sufficientarianism in health care plays its own distinctive role only when the health-related quality of life is considered alongside the overall quality of life.

7.6 Age and health care distribution

In chapter 6, we examined the temporal unit of distributive judgment. More specifically, we examined the contrast between the time-slice view and the lifetime view. The issue of the appropriate temporal unit is one of the focal points in the context of the distribution of health care.

Let me start by explaining one of the major (alleged) objections to QALY maximization. Imagine that two patients with heart disease need a heart transplant. They will die unless they receive a new heart. But if they receive the new heart, they will recover their full health. As always, there are no morally relevant differences between the two patients. The only difference this time is that one patient is 20 years old and the other is 60 years old. Now imagine that there is one donor. We must choose the 20-year-old or the 60-year-old. Which patient should we choose? In this case, QALY maximization claims that we should give the new heart to the 20-year-old. Why? Let us assume that the improvement in the health-related quality of life is the same. The only difference is the number of years that we can extend their lives by the transplant. Let us assume that the life expectancy at birth is 80 years. The 20-year-old can continue to live for 60 extra years, whereas the 60-year-old can continue to live for only 20 extra years. We can obtain more QALYs from giving the heart to the 20-year-old. This is why QALY maximization would recommend giving the heart to the 20-year-old.

Here is the objection to QALY maximization. QALY maximization discriminates against the old and therefore is unjust. In this example, age determines who receives the heart. Given the same size of improvement in the health-related quality of life, the consideration of age tips the balance in favor of the 20-year-old, and the older patient receives lower priority than the younger one. According to the objection, this is discrimination against the old, and therefore wrong. Call this objection the *anti-ageism objection* to QALY maximization. The implication of the ageism objection is that the old and the young must be treated equally, and that we should flip a fair coin to decide who receives the heart in this example.

A quick response can be made to the ageism objection. The fact is that everyone ages. The unequal treatment of the old and the young in QALY maximization implies that everyone receives lower priority when he or she ages. Given that everyone ages, everyone is treated equally. Therefore, treating the young and the old differently is not an unjustifiable form of unequal treatment. This response sounds effective.

Still, the fundamental question of the appropriate temporal unit in health care distribution remains intact. Should we take the lifetime view or time-slice view? If we take the time-slice view in health care, we would flip a fair coin to decide which one we save in the case of the two heart-failure patients, thus opposing QALY maximization. The objection to QALY maximization on the basis of age discrimination is not promising. But the objection on the basis of the time-slice view still makes sense.

Let us go back to the example of the two heart-failure patients. QALY maximization claims that we should give the heart to the 20-year-old rather than the 60-year-old. Intuitively, many people support such a claim. Why? The reason is not merely that doing so produces more health benefits measured by QALYs. There seems to be at least one other reason. The 60-year-old has already completed a significant part of his or her life, and has had a lot of opportunities to pursue his or her life project. With all due respect, not much time will be left to the 60-year-old, even if he or she receives a new heart. In contrast, the 20-year-old is at the early stage of his or her life and has not had much opportunity for pursuing his or her life project. In terms of opportunity for pursuing a life project, it seems fair to give the new heart to the 20-year-old.

Whatever their reasoning might be, many people support the unequal treatment of the young and the old. Yet, should we support it on the basis of QALY maximization? Here is John Harris's example, where the reason given for favoring the young on the basis of QALY maximization appears counterintuitive (Harris 1985: 89–90). Imagine that a large class of students are trapped in a lecture theater on fire. As always, there are no morally relevant differences among the students, except their ages. Suppose that only 20 students could be rescued in time. The rescuers, if they are motivated by QALY maximization, would shout "youngest first!" In this example, age does not seem to provide a plausible criterion for determining who is rescued. At least, the strict application of QALY maximization does not seem to be compelling in this example.

Two conflicting intuitions bear on the relevance of age in health care distribution. Age seems relevant in some cases and not in others. QALY maximization always takes age to be relevant. Is there any way to find a compromise between these two conflicting intuitions? There is one. That is the *fair innings argument* (Harris 1985; Alan Williams 1997). The fair innings argument is the view that everyone should be entitled to a fair share of the resources needed to live for some reasonable span of years. For example, many people would take 70 years to be the reasonable span of life years. Until one reaches the fair innings, he or she should be treated equally with others who have also not reached the fair innings. When one reaches the fair innings, he or she has received their fair share of health care resources, and his or her remaining life is a bonus that may be cancelled if it is necessary to extend other people's life to the fair innings. It is not clear how many life years should be considered to amount to a fair innings. For the sake of argument, however, let us assume 70 years to be the span that we consider a reasonable life. According to the fair innings argument, patients below 70 should be given an equal chance to receive health care resources insofar as their health-related quality of life is the same. Patients above 70, on the other hand, have less of a claim than those below 70. Thus, the fair innings argument takes age as a threshold, but does not see age as a relevant consideration in the distribution of health care resources among patients who have not reached that threshold.

The fair innings argument, however, encounters objections. Let us consider just one of these – John Harris's. Imagine that there are two patients who will die if a treatment is not given to them immediately. The only difference is that one patient is 30 years old, and the other 40 years old. In this example, the fair innings argument holds that the two patients should be treated equally because they are below the threshold, and are entitled to an equal chance of reaching it:

> However, the 30-year-old can argue that the considerations which support the fair innings argument require that she be given the place. After all, what's fair about the fair innings argument is precisely that each individual should have an equal chance of enjoying the benefits of a reasonable lifespan. The younger patient can argue that from where she's standing, the age of 40 looks much more reasonable a span than that of 30, and that she should be given the chance to benefit from those ten extra years. ... It is difficult to stop whatever span is taken to be a fair innings collapsing towards zero under pressure from those younger candidates who see their innings as less fair than that of those with a larger share.
>
> (Harris 1985: 92–93)

Harris's point is that there is no way to determine how long the fair innings should be that is fair to everyone. The fair innings argument cannot be perfectly fair to everyone.

7.7 The lifetime view for health care distribution?

To be precise, QALY maximization is not a version of the lifetime view. It only considers the health benefits from the point of treatment onward, and does not take any past health condition into account. To see this, consider the simple two-person, two-period case in table 7.1.

The numbers in the results columns represent the health-related quality of life of each patient in each year. In the past 40 years, patient 1 was perfectly healthy, whereas patient 2 had a disease. Obviously, we cannot change their past health conditions. At the present moment, patients 1 and 2 have the same disease and their health-related quality of life in the next 40 years will be 0.8 unless they receive a given treatment. For some reason, we can offer the treatment to only one patient. In this case, QALY maximization, which considers the health benefits from the present moment onward, is indifferent between alternatives 1 and 2 because the expected health benefits are the same. However, the lifetime view of PD-ism, be it telic egalitarianism or prioritarianism, would judge that alternative 1 is strictly better than alternative 2. Thus, there is a clear difference between the lifetime view and QALY maximization. QALY maximization is not committed to the time-slice view or the lifetime view.

Few attempts have been made to apply the lifetime view to the distribution of health care. The most sophisticated in the literature was made first by Norman Daniels (1988, 2008a) and subsequently by Ronald Dworkin (2000) and Dan Brock (1993). In what follows, I will concentrate on Daniels' argument, which he calls the *prudential lifespan account*. The prudential lifespan account does not apply the lifetime view directly to the distribution of health care. Rather, it appeals to a sort of lifetime view in order to

Table 7.1

	Past 40 years	Future 40 years		Past 40 years	Future 40 years
Person 1	1.0	0.8	Person 1	1.0	1.0
Person 2	0.8	1.0	Person 2	0.8	0.8
Alternative 1			Alternative 2		

ground the just distribution of health care between the young and the old. Daniels does not see the distribution of health care between the young and the old as an intergenerational (and hence not as an interpersonal) conflict, but as the problem of distributing health care resources across the different temporal stages within one life.

> We must not look at the problem as one of justice between distinct groups in competition with each other, for example, between working adults who pay high premiums and the frail elderly who consume so many services. Rather, we must see that each group represents a stage of our lives. We must view the prudent allocation of resources through the stages of life as our guide to justice between groups.
>
> (Daniels 1988: 45)

The basic strategy is thus to reduce the interpersonal problem for the young and the old to an intrapersonal problem for a rational planner. How does it work? The prudential lifespan account first allocates the same lifetime share of resources to each person. This means that the prudential lifespan account starts from equality of lifetime resources. Then, Daniels invites us to imagine how a rational and prudent planner, acting on behalf of society in general, would allocate the lifetime share of resources across the different temporal stages within one life.

There is one important assumption made about the rational and prudent planner. The planner is deprived of information about his or her actual age. If I knew my actual age and allocated resources only from the perspective of what I take to be important at this point in my life, I would make a biased allocation. To ensure that he or she is impartial between different age groups, the planner is assumed to be ignorant about his or her actual age group, birth cohort, genetic make-up, gender, socioeconomic group, the history of his or her family members' illnesses, and any other factors that would affect an impartial judgment regarding the allocation of health-care-resources over his or her complete life. How would such a rational and prudent planner allocate resources across the different stages of one life?

To make this question more vivid, imagine the following situation. Suppose that you do not know how old you are. You are given $100,000 and 10 envelopes, each of which is clearly labeled with a 10-year stage of your life (e.g. "0–10," "10–20," "20–30," … , "90–100"). You are asked to put a certain amount of money in each envelope so that you can use the money in each to pay the cost of the health care you would need at the life stage that the envelope refers to. For instance, if you develop a certain type of disease at the age of 24, you will fund your health care costs from the envelope labeled as "20–30." The goal is to decide on an allocation that is likely to achieve the best possible results over a lifetime. How much would you put in each envelope? You would likely put little money in the envelope labelled "90–100," because it is highly unlikely you will live that long. You may be tempted to put some money in the envelopes picking out very early ages of your life (say, "0–10" and "10–20") because ill-health at very early stages would have long and significant effects on the rest of your life. But you would also consider the general fact that, in your younger stages, you are unlikely to develop serious major diseases such as cardiovascular disease and cancer. You would think that you should spare a lot of money for "50–60" and "60–70" to cover the health care costs of these diseases.

It is not clear exactly how much a rational and prudent planner would allocate across the different life stages. But it seems that the planner would put a lot more money in "40–50" and "50–60" than "90–100." The main claim of the prudential lifespan account is that the distribution of health care resources is unfair if elderly people receive less than a prudent planner would have assigned to that temporal stage of life. This claim has an important implication. Given that the planner would spare less money in the very late life stages, unequal distribution between the young and old can be justified insofar as elderly people receive what the prudent planner would have assigned.

The prudential lifespan account, grounded on the lifetime view, encounters objections. One objection is that the appeal to prudence is not the right way to tackle the problem of the distribution of health care resources between different age groups. For example, Dennis McKerlie (2001b, 2013) thinks that the upshot of the prudential lifespan account would be unacceptable to elderly people. McKerlie points out that the rational and prudent planner would spare few resources for very old age. Even if this upshot may be rational and prudent for anyone who would occupy the planner's position, the elderly people would end up very badly off, and this situation would be hard for them to accept. McKerlie's reason for rejecting the prudential lifespan view is not that it permits inequality between the young and the old, but that it might justify extreme inequality and an extremely bad situation for the elderly. McKerlie thinks that the prudential lifespan account does not help to solve the conflict between the young and the old, and hence that the appeal to prudence (and the reduction of the interpersonal problem to the intrapersonal problem) is not the right way to deal with the problem.

Chapter summary

This chapter considered what the egalitarian principles we examined in chapters 1 through 6 have to say about the distribution of health and health care. Health is an important part of the quality of life, and is a major domain of public policy. Therefore, egalitarian principles are expected to say some substantive things about it. In the context of the distribution of health, there are three major questions, and the choice of principles may depend on how we answer these questions: (1) should the notion of responsibility play a central role; (2) is health just one part of well-being or something special; (3) how should we understand the relation between inequalities in health and in other socioeconomic conditions. In the context of the distribution of health care, the standard utilitarian method of QALY aggregation can be modified in order to accomodate telic egalitarianism and prioritarianism. However, there is no clear consensus among ethicists on the issue of the appropriate temporal unit of distributive judgment.

Further reading

The study of distributive justice in health and health care is part of what has become known as population-level bioethics. Although population-level bioethics is a relatively new area of research, there are a few comprehensive books. One must start by reading the seminal works by Daniels (1985, 2008a). Segall (2010) puts forward luck egalitarianism in health and health care. The literature on the social determinants of health is enormous: I would recommend starting with Hausman (2009) and Hausman et al. (2002), Marmot (2004), Pickett and Wilkinson (2009), and Deaton (2013). Harris (1985) and Bognar and Hirose (2014) may be a good starting point for studying the ethics of health care rationing. Nord (1999) is a standard textbook on QALY. Norheim (2009) examines how telic egalitarianism and prioritarianism operate in the evaluation of health outcomes. The anti-ageism objection is discussed in Broome (1988), Harris (1985), and Kappel and Sandøe (1992). For the debate concerning the prudential lifespan account, see Daniels (1988, 2008a, 2008b), Lazenby (2011), and McKerlie (2001b, 2013).

Note

1 Observational research is based on the direct observation of phenomena in their natural setting. It is distinguished from quantitative research and experimental research. Contrary to observational research on the social gradient in health, some quantitative studies report that there is no significant correlation between income inequalities and health inequalities (see Leigh *et al.* 2009).

CONCLUDING REMARKS

I shall not attempt to summarize the arguments presented in this book, but will make four general remarks to put the discussion in perspective.

Giving priority to the worse off

It is clear that all the egalitarian distributive principles examined in this book share one common feature. That is "give priority to the worse off." Of course, utilitarianism does not give priority to anyone in particular. But the other principles give it to the worse off in one way or another. Rawls's difference principle gives complete priority to benefiting the worst off group in society. Nagel's pairwise comparison gives complete priority to benefiting the person whose possible loss would be greatest. Telic egalitarianism gives priority to benefiting those who are worse off than others. Prioritarianism gives relative priority to benefiting those who are at a lower absolute level of well-being. Likewise, luck egalitarianism gives relative priority to benefiting the worse off if he or she cannot be held responsible for his or her position. Sufficientarianism gives priority to benefits to the badly off and to the worse off below the sufficiency level. Thus, it is safe to say that "priority to the worse off" is a common denominator of all egalitarian theories of distributive justice.

And yet, the focus on this common denominator does not help us to understand the contemporary debates concerning egalitarian theories of distributive justice. The phrase "giving priority to the worse off" is closely associated with prioritarianism simply because it was the title of an early draft of Parfit's "Equality or Priority?" (1995), which had been circulated widely for several years before its publication. Sometimes, it is conceived that an ethical principle is a version of prioritarianism if it can be phrased as "giving priority to X," where X stands for some person who can be understood as worse/worst off in some sense. But this is incorrect and misleading. Nozick's side-constraint theory can be phrased as "giving priority to individual rights," but it is not prioritarian at all. Also, because prioritarianism and telic egalitarianism are always contrasted, it is widely concluded that telic egalitarianism does not give priority to the worse off. As we saw in chapter 3, that is not the case. The real contrast between prioritarianism and telic egalitarianism is the difference in their interpretations of what it is to be worse off. Thus, the focus on "giving priority to the worse off" may obscure many important points about different distributive principles. The phrase "giving priority to the worse off" is meaningful only when the differences in the theoretical structure of different distributive principles are properly examined. This is why I devoted significant parts of my discussion to elucidating the theoretical structure of each principle in this book.

Once we start examining the theoretical structure of distributive principles, the results from economic theory become very important. As I said in my Introduction, distributive justice is an area of economics, as well as philosophy and political theory. Many results in economics are very useful when we are analyzing the structure of distributive principles. However, the results from economics have not been appreciated sufficiently by philosophers. This unfortunate fact is partly a result of some philosophers being allergic to math and formal methods, and partly a result of some economists not explaining the normative implications of their assumptions, axioms, and theorems, and the normative significance of their results for philosophy. Of course, a critical mass of economists have been making an effort to bridge the gap between economics and philosophy, and the gap has been closing as the number of scholars in the overlapping areas of economics and philosophy is steadily increasing. Research on egalitarian theories of distributive justice will benefit from the increased interaction between economics and philosophy.

Basic structure or particular cases?

There are a few issues that I did not discuss in this book but that must be addressed in future research. I will refer to two such issues here.

The first issue concerns the aim of egalitarian distributive justice. More specifically, it concerns the following question. Should egalitarian theories of distributive justice be about basic socioeconomic structure or evaluative judgments in particular cases? This question is rarely discussed in the literature. But I think that whether a distributive principle is plausible or not depends on how one answers this question. Let me explain the question I am raising.

As I explained in section 1.1, by the basic structure of society, Rawls refers to the major social, economic, and political institutions that distribute fundamental rights and duties and determine the division of advantages arising from the cooperative venture. Rawls's difference principle applies to the basic structure of society, not to the distributive judgments made in particular cases. Some people find the difference principle implausible, partly because the maximin rule, which underlies the difference principle, appears counterintuitive in particular cases of distributive judgment. However, as Rawls clearly states, the difference principle is quite different from the maximin rule. The maximin rule is a decision-theoretic axiological principle whereas the difference principle identifies the instances where socioeconomic inequalities among different groups in society can be tolerated. Even if the maximin rule appears counterintuitive in particular cases of distributive judgment, the difference principle may well be plausible enough as a principle that governs the basic structure of society.

A similar point can be made about sufficientarianism. If sufficientarianism is applied to particular cases of distributive judgment, then it may be counterintuitive. For example, Crisp's version of sufficientarianism implies that any loss to a large number of people above the sufficiency level, no matter how large, can be justified for the sake of a small gain to one person below the sufficiency level. This implication may well be seen as counterintuitive. However, if sufficientarianism is understood as a theoretical framework within which the basic economic, social, and political systems may be designed, it may become less counterintuitive. As I reported in section 6.1, the overwhelming majority of subjects in experiments favor utilitarianism with a floor when they are asked to choose the basic structure of society, as opposed to a distributive principle that applies to particular instances of distribution.

Presumably, telic egalitarianism and prioritarianism are each supposed to serve as a distributive principle that applies to particular instances, although each may well be generalized to serve as a principle for the basic structure of society. Just as my plan for my entire life is quite different from my plan for Saturday night, a distributive principle for the basic structure of society may well be quite different from a distributive principle that applies to particular instances of distributive judgment. I think it is unfair to reject the difference principle or sufficientarianism on the basis that these principles may not work in everyday distributive contexts.

It may be claimed that the distinction between principles for the basic structure of society and those for particular cases is the point at which political philosophy and ethics part ways. On the one hand, political philosophers are primarily concerned with the normative grounds for designing and reforming the basic structure of society such as the economic system, social organizations, and political institutions. On the other hand, ethicists are primarily concerned with the normative grounds for judging the relative goodness of states of affairs. Such a claim may be correct, or it may not be. There is at least one danger in such a claim. Dividing the research on egalitarian theories of distributive justice into two areas will only lead to an unprofitable divide between political philosophy and ethics. This is an undesirable consequence we ought to avoid.

Well-being, measurement, and distributive principles

The second issue, which I did not discuss in this book, is the relation between the equalisandum, measurement, and distributive principles. In many parts of the book, I examined the distribution of well-being, and left the notion of well-being unspecified. Furthermore, I simply assumed the interpersonal comparability of the equalisandum in general and well-being in particular. The issue I want to raise is the relation between the equalisandum, measurement, and principles. The issue in question can be expressed in various forms. If I commit to a certain notion of the equalisandum among others, must I commit to a particular theory of measurement and/or a particular type of distributive principle? If I commit to a particular theory of measurement, then must I commit to a particular distributive principle and/or a particular notion of the equalisandum? If I commit to a particular distributive principle, must I commit to a particular notion of the equalisandum and/or a particular theory of measurement? My analysis of distributive principles in this book is independent of any particular notion of the equalisandum. For example, even if I commit to telic egalitarianism, I can still choose my preferred notion of well-being. That is, assuming telic egalitarianism, the notion of well-being could be pleasure, resources, social primary goods, the capability to function, income, and so on.

Some philosophers claim that there is nonetheless a strong connection. Rawls, for example, contends that the difference principle compares the ordinal measure of social primary goods. He would claim that some notions of well-being, such as pleasure or other mental states, would not serve as the basis for the difference principle when it comes to the choice of the basic structure of society by the parties behind the veil of ignorance. In contrast, Parfit seems to believe that prioritarianism does not commit its proponents to a particular notion of well-being, although it requires a well-defined cardinal measure of well-being. In other words, prioritarianism must be able to measure the absolute level of people's well-being, but it can accept any account of well-being. If a proponent of prioritarianism wants to argue for a particular account of well-being, that argument is independent of the basic theoretical features of prioritarianism.

That said, little research has been done with regard to the relation between the equalisandum, measurement, and distributive principles. This is partly because, as I mentioned in chapter 1, it is considered that a complete study of distributive justice takes four sequential steps. The first step is to identify the most plausible account of the equalisandum. The second is to establish the measurability of the equalisandum. The third is to establish the interpersonal comparability of the equalisandum. The fourth and final step is to identify the most plausible distributive principle. Usually, it is believed that we must start our analysis with the first step and then follow through with the other three steps in sequence. This means that we cannot analyze distributive principles unless we settle the discussion in the first three steps. It is true that a complete theory of distributive justice must go through all four steps. However, I do not believe that our analysis needs to start with the first step and end with the fourth. I believe that our analysis can start with any step. For example, we can start with the fourth step, and consider what kind of conditions a particular distributive principle would impose on the notion of the equalisandum, measurability, and interpersonal comparability. I am almost certain that this departure from the conventional step-by-step study will bring new perspectives to bear on the analysis of egalitarian theories of distributive justice.

Final thought

Up to this point, I have not expressed my own view, because this book has aimed to offer a balanced overview of egalitarian theories of distributive justice. Of course, some parts of this book include my own interpretation and understanding of the literature, which some people would disagree with. That being said, I have tried to be as neutral as possible.

At this time, I would like to express my own view. My preferred distributive principle is the aggregate view of telic egalitarianism. I am not willing to support Rawls's difference principle, because I agree with Harsanyi (1975) that the difference principle in practice ignores the benefits to the non-worst off groups and therefore fails to secure the stability of the basic structure of society. This stands in opposition to Rawls's claim that the difference principle, together with other principles of justice, guarantees a satisfactory minimum, and therefore secures the stability of the basic structure.

I am fairly neutral about luck egalitarianism. I do not have a strong argument against it. At the same time, I am not willing to endorse it, because I worry that luck egalitarianism might collapse into a desert theory of distribution and thus become too moralistic. I think that responsibility is not a matter of all/nothing, yes/no, one/zero, or black/white. Responsibility comes in degrees. One person may be more responsible than another although both may be worse off as a consequence of the differential effects of their choices. For example, a cancer patient who smoked 40 cigarettes each day seems to be more responsible for his illness than another cancer patient who smoked 10 cigarettes each day. If we take the degree of responsibility seriously and treat these two cancer patients differently, then luck egalitarianism has to strive to match their well-being to their level of responsibility. If this is all correct, then luck egalitarianism may become responsibility-oversensitive.

I am also neutral with regard to sufficientarianism. It all depends on how sufficientarianism is formulated. If the sufficiency level is set so high that very few people are eliminated from the scope of distributive judgments, sufficientarianism seems to come close to telic egalitarianism or prioritarianism. If that is the case, I have nothing against sufficientarianism. However, if the sufficiency level is set very low, I would disagree with sufficientarianism because I do care about inequality between people just above the sufficiency level and people far above.

I prefer telic egalitarianism to prioritarianism. The leveling down objection, although many philosophers take it seriously, does not bother me, for the reasons I discussed in section 3.3. The reason why I prefer telic egalitarianism is abstract and formal. I believe that the goodness of states of affairs should be a linear combination of people's well-being. According to prioritarianism, the goodness of a state of affairs is given by a strictly concave function of people's well-being – that is, a non-linear combination of people's well-being. On the other hand, according to telic egalitarianism, the goodness of states of affairs is a linear combination of people's well-being. What is all the fuss about the linear/non-linear distinction? The distinction is closely related to the point I discussed in section 4.4. In that section, I pointed out that the change in the numerical representation of the level of well-being affects the distributive judgments of prioritarianism but not those of telic egalitarianism. Once again, consider the two binary comparisons we examined in section 4.4. Remember that we just alter the numerical representation of the same state of two persons.

$$X = (5, 20) \quad X' = (105, 120)$$
$$Y = (12, 12) \quad Y' = (112, 112)$$

If the prioritarian function is a square-root function, prioritarianism judges that Y is strictly better than X. However, if we alter the numerical representation and add 100 to the numerical value of each person's well-being, prioritarianism with a square-root function judges that X' is strictly better than Y' although the state of the two persons remains unchanged. In contrast, telic egalitarianism judges that Y is strictly better than X, and that Y' is strictly better than X'. This means that telic egalitarianism is consistent and unaffected by the change in the numerical representation of the level of people's well-being. The ultimate question that this contrast poses is this: Is well-being something we can measure in an absolute scale like weight and height? Or is well-being something to which we can only assign some numerical scale to represent its relative level, such as temperature or cuteness?

Proponents of prioritarianism would say that well-being can be measured in absolute terms, like weight and height. If well-being can be measured in absolute terms, prioritarianism must reject some accounts of well-being, such as those which take it to consist in pleasure or happiness, because these mental states are difficult to measure in absolute terms. On the other hand, telic egalitarianism can be neutral with respect to different accounts of well-being because it does not matter whether well-being can be measured in absolute or relative terms. The point is that prioritarianism requires a tighter measure of well-being and therefore a narrower notion of well-being, whereas telic egalitarianism does not. I think that well-being is something we cannot measure in absolute terms. This is why I prefer telic egalitarianism to prioritarianism. However, I also believe that my point is not a knock-down argument against prioritarianism. Prioritarianism may well come up with an argument for a tighter measure of well-being and a specific notion of well-being.

GLOSSARY

abandonment objection An objection to luck egalitarianism, according to which it is unjustifiably harsh that luck egalitarianism permits not assisting negligent victims of option luck, no matter how dire their states.

aggregate view An interpretation of telic egalitarianism. The view contends that the goodness of a state of affairs is given by a weighted sum of people's well-being levels, with the weights determined by the rank-order position of the person in a ranking by well-being level.

axiology The philosophical study of value.

brute luck Luck that is not within the control of a person and could not be avoided by his or her choice.

conditional egalitarianism A version of telic egalitarianism, according to which equality is valuable for its own sake only if it benefits some people.

consequentialism The thesis that the rightness or wrongness of an act is determined solely by the goodness of its consequences.

crude choice view A view about responsibility in luck egalitarianism. The view contends that a person should be held responsible for the bad effects of his or her choice, even if the choice is based on tastes and preferences that are shaped by unchosen circumstances.

deontic egalitarianism The view that we should aim for equality of well-being, not to make the outcome better, but for some other moral reason.

deontology The thesis that the notion of rightness and wrongness can be determined independently of the notion of good and bad.

difference principle A principle in John Rawls's theory of justice. It holds that socioeconomic inequalities are permitted only when, and only because, these inequalities maximize the long-term holdings of social primary goods for the members of the worst-off group in terms of social primary goods.

egalitarianism A class of distributive principles, which claim that individuals should have equal quantities of well-being or morally relevant factors that affect their lives.

equalisandum The preferred concept of morally relevant factors to be equalized among different individuals.

fair equality of opportunity A principle in John Rawls's theory of justice. It holds that the basic structure of society should be arranged so that any two individuals with the same native talent and the same ambition should have the same prospects of success in the competition for positions that affect the distribution of social primary goods.

fair innings argument The claim that every individual is entitled to sufficient health care resources to provide him or her with the opportunity to live in good health for a reasonable span of years.

genuine choice view A view about responsibility in luck egalitarianism. The view contends that a person should be held responsible for the bad effects of his or her choice, but not if the choice is based on tastes and preferences that are shaped by unchosen circumstances.

harshness objection See **abandonment objection**.

head-count method A criterion for estimating the badness associated with sub-sufficiency well-being in sufficientarianism. It judges that it is worse if the incidence of sub-sufficiency well-being is greater.

impartiality Two states are equally good if they differ only with regard to the identities of the people in question.

intrinsic view An interpretation of telic egalitarianism. The view contends that equality of well-being is valuable in itself, independently of any other feature external to equality.

law of diminishing moral goodness An essential feature of prioritarianism, according to which the marginal moral importance of well-being diminishes as the absolute level of well-being gets higher.

leveling down objection An objection to telic egalitarianism, according to which it is absurd for telic egalitarianism to judge that it is, at least in one respect, better if the well-being of a better off person is reduced to the level of a worse off person without benefiting anyone.

leximin (the lexicographic extension of the maximin rule) A non-aggregative principle, according to which the best outcome is that which maximizes the well-being of the worst off; or that which maximizes the well-being of the second worst off if the well-being levels of the worst off are the same in all outcomes; or that which maximizes the well-being of the third worst off if the well-being levels of the worst off and the second worst off are the same in all outcomes – and so on.

lifetime view The thesis that we should evaluate the distribution of people's well-being over their entire life.

luck egalitarianism The view that inequality is bad or unjust if it reflects the differential effects of brute luck and that inequality is not bad or unjust if it reflects the differential effects of option luck.

maximin rule A non-aggregative principle, according to which the best outcome is the one that maximizes the well-being (or morally relevant factor that affects people's life) of the worst off.

negative thesis An essential claim of sufficientarianism. It contends that no priority is to be given to benefits among those above the sufficiency level.

option luck Luck that is within the control of a person and could be avoided by his or her choice.

Pareto principle If one alternative is better for some person than another alternative, and if it is worse for no one, then it is better than the other.

person-affecting restriction A state of affairs cannot be better (or worse) than another state if there is no one for whom it is better (or worse).

Pigou-Dalton condition A transfer of benefit from a better off person to a worse off person makes the outcome strictly better if (1) there is no net loss of well-being in this transfer, (2) well-being of all other people remains constant, and (3) the relative position of the better off and the worse off is not altered.

positive thesis An essential feature of sufficientarianism. It contends that priority is given to benefits to those below the sufficiency level over those above the sufficiency level.

principle of equality It is in itself bad if some people are worse off than others.

principle of utility It is in itself better if people are better off.

principle of unanimity A non-aggregative principle that chooses the outcome in which the maximum loss is minimized from individual standpoints.

prioritarianism The view that the goodness of a state of affairs is given by the sum of weighted well-being, where the weights are determined by an increasing, strictly concave function. That is, the weight of well-being diminishes as the absolute level of well-being gets higher.

prudential lifespan account The view that the problem of justice between age groups should be conceived as the problem of budgeting a prudential planner's fair share of health care over his or her lifetime in order to protect the age-relative normal opportunity range.

quality-adjusted life year (QALY) A measure of the value of health outcomes that combines the health-related quality of life associated with a health outcome and the number of years during which a person lives with that health outcome.

reasonable avoidability view An interpretation of responsibility in luck egalitarianism. The view contends that a person should be held responsible for the bad effects of his or her act when and because he or she is reasonably expected to refrain from choosing this act.

repugnant conclusion For any possible population, all with a very high quality of life, there must be some much larger imaginable population whose existence, other things being equal, would be better even though its members had lives that were barely worth living.

scope problem A problem for telic egalitarianism. The problem is that, on telic egalitarianism, it is in itself bad if (1) there is inequality between two populations that are each unaware of each other's existence, or (2) there is inequality between deceased Inca peasants and present people.

social gradient in health A body of epidemiological findings that there is a correlation between socioeconomic inequalities and health inequalities within the population. The lower the socioeconomic status, the worse the health outcome.

social primary goods The basis for intergroup comparisons in Rawls's difference principle. Social primary goods are things that every rational person is presumed to want in the choice of the basic structure of society. Those goods include liberties, income and wealth, the social bases of self-respect, and so on.

specialness thesis The claim that health has a special moral importance because it protects a range of opportunities open to individuals.

strong separability The relative goodness of states of affairs depends on the relative goodness of the well-being of people affected by a choice of outcomes.

sub-sufficiency priority thesis Relative priority is to be given to benefits to the worse off below the sufficiency level.

sufficientarianism The view that priority is to be given to benefits to those below the sufficiency level over those above the sufficiency level, while no priority is to be given to benefits among those above the sufficiency level.

teleology The thesis that the notion of rightness and wrongness is determined by the notion of good and bad.

telic egalitarianism The view that equality of well-being makes an outcome better.

time-slice view The thesis that we should evaluate the distribution of well-being for a period, independently of distributions for other periods.

total shortfall method A criterion for estimating the badness associated with sub-sufficiency well-being in sufficientarianism. It judges that it is worse if the sum of each person's shortfall from the sufficiency level is greater.

utilitarianism The view that an act is right if and only if it maximizes the sum (or the average) of people's well-being.

BIBLIOGRAPHY

Adler, Matthew D. (2011). *Well-Being and Fair Distribution: Beyond Cost-Benefit Analysis.* New York: Oxford University Press.

Anderson, Elizabeth (1999). "What Is the Point of Equality?," *Ethics*, 109: 287–337.

——(2007). "Fair Opportunity in Education: A Democratic Equality Perspective," *Ethics*, 117: 595–622.

——(2010). "The Fundamental Disagreement between Luck Egalitarians and Relational Egalitarians," *Canadian Journal of Philosophy, Supplementary Volume*, 36: 1–23.

Arneson, Richard J. (1989). "Equality and Equal Opportunity for Welfare," *Philosophical Studies*, 56: 77–93.

——(2000). "Luck Egalitarianism and Prioritarianism," *Ethics*, 110: 339–49.

——(2002). "Why Justice Requires Transfers to Offset Income and Wealth Inequalities," *Social Philosophy and Policy*, 19: 172–200.

——(2004). "Luck Egalitarianism Interpreted and Defended," *Philosophical Topics*, 32: 1–20.

——(2006). "Distributive Justice and Basic Capability Equality: 'Good Enough' Is Not Good Enough," in Alexander Kaufman (ed.) *Capabilities Equality: Basic Issues and Problems.* London: Routledge, 17–43.

——(2007). "Equality," in Robert E. Goodin, Philip Pettit, and Thomas W. Pogge (eds.) *A Companion to Contemporary Political Philosophy*, 2nd ed., vol. 2. Oxford: Blackwell, 593–611.

Arrhenius, Gustaf (2000). "An Impossibility Theorem for Welfarist Axiologies," *Economics and Philosophy*, 16: 247–66.

——(2008). "Life Extension versus Replacement," *Journal of Applied Philosophy*, 25: 211–27.

——(2009). "Egalitarianism and Population Change," in Axel Gosseries and Lukas H. Meyer (eds.) *Intergenerational Justice*. Oxford: Oxford University Press, 323–46.

Arrow, Kenneth J. (1973). "Some Ordinalist-Utilitarian Notes on Rawls's Theory of Justice," *Journal of Philosophy*, 70: 245–63.

Atkinson, Anthony B. (1970). "On the Measurement of Inequality," *Journal of Economic Theory*, 2: 244–63.

Barry, Brian M. (1973). *The Liberal Theory of Justice: A Critical Examination of the Principal Doctrines in "A Theory of Justice" by John Rawls*. Oxford: Clarendon Press.

Barry, Nicholas (2006). "Defending Luck Egalitarianism," *Journal of Applied Philosophy*, 23: 89–107.

——(2008). "Reassessing Luck Egalitarianism," *Journal of Politics*, 70: 136–50.

Benbaji, Yitzhak (2005). "The Doctrine of Sufficiency: A Defence," *Utilitas*, 17: 310–32.

——(2006). "Sufficiency or Priority?," *European Journal of Philosophy*, 14: 327–48.

Blackorby, Charles, Walter Bossert, and David Donaldson (1995). "Intertemporal Population Ethics: Critical-level Utilitarian Principles," *Econometrica*, 63: 1303–20.

——(2005). *Population Issues in Social Choice Theory, Welfare Economics, and Ethics*. Cambridge: Cambridge University Press.

Bleichrodt, Han, Enrico Diecidue, and John Quiggin (2004). "Equity Weights in the Allocation of Health Care: The Rank-Dependent QALY Model," *Journal of Health Economics*, 23: 157–72.

Bognar, Greg, and Iwao Hirose (2014). *The Ethics of Health Care Rationing*. London: Routledge.

Bradley, Ben (2009). *Well-Being and Death*. Oxford: Oxford University Press.

Braybrooke, David (1987). *Meeting Needs*. Princeton: Princeton University Press.

Brink, David O. (1993). "The Separateness of Persons, Distributive Norms, and Moral Theory," in Christopher W. Morris and Raymond G. Frey (eds.) *Value, Welfare, and Morality*. New York: Cambridge University Press, 252–89.

Brock, Dan W. (1993). *Life and Death: Philosophical Essays in Biomedical Ethics*. Cambridge: Cambridge University Press.

Broome, John (1988). "Good, Fairness and QALYs," in John Martin Bell and Susan Mendus (eds.) *Philosophy and Medical Welfare*. Cambridge: Cambridge University Press, 57–73.

——(1991). *Weighing Goods: Equality, Uncertainty and Time*. Oxford: Blackwell.

——(2002). "Respects and Levelling Down," Oxford University website, available online at http://users.ox.ac.uk/~sfop0060/pdf/respects%20and%20levelling%20down.pdf

——(2004). *Weighing Lives*. Oxford: Oxford University Press.

Brown, Campbell (2003). "Giving Up Levelling Down," *Economics and Philosophy*, 19: 111–34.

——(2005). "Priority or Sufficiency, or Both?," *Economics and Philosophy*, 21: 199–220.

——(2007). "Prioritarianism for Variable Populations," *Philosophical Studies*, 134: 325–61.

Buchanan, Allen, Dan W. Brock, Norman Daniels, and Daniel Wikler (2001). *From Chance to Choice: Genetics and Justice*. Cambridge: Cambridge University Press.

Caney, Simon (2005). *Justice beyond Borders: A Global Political Theory*. Oxford: Oxford University Press.

Cappelen, Alexander W., and Olle F. Norheim (2005). "Responsibility in Health Care: A Liberal Egalitarian Approach," *Journal of Medical Ethics*, 31: 476–80.

Casal, Paula (2007). "Why Sufficiency Is Not Enough," *Ethics*, 117: 296–326.

Christiano, Thomas (1996). *The Rule of the Many: Fundamental Issues in Democratic Theory*. Boulder, CO: Westview Press.

Christiano, Thomas, and Will Braynen (2008). "Inequality, Injustice and Levelling Down," *Ratio*, 21: 392–420.

Clayton, Matthew (2000). "The Resources of Liberal Egalitarianism," *Imprints*, 5: 63–84.

Cohen, G. A. (1989). "On the Currency of Egalitarian Justice," *Ethics*, 99: 906–44.

——(1992). "Incentives, Inequality, and Community," in Grethe B. Peterson (ed.) *The Tanner Lectures on Human Values*, vol. 13. Salt Lake City, UT: University of Utah Press, 263–329.

——(1995). "The Pareto Argument for Inequality," *Social Philosophy and Policy*, 12: 160–85.

——(2004). "Expensive Taste Rides Again," in Justine Burley (ed.) *Dworkin and His Critics*. Oxford: Blackwell, 3–29.

——(2006). "Luck and Equality: A Reply to Hurley," *Philosophy and Phenomenological Research*, 72: 439–46.

——(2008). *Rescuing Justice and Equality*. Cambridge, MA: Harvard University Press.

Cohen, Joshua (2001). "Taking People as They Are?," *Philosophy and Public Affairs*, 30: 363–86.

Cowell, Frank (2011). *Measuring Inequality*, 3rd ed. Oxford: Oxford University Press.

Crisp, Roger (2003). "Equality, Priority, and Compassion," *Ethics*, 113: 745–63.

——(2011). "In Defence of the Priority View: A Response to Otsuka and Voorhoeve," *Utilitas*, 23: 105–8.

d'Aspremont, Claude, and Louis Gevers (1977). "Equity and the Informational Basis of Collective Choice," *Review of Economic Studies*, 44: 199–209.

Daniels, Norman (1985). *Just Health Care*. Cambridge: Cambridge University Press.

——(1988). *Am I My Parents' Keeper? An Essay on Justice between the Young and the Old*. New York: Oxford University Press.

——(2003). "Democratic Equality: Rawls's Complex Egalitarianism," in Samuel Freeman (ed.) *The Cambridge Companion to Rawls*. Cambridge: Cambridge University Press, 241–77.

——(2008a). *Just Health: Meeting Health Needs Fairly*. Cambridge: Cambridge University Press.

——(2008b). "Justice between Adjacent Generations: Further Thoughts," *Journal of Political Philosophy*, 16: 476–94.

——(2012). "Reasonable Disagreement about Identified vs. Statistical Victims," *Hastings Center Report*, 42: 35–45.

Darwall, Stephen (ed.) (2002). *Contractarianism/Contractualism*. Oxford: Blackwell.

Dasgupta, Partha, Amartya K. Sen, and David Starrett (1973). "Notes on the Measurement of Inequality," *Journal of Economic Theory*, 6: 180–87.

Deaton, Angus (2002). "Policy Implications of the Gradient of Health and Wealth," *Health Affairs*, 21: 13–30.

——(2013). *The Great Escape: Health, Wealth, and the Origin of Inequality*. Princeton: Princeton University Press.

Diamond, Peter A. (1967). "Cardinal Welfare, Individualistic Ethics, and Interpersonal Comparison of Utility: Comment," *Journal of Political Economy*, 75: 765–66.

Dworkin, Ronald (1981). "What Is Equality? Part 2: Equality of Resources," *Philosophy and Public Affairs*, 10: 283–345.

——(2000). *Sovereign Virtue*. Cambridge, MA: Harvard University Press.

——(2002). "Sovereign Virtue Revisited," *Ethics*, 113: 106–43.

Elster, Jon, and John E. Roemer (eds.) (1991). *Interpersonal Comparisons of Well-Being*. Cambridge: Cambridge University Press.

Epstein, Larry G., and Uzi Segal (1992). "Quadratic Social Welfare Functions," *Journal of Political Economy*, 100: 691–712.

Estlund, David (1998). "Debate: Liberalism, Equality, and Fraternity in Cohen's Critique of Rawls," *Journal of Political Philosophy*, 6: 99–112.

Fleurbaey, Marc (1995). "Equal Opportunity or Equal Social Outcome?," *Economics and Philosophy*, 11: 25–55.

——(2001). "Egalitarian Opportunities," *Law and Philosophy*, 20: 499–530.

——(2005). "Freedom with Forgiveness," *Politics, Philosophy and Economics*, 4: 29–67.

——(2008). *Fairness, Responsibility, and Welfare*. New York: Oxford University Press.

Fleurbaey, Marc, and Peter Hammond (2004). "Interpersonally Comparable Utility," in Salvador Barbera, Peter Hammond and Christian Seidl (eds.) *Handbook of Utility Theory*, vol. 2: *Extensions*. Dordrecht: Kluwer, 1179–1285.

Fleurbaey, Marc, Bertil Tungodden, and Peter Vallentyne (2009). "On the Possibility of Nonaggregative Priority for the Worst Off," *Social Philosophy and Policy*, 26: 258–85.

Frankfurt, Harry (1987). "Equality as a Moral Ideal," *Ethics*, 98: 21–43.

——(1997). "Equality and Respect," *Social Research*, 64: 3–15.

——(2000). "The Moral Irrelevance of Equality," *Public Affairs Quarterly*, 14: 87–103.

Frohlich, Norman, and Joe A. Oppenheimer (1993). *Choosing Justice: An Experimental Approach to Ethical Theory*. Berkeley: University of California Press.

Gaertner, Wulf, and Erik Schokkaert (2011). *Empirical Social Choice: Questionnaire-Experimental Studies on Distributive Justice*. Cambridge: Cambridge University Press.

Gevers, Louis (1979). "On Interpersonal Comparability and Social Welfare Orderings," *Econometrica*, 47: 75–89.

Gibbard, Allan (2008). *Reconciling Our Aims: In Search of Bases for Ethics*. New York: Oxford University Press.

Gilabert, Pablo (2012). *From Global Poverty to Global Equality: A Philosophical Exploration*. Oxford: Oxford University Press.

Griffin, James (1986). *Well-Being: Its Meaning, Measurement, and Moral Importance*. Oxford: Oxford University Press.

Hammond, Peter J. (1976). "Equity, Arrow's Conditions, and Rawls' Difference Principle," *Econometrica*, 44: 793–804.

Hare, R. M. (1973). "Rawls' Theory of Justice I," *Philosophical Quarterly*, 23: 144–55.

——(1996). *Essays on Bioethics*. Oxford: Clarendon Press.

Harper, S., D. Rushani, and J. S. Kaufman (2012). "Trends in the Black-White Life Expectancy Gap, 2003–8," *JAMA*, 307: 2257–59.

Harris, John (1985). *The Value of Life*. London: Routledge.

Harsanyi, John C. (1953). "Cardinal Utility in Welfare Economics and in the Theory of Risk-Taking," *Journal of Political Economy*, 61: 434–35.

——(1955). "Cardinal Welfare, Individualistic Ethics, and Interpersonal Comparisons of Utility," *Journal of Political Economy*, 63: 309–21.

——(1975). "Can the Maximin Principle Serve as a Basis for Morality? A Critique of John Rawls's Theory," *American Political Science Review*, 69: 594–606.

——(1977). *Rational Behaviour and Bargaining Equilibrium in Games and Social Situations*. Cambridge: Cambridge University Press.

Hausman, Daniel M. (2009). "Benevolence, Justice, Well-Being and the Health Gradient," *Public Health Ethics*, 2: 235–43.

Hausman, Daniel M., Yukiko Asada, and Thomas Hedemann (2002). "Health Inequalities and Why They Matter," *Health Care Analysis*, 10: 177–91.

Hirose, Iwao (2005). "Intertemporal Distributive Judgment," *Ethical Theory and Moral Practice*, 8: 371–86.

——(2009). "Reconsidering the Value of Equality," *Australasian Journal of Philosophy*, 87: 301–12.

——(2014). *Moral Aggregation*. New York: Oxford University Press.

Holtug, Nils (2007). "Prioritarianism," in Nils Holtug and Kasper Lippert-Rasmussen (eds.) *Egalitarianism: New Essays on the Nature and Value of Equality*. Oxford: Oxford University Press, 125–56.

——(2010). *Persons, Interests, and Justice*. Oxford: Oxford University Press.

Hurley, Susan L. (2003). *Justice, Luck, and Knowledge*. Cambridge, MA: Harvard University Press.

Huseby, Robert (2010). "Sufficiency: Restated and Defended," *Journal of Political Philosophy*, 18: 178–97.

Jensen, Karsten Klint (2003). "What Is the Difference between (Moderate) Egalitarianism and Prioritarianism?," *Economics and Philosophy*, 19: 89–109.

Kappel, Klemens (1997). "Equality, Priority, and Time," *Utilitas*, 9: 203–25.

Kappel, Klemens, and Peter Sandøe (1992). "QALYs, Age and Fairness," *Bioethics*, 6: 297–316.

Karni, Edi, and Zvi Safra (2002). "Individual Sense of Justice: A Utility Representation," *Econometrica*, 70: 263–84.

Knight, Carl, and Zofia Stemplowska (eds.) (2011). *Responsibility and Distributive Justice*. Oxford: Oxford University Press.

Konow, James (2003). "Which Is the Fairest One of All? A Positive Analysis of Justice Theories," *Journal of Economic Literature*, 41: 1188–1239.

Korsgaard, Christine M. (1983). "Two Distinctions in Goodness," *Philosophical Review*, 92: 169–95.

Krantz, David H., R. Duncan Luce, Patrick Suppes, and Amos Tversky (1971). *Foundations of Measurement*, vol. I. San Diego and London: Academic Press.

Kymlicka, Will (1988). "Rawls on Teleology and Deontology," *Philosophy and Public Affairs*, 17: 173–90.

Lazenby, Hugh (2011). "Is Age Special? Justice, Complete Lives and the Prudential Lifespan Account," *Journal of Applied Philosophy*, 28: 327–40.

Leigh, Andrew, Christopher Jencks, and Timothy M. Smeeding (2009). "Health and Economic Inequality," in Wiemer Salverda, Brian Nolan, and Timothy M. Smeeding (eds.) *The Oxford Handbook of Economic Inequality*. Oxford: Oxford University Press, 384–405.

Lippert-Rasmussen, Kasper (2001). "Egalitarianism, Option Luck, and Responsibility," *Ethics*, 111: 548–79.

——(2005). "Hurley on Egalitarianism and the Luck-neutralizing Aim," *Politics, Philosophy and Economics*, 4: 249–65.

——(2007). "The Insignificance of the Distinction between Telic and Deontic Egalitarianism," in Nils Holtug and Kasper Lippert-Rasmussen (eds.) *Egalitarianism: New Essays on the Nature and Value of Equality*. Oxford: Oxford University Press, 101–24.

——(2009). "Justice and Bad Luck," in Edward N. Zalta (ed.) *Stanford Encyclopedia of Philosophy*, available online at http://plato.stanford.edu/entries/justice-bad-luck/

——(2012). "Democratic Egalitarianism versus Luck Egalitarianism: What Is at Stake?," *Philosophical Topics*, 40: 117–34.

Marmot, Michael (2004). *The Status Syndrome: How Social Standing Affects Our Health and Longevity*. New York: Henry Holt & Co.

Marmot, M. G., M. J. Shipley, and Geoffrey Rose (1984). "Inequalities in Health-Specific Explanations of a General Pattern?," *Lancet*, 323: 1003–6.

Maskin, Eric (1978). "A Theorem on Utilitarianism," *Review of Economic Studies*, 46: 93–96.

Mason, Andrew (2001). "Egalitarianism and the Levelling Down Objection," *Analysis*, 61: 2456–2254.

McCarthy, David (2006). "Utilitarianism and Prioritarianism I," *Economics and Philosophy*, 22: 335–63.

——(2008). "Utilitarianism and Prioritarianism II," *Economics and Philosophy*, 24: 1–33.

——(2013). "Risk-Free Approaches to the Priority View," *Erkenntnis*, 78: 421–49.

McKerlie, Dennis (1989). "Equality and Time," *Ethics*, 99: 475–91.

——(1994). "Equality or Priority," *Utilitas*, 6: 25–42.

——(1997). "Priority and Time," *Canadian Journal of Philosophy*, 27: 287–309.

——(2001a). "Dimensions of Equality," *Utilitas*, 13: 263–288.

——(2001b). "Justice between the Young and the Old," *Philosophy and Public Affairs*, 30: 152–77.

——(2013). *Justice between the Young and the Old*. New York: Oxford University Press.

Moore, G. E. (1922). "The Conception of Intrinsic Value," in *Philosophical Studies*. London: Routledge & Kegan Paul, 253–75.

Nagel, Thomas (1979). "Equality," in *Mortal Questions*. New York: Cambridge University Press, 106–27.

——(1991). *Equality and Partiality*. New York: Oxford University Press.

Nord, Erik (1999). *Cost-Value Analysis in Health Care: Making Sense Out of QALYs*. Cambridge: Cambridge University Press.

Nord, Erik, Jose Luis Pinto, Jeff Richardson, Paul Menzel, and Peter Ubel (1999). "Incorporating Societal Concerns for Fairness in Numerical Valuations of Health Programmes," *Health Economics*, 8: 25–39.

Norheim, Ole F. (2009). "A Note on Brock: Prioritarianism, Egalitarianism and the Distribution of Life Years," *Journal of Medical Ethics*, 35: 565–69.

Nozick, Robert (1974). *Anarchy, State, and Utopia*. Oxford: Basic Books.

Nussbaum, Martha C. (2009). *Frontiers of Justice: Disability, Nationality, Species Membership*. Cambridge, MA: Harvard University Press.

Olson, Jonas (2004). "Intrinsicalism and Conditionalism about Final Value," *Ethical Theory and Moral Practice*, 7: 31–52.

Otsuka, Michael (2000). "Scanlon and the Claims of the Many versus the One," *Analysis*, 60: 288–93.

——(2001). "Luck, Insurance, and Equality," *Ethics*, 113: 40–54.

Otsuka, Michael, and Alex Voorhoeve (2009). "Why It Matters That Some Are Worse Off Than Others: An Argument against the Priority View," *Philosophy and Public Affairs*, 37: 171–99.

——(2011). "Reply to Crisp," *Utilitas*, 23: 109–14.

Parfit, Derek (1984). *Reasons and Persons*. Oxford: Clarendon Press.

——(1995). *Equality or Priority?* Lindley Lecture. Lawrence, KS: University of Kansas.

——(2000). "Equality or Priority?," in Matthew Clayton and Andrew Williams (eds.) *The Ideal of Equality*. Basingstoke: Macmillan, 81–125.

——(2012). "Another Defence of the Priority View," *Utilitas*, 24: 399–440.

Peterson, Martin, and Sven Ove Hansson (2005). "Equality and Priority," *Utilitas*, 17: 299–309.

Pickett, Kate, and Richard Wilkinson (2009). *The Spirit Level: Why Greater Equality Makes Societies Stronger*. New York: Bloomsbury Publishing.

Pogge, Thomas W. (2000). "On the Site of Distributive Justice: Reflections on Cohen and Murphy," *Philosophy and Public Affairs*, 29: 137–69.

——(2008). *World Poverty and Human Rights*, 2nd ed. Cambridge: Polity Press.

Rabinowicz, Wlodek (2001). "Prioritarianism and Uncertainty: On the Inter-personal Addition Theorem and the Priority View," in Dan Egonsson, Jonas Josefsson, Björn Peterson, and Toni Rønnow-Rasmussen (eds.) *Exploring Practical Philosophy: From Action to Values*. Aldershot: Ashgate, 139–65.

——(2002). "Prioritarianism for Prospects," *Utilitas*, 14: 2–21.

Rabinowicz, Wlodek, and Toni Rønnow-Rasmussen (2000). "A Distinction in Value: Intrinsic and for Its Own Sake," *Proceedings of the Aristotelian Society*, 100: 33–51.

Rakowski, Eric (1991). *Equal Justice*. Oxford: Oxford University Press.

Rawls, John (1971). *A Theory of Justice*. Cambridge, MA: Harvard University Press.

Raz, Joseph (2009). "On the Value of Distributional Equality," in Stephen De Wijze, Matthew H. Kramer, and Ian Carter (eds.) *Hillel Steiner and the Anatomy of Justice: Themes and Challenges*. London: Routledge, 22–33.

Roberts, Fred S. (1985). *Measurement Theory: With Applications to Decision-making, Utility, and the Social Sciences*. Cambridge: Cambridge University Press.

Roberts, Kevin W. S. (1980). "Interpersonal Comparability and Social Choice Theory," *Review of Economic Studies*, 47: 421–39.

Roberts, Melinda A., and David T. Wasserman (eds.) (2009). *Harming Future Persons: Ethics, Genetics and the Nonidentity Problem*. Dordrecht: Springer.

Roemer, John E. (1998a). *Equality of Opportunity*. Cambridge, MA: Harvard University Press.

——(1998b). *Theories of Distributive Justice*. Cambridge, MA: Harvard University Press.

Ryberg, Jesper, and Tännsjö Torbjörn (eds.) (2004). *The Repugnant Conclusion: Essays on Population Ethics*. Dordrecht: Springer.

Sandbu, Martin E. (2004). "On Dworkin's Brute-Luck–Option-Luck Distinction and the Consistency of Brute-Luck Egalitarianism," *Politics, Philosophy and Economics*, 3: 283–312.

Satz, Debra (2007). "Equality, Adequacy, and Education for Citizenship," *Ethics*, 117: 623–48.

Savage, Leonard J. (1972). *The Foundations of Statistics*. New York: Dover Publications.

Scanlon, T. M. (1982). "Contractualism and Utilitarianism," in Amartya K. Sen and Bernard Williams (eds.) *Utilitarianism and Beyond*. Cambridge: Cambridge University Press, 103–28.

——(1998). *What We Owe to Each Other*. Cambridge, MA: Belknap Press.

Scheffler, Samuel (2003a). "Rawls and Utilitarianism," in Samuel Freedman (ed.) *The Cambridge Companion to Rawls*. Cambridge: Cambridge University Press, 426–59.

——(2003b). "What Is Egalitarianism?," *Philosophy and Public Affairs*, 31: 5–39.

——(2005). "Choice, Circumstance, and the Value of Equality," *Politics, Philosophy and Economics*, 4: 5–28.

——(2006). "Is the Basic Structure Basic?," in Christine Sypnowich and G. A. Cohen (eds.) *The Egalitarian Conscience: Essays in Honour of G. A. Cohen*. New York: Oxford University Press, 102–29.

Segall, Shlomi (2007). "Is Health Care (Still) Special?," *Journal of Political Philosophy*, 15: 342–61.

——(2010). *Health, Luck, and Justice*. Princeton, NJ: Princeton University Press.

Sen, Amartya K. (1970). *Collective Choice and Social Welfare*. San Francisco, CA: Holden-Day.

——(1976). "Poverty: An Ordinal Approach to Measurement," *Econometrica*, 44: 219–31.

——(1979). "Utilitarianism and Welfarism," *Journal of Philosophy*, 76: 463–89.

——(1982). *Poverty and Famines: An Essay on Entitlement and Deprivation*. Oxford: Oxford University Press.

——(1985). *Commodities and Capabilities*. Amsterdam: North-Holland.

——(1995). *Inequality Reexamined*. Cambridge, MA: Harvard University Press.

——(1999). *Development as Freedom*. New York: Oxford University Press.

Sen, Amartya K., and James E. Foster (1997). *On Economic Inequality: Enlarged Edition with a Substantial Annexe*. Oxford: Clarendon Press.

Sen, Amartya K., and Bernard Williams (eds.) (1982). *Utilitarianism and Beyond*. Cambridge: Cambridge University Press.

Shields, Liam (2012). "The Prospects for Sufficientarianism," *Utilitas*, 24: 101–17.

Singer, Peter (1972). "Famine, Affluence, and Morality," *Philosophy and Public Affairs*, 1: 229–43.

Skorupski, John (1999). "Value and Distribution," in *Ethical Explorations*. Oxford: Oxford University Press, 85–101.

Strasnick, Steven (1976). "Social Choice and the Derivation of Rawls's Difference Principle," *Journal of Philosophy*, 73: 85–99.

Tan, Kok-Chor (2012). *Justice, Institutions, and Luck: The Site, Ground, and Scope of Equality.* Oxford: Oxford University Press.

Taurek, John (1977). "Should the Numbers Count?," *Philosophy and Public Affairs*, 6: 293–316.

Temkin, Larry S. (1993). *Inequality.* New York: Oxford University Press.

——(2000). "Equality, Priority, and the Levelling Down Objection," in Matthew Clayton and Andrew Williams (eds.) *The Ideal of Equality.* Basingstoke: Macmillan, 126–61.

——(2003a). "Egalitarianism Defended," *Ethics*, 113: 764–82.

——(2003b). "Equality, Priority or What?," *Economics and Philosophy*, 19: 61–87.

——(2009). "Illuminating Egalitarianism," in Thomas Christiano and John Christman (eds.) *Contemporary Debates in Political Philosophy.* Oxford: Blackwell, 155–78.

Tungodden, Bertil (2003). "The Value of Equality," *Economics and Philosophy*, 19: 1–44.

Vallentyne, Peter (2002). "Brute Luck, Option Luck, and Equality of Initial Opportunities," *Ethics*, 112: 529–57.

——(2007). "Distributive Justice," in Robert E. Goodin, Philip Pettit, and Thomas W. Pogge (eds.) *A Companion to Contemporary Political Philosophy*, 2nd ed., vol. 2. Oxford: Blackwell, 548–62.

Vallentyne, Peter, and Bertil Tungodden (2007). "Paretian Egalitarianism with Variable Population Size," in John Roemer and Kotaro Suzumura (eds.) *Intergenerational Equity and Sustainability.* Basingstoke: Palgrave Macmillan.

van Parijs, Philippe (2003). "Difference Principles," in Samuel Freeman (ed.) *The Cambridge Companion to Rawls.* Cambridge: Cambridge University Press, 200–240.

Weirich, Paul (1983). "Utility Tempered with Equality," *Noûs*, 17: 423–39.

Weymark, John A. (1991). "A Reconsideration of the Harsanyi-Sen Debate on Utilitarianism," in Jon Elster and John E. Roemer (eds.) *Interpersonal Comparisons of Well-Being.* Cambridge: Cambridge University Press, 255–320.

White, Stuart (2007). *Equality.* Cambridge: Wiley.

Wiggins, David (1998). *Needs, Values, Truth: Essays in the Philosophy of Value*. Oxford: Oxford University Press.

Williams, Alan (1997). "Intergenerational Equity: An Exploration of the 'Fair Innings' Argument," *Health Economics*, 6: 117–32.

Williams, Andrew (1998). "Incentives, Inequality, and Publicity," *Philosophy and Public Affairs*, 27: 225–47.

——(2002). "Equality for the Ambitious," *Philosophical Quarterly*, 52: 377–89.

Wolff, Jonathan (1998). "Fairness, Respect, and the Egalitarian Ethos," *Philosophy and Public Affairs*, 27: 97–122.

World Health Organization (2008). *Closing the Gap in a Generation: Health Equity through Action on the Social Determinants of Health*. Geneva: World Health Organization.

INDEX

abandonment objection 58–61,
  158–60
aggregate view (telic egalitarianism)
  7, 64, 74–80, 92–95, 103, 106–9,
  140, 145, 184; compared with
  intrinsic view 78–80; compared
  with prioritarianism 92–95, 106–9;
  defined 74–78
ambition-sensitivity 43–44
Anderson, E. 9, 58–61, 128, 158–60
Arneson, R. 7, 42, 47, 128–29
Arrhenius, G. 143, 148
Arrow, K. J. 154–55, 158
Atkinson, A. B. 99
axiology 11–13, 16–17, 71

Barry, N. 51, 53
basic social structure 22–23, 29–30,
  180–82
Benbaji, Y. 128
Blackorby, C. et al 82

Bleichrodt, H. et al 168
bottomless pit objection 167
Braybrooke, D. 120
Brock, D. 174
Broome, J. 18, 73–74, 99–100,
  141–43
brute luck 42, 44–48, 51–55, 57,
  157–58, 161 see also option luck
Buchanan, A. 155

Caney, S. 10
Cappelen, A. W. and Norheim, O. F.
  159–60
cardinal measure 12, 19–20,
  90–91, 183
Casal, P. 116
Christiano, T. 9
Cohen, G.A. 7, 29–30, 42, 47, 48–49,
  55–56, 59–60, 161
compassion principle 121–24, 126,
  129–34

conditional egalitarianism 71–73
consequentialism 11, 16–17, 37, 81–82, 90–91
contractarianism 15–16, 34–35
contractualism 7, 15–16, 31, 34–38
Cowell, F. 76
Crisp, R. 112, 121–24, 126, 129–32, 181

Daniels, N. 9–10, 23, 155–57, 158, 163–64, 174–76
Darwall, S. 15–16
Deaton, A. 163
democratic equality XII, 9–10
deontic egalitarianism 63–65, 81, 83–84
deontology 10–11
difference principle 6–7, 13, 15, 22–34, 41–44, 97–98, 113–15, 154–58, 179, 181–84; defined 22–26; egalitarian criticisms 29–33, 41–44; in experimental economics 113–15; in health 154–58; non-egalitarian criticisms 27–29; priority among Rawlsian principles 23 see also Rawls, J.
diminishing marginal utility 20–22, 88
downstream factors 160
Dworkin, R. 3, 7, 12, 41–49, 54, 56, 59, 137, 161, 174; and brute/option luck 44–45, 47–49, 54; and the fresh-start view 56; criticism of difference principle 41–44; on the lifetime view 137; on health-care 161, 174; resource egalitarianism 3, 7, 12, 41–49, 59

egalitarianism (definition) 1–6
endowment-insensitivity 42–44

equal initial opportunities view (luck egalitarianism) 54–55
equalisandum 2–3, 12, 182–83 see also well-being
equity weights 168
expensive tastes 48–49, 161

fair equality of opportunity 23, 154–58, 163–64
fair innings argument 173–74
final value 70–71
Fleurbaey, M. 51, 55–56, 58
Frankfurt, H. 112, 116–20, 123, 131
fresh start view (luck egalitarianism) 55–56, 61, 159
Frohlich, N. et al 113–14

Gaertner, W. and Schokkaert, E. 114
Gilabert, P. 10
global justice XII, 10

Hammond equity condition 97
Hammond, P. J. 97
Hare, R. M. 153
Harper, S. et al 156
Harris, J. 172–74
Harsanyi, J. C. 27–28, 113, 184
harshness objection see abandonment objection
head-count method 116–19, 123, 124–27
Hirose, I. 143
Holtug, N. 69, 71–73
Hurley, S. 57–58

Impartial Spectator Theorem 27–28
impartiality 17–18, 34, 90–91, 126

impersonal good 69–70, 73–74, 77;
the person-affecting restriction
69–70
incentive argument 26, 29–30
interpersonal aggregation 33, 37–38,
138, 140–41, 144–45, 167
interpersonal comparability XII, 3,
12–13, 19–20, 25, 91, 154, 182–83;
full comparability 13, 19–20,
91; level comparability 13, 25,
91; unit comparability 13, 19–20,
25, 91
intrinsic value 67, 69, 70–71,
80, 82
intrinsic view (telic egalitarianism) 7,
64–84, 87, 106; and alternative
interpretations 71–80; and the
leveling down objection 67–70;
and the scope problem 80–84;
defined 64–67

Kantian ethics 11
Konow, J. 115
Korsgaard, C. 71
Kymlicka, W. 11

law of diminishing moral goodness
87–89, 97
leveling down objection 7–8, 63–64,
67–77, 87, 90, 98–100, 106, 121,
184; and aggregation view 74–77;
and conditional egalitarianism
70–73; and prioritarianism 87, 90,
98–100, 106
leximin 25–26, 95–98, 101, 120–21,
130, 148, 167
Lippert-Rasmussen, K. 51, 57, 83
luck egalitarianism 6–7, 9, 30, 41–61,
63, 84, 153, 157–61, 179, 184;

abandonment objection 58–61,
158–60; axiological and deontic
45–47, 84; defined 45; Hurley's
objections 57–58; interpretation
47–57; in health 153, 157–61

Marmot, M. G. et al 162
Mason, A. 71
maximin rule 24–26, 28, 95–96, 101,
130, 167, 181
McCarthy, D. 103
McKerlie, D. 8, 138, 140, 143, 176–77
minimax rule 33
Moore, G.E. 67, 70

Nagel, T. 7, 15, 30–37, 46–47, 137,
167, 179
negative thesis (sufficientarianism)
116–21, 124, 131–33; defined 116;
neutral 119–20; strong 118, 120,
131; weak 118–19, 121, 131
non-health-related quality of life
169–71
non-identity case 146–49
non-relationality 8, 19, 87, 90–91,
94–95, 96–98
Nord, E. et al 168
Norheim, O. F. 159–60
Nozick, R. 4–5, 11, 20, 86, 180
number problem 37–38

Olson, J. 71
option luck 42, 44–45, 51–52, 53–54,
59, 61; all-luck view 51–54, 61, 159;
crude choice view 47–48; genuine
choice view 48–49; no-luck
view 51,54; reasonable avoidability
view 50–51 see also luck
egalitarianism

ordinal measure 12–13, 183
original position 22–23, 26, 27–28,
  35, 42, 113–14, 137
Otsuka, M. 38, 51; and Voorhoeve,
  A. 104–6

pairwise comparison 32–34,
  167, 179
Pareto argument for inequality *see*
  incentive argument
Pareto principle 8, 17–18, 25–26, 27,
  90–91
Parfit, D. 7–9, 63–106, 142, 147–49;
  formulation of the priority view 8,
  86–95; formulation of telic
  egalitarianism 7,63–67, 73–80;
  objections to the priority view
  98–106; objections to telic
  egalitarianism 7, 63–64, 67–76,
  80–84; reductionism about
  personal identity 142; the
  repugnant conclusion 9, 147–49
PD-ism 94–95, 99–100, 116, 168,
  170, 174
Pigou-Dalton condition 8, 93–95,
  126–27, 132–33, 168
pluralism 59–60, 66, 77–78, 159; and
  the abandonment objection
  59–60, 159; and telic
  egalitarianism 66, 77–78
Pogge, T. 10
population axiology 9, 146–49
population invariance condition 76
positive thesis (sufficientarianism)
  116–18, 120–21
poverty measurement 112, 124–27
principle of equality (telic
  egalitarianism) 65, 78
principle of unanimity 7, 31, 31–37

principle of utility (telic
  egalitarianism) 66, 78–79
prioritarianism 3, 7–9, 19, 63, 82,
  86–111, 112, 116, 121, 131–33,
  136–49, 168, 174, 179–85; and
  leveling down objection 98–100;
  and maximin/leximin 95–98; and
  the one-person case 102–6; and
  time 136–46; and variable
  population sizes 146–49; and
  well-being measurement 100–102,
  184–85; defined 87–95; in health
  168, 174; versus telic
  egalitarianism 106–9, 184–85
priority: complete 33, 95–98, 117–20,
  122–23, 129, 167, 179; lexical 23,
  95, 95–97, 117, 123, 129, 133,
  156–57; relative 117, 122–24, 179
prudential lifespan account 174–77

quality-adjusted life year (QALY)
  164–74; and non-health-related
  quality-of-life 169–71; anti-ageism
  objection 171–74; and time 174;
  defined 164–66; objections to
  aggregation 166–68

Rabinowicz, W. 71, 97–98, 103
Rakowski, E. 51
Rawls, J. 3, 6–7, 9, 10–11, 12, 13,
  15–44, 63, 97–98, 105–6, 113–15,
  121, 137–38, 153–58, 179, 181,
  183–84; characterization of
  teleology/deontology 10–11; to
  Rawlsian egalitarianism 26–44;
  Rawlsian egalitarianism 6–7,
  22–26, 97–98; Rawlsian
  egalitarianism and experimental
  economics 113–15; Rawlsian

egalitarianism and health care 9,153–58; separateness of persons objection to classical utilitarianism 105–6, 137–38

Representation Theorem 27–28, 113

repugnant conclusion 9, 147–49

responsibility-sensitivity 7, 41–45, 57–58, 157–60, 184 see also luck egalitarianism

Rønnow-Rasmussen, T. 71

Satz, D. 128

Savage, L. 12

Scanlon, T. M. 7, 15, 30–31, 34–38

Scheffler, S. 9

scope problem 7, 63–64, 80–83; and divided world case 80–81, 83; and Inca case 80–82

Segall, S. 50, 59–60, 156, 159, 161

Sen, A. K. 10, 20, 112, 124–27

separability of time 141–43

separateness of persons 105–6, 137–38

side-constraint theory 4–5, 20, 86, 180

Singer, P. 21

Skorupski, J. 120–22

social gradient in health 153, 160–64

social primary goods 3, 12, 13, 24, 30, 33, 42–43, 114, 154–58, 182–83 see also Rawls, J.

specialness thesis 155–57, 164

strong separability 18–19, 24–25, 78, 90–91, 95–98 see also non-relationality

sub-sufficiency priority thesis 123–24

sufficiency level 8, 112, 116–27; criticism of 127–33 see also sufficientarianism

sufficientarianism 8, 112–35, 170–71, 179, 181–82; and experimental economics 113–16; in health 170–71; interpretation 116–27; objections to 127–34

Tan, K. 10

Taurek, J. 37

teleology 10–13, 64–65, 81, 84

telic egalitarianism 7–9, 19, 63–87, 92–95, 98, 101–3, 106–9, 138–39, 148–49, 164, 168, 174, 179–82, 184–85; and time 138–39; and variable population sizes 148–49; in health 164, 168, 174; interpretation 64–84; objections to 67–70, 80–84, 106–7

Temkin, L. 69–70, 83–84, 131–32

temporal unit of distributive judgment 8, 136–46, 171–77; hybrid view 143–46; in health 171–77; lifetime view 137–39, 142, 143–44, 146, 171–77; time-slice view 139–44, 171–74

threshold level see sufficiency level

total shortfall method 125–27

transitivity 13, 34, 71–73

upstream factors 160–64

utilitarianism 4, 6, 11, 15–22, 24, 26–30, 33–34, 36–38, 67, 78, 82, 88, 90–92, 101, 103, 105–6, 109, 113, 115, 116, 120–22, 131, 137–38, 147–49; average 16–22; classical 4,11, 16–22; defining features of 16–22; arguments for 27–29; objections to 21–22, 33,37,105–6,

137–38; and variable population sizes 147–49
utilitarianism with a floor 113–16, 120–24

Vallentyne, P. 50, 54–55, 161
veil of ignorance 23, 27–28, 31–32, 35, 42, 115, 183 *see also* Rawls, J.

welfarism 16–17, 90–91
well-being 2–3, 11–12, 182–83
Weymark, J. A. 28
Whitehall studies 162–63
Wiggins, D. 119–20
Williams, Alan 168, 173
World Health Organization 163